Annie C. Kane-

1923.

6668
dup

BELIEF IN CHRIST

BELIEF IN CHRIST

BY CHARLES GORE, D.D.

HON. D.D. EDIN. AND DURHAM, HON. D.C.L. OXFORD, HON. LL.D. CAMBRIDGE
AND BIRMINGHAM, HON. FELLOW OF BALLIOL AND TRINITY COLLEGES,
OXFORD, AND FELLOW OF KING'S COLLEGE, LONDON

NEW YORK
CHARLES SCRIBNER'S SONS
1922

Printed in Great Britain by
Hazell, Watson & Viney, Ld., London and Aylesbury.

PREFACE

1. THIS volume is, again, an appeal to men to think for themselves, and to think freely. It does not concern itself with any question of orthodoxy, that is of ecclesiastical authority. Such questions are deferred to the next volume, which will concern the Church, where they will be wholly in place. But in this volume they are quite omitted.

It is not that I am under the illusion that my own beliefs, or those of other men, orthodox or unorthodox, with very few exceptions, have been actually reached purely or mainly by an argumentative process. They have been the result of a complex of movements within the soul, and of influences from without it, which are largely emotional, moral and social, and not in the narrower sense intellectual. But if the resultant belief or theory is to be described as rational, that must mean that it can account for the relevant experience in its widest sense, and the facts of nature and history, better than any other theory ; and the best way to test the ability of any theory to do this is not mainly by attacking other theories, but by approaching the facts constructively and critically and seeing what theory appears to emerge out of their free consideration.

Accordingly this volume is an attempt to take a critical estimate of all the evidence which concerns the person of Christ, and to show that the belief about Him which really grows out of the evidence, taken all together, and which best accounts for all

v

the facts, is just the traditional belief in the incarnation of the eternal Son of God. I seem to see the intellectuals of my generation, and of the generations below me, as, for the most part, the victims of a delusion. What is called " free thought " is really thought enslaved to a negative dogma, which is not really valid ; viz. that the sort of redemptive action of a personal God, which the Bible professes to record, cannot really have occurred. If the inhibition of this negative dogma is removed—if the enquirer is again really open-minded—then I believe that free enquiry will be found to establish what is substantially the traditional belief. That is the thesis of this volume. And, as I say, it is a challenge to men to think for themselves.

2. The argument of this volume does not begin at the beginning. It presupposes the conclusion of the first volume on Belief in God. Every year of my life makes me more firmly convinced that all the questions which concern the person of Christ are really secondary to the question whether the teaching about God, which was the message of the Hebrew prophets and of Jesus Christ and His apostles, is true—whether it rests upon a real self-disclosure of God to men. I have not of course in this volume repeated the arguments which convince me that so it is. They constitute the substance of my first volume. But I should like to call the attention of my readers to the admirable article on " Theism " by Dr. A. E. Taylor in Hastings' *Encyclopædia of Religion and Ethics*, and particularly to its conclusion. " In the present generation," he says, " the issues seem to be clearing. Philosophers are certainly tending, though not without exception, to range themselves in two camps. Those to whom the business of philosophy seems to consist mainly, if not exclusively, in providing a logical basis and a

methodology for exact science appear to be identifying themselves with the doctrine of logical pluralism
and taking up a definitely atheistic attitude which
involves the denial of the objectivity of judgments
of value ; those on the other hand who are convinced that the business of philosophy is to make
life, as well as science, intelligible, and consequently
find themselves obliged to maintain the validity of
those categories of worth apart from which life would
have no significance, are, in the main, declared
Theists." This is, I believe, true. But I would add
that philosophy, though it can, working by itself,
substantiate Theism, cannot substantiate the equivalent of the Biblical idea of God without the
postulate of a positive self-revelation of God. Nor
can it show the idea of a self-revealing God to be
untenable. And that God has in fact so revealed
Himself, especially through the prophets of Israel and
Jesus Christ, seems to me to be established by the
most cogent reasons. Also the conviction that God
had so done is so manifestly the ground on which
Jesus stood, and on which His Church has always
stood, that I find it very difficult to understand how
any of those who reject this foundation, and deprecate the very idea of a positive revelation, can
suppose that the fabric of Christianity would remain
standing.

It is quite true that there were elements in Baby-
lonian, Persian and Greek thought which the Jews
had assimilated before our Lord's time, and that
they were the richer for the assimilation. And it is
true also that Christianity, which is the flower of
Judaism, assimilated more from Hellenism than the
Jews had previously done ; and that it must learn
in like manner to assimilate important elements from
Indian and Chinese and Japanese thought and art
and religion. But this was done of old, and must

still be done, so as to leave as the main constructive element in the fabric the specific belief in God which came from Israel. On this Christianity was built and must stand. This is the *assumption* of this volume which I did my best to *prove* in its predecessor.

But if I live long enough to accomplish my design I should wish to come back upon the argument of the first volume and consider at length some of the criticisms made upon it.

I have done my best to make the argument in this volume intelligible to those of my readers who are not used to books of biblical criticism, by putting into footnotes and appended notes, which they can omit, some of the more detailed critical enquiries.

Perhaps I ought to apologize for the frequency with which, at certain points in this book, I have referred to other writings of mine. But where I had nothing new to say of much importance, it seemed better to refer to what I had written elsewhere than to increase the bulk of this book by repeating it.

C. G.

St. Luke's Day, 1922.

CONTENTS

CHAPTER I

ix

CHAPTER VII

CHAPTER VIII

CHAPTER IX

CHAPTER X

CHAPTER XI

BELIEF IN CHRIST

CHAPTER I

THE JEWISH BACKGROUND

TWICE in the Gospels Jesus is represented as asking a question bearing upon His own person. The first occasion was at the opening of what we may call the second stage of His mission, when an intense opposition centring in the religious leaders of Israel, the scribes and Pharisees, had declared itself openly in Galilee, and the faith of His first eager disciples was beginning to be deeply tested.[1] Then it was that, away from the centres of the life of Israel, almost as a fugitive, in the neighbourhood of a city beyond the Jordan, whose very name—Caesarea Philippi—would strike upon Jewish ears as repulsively alien, He pressed upon His disciples the direct question: "Who do ye say that I am?" He had asked them first what people in general were saying about Him, and that question was easily answered. It was generally believed that He was someone extraordinary, of prophetic character and divine commission.[2] But more than such vague answers is

[1] Mark iii 6, 22, vii 1-13, viii 11, 15. The great question is recorded in viii 27 ff.

[2] What exactly was meant by saying He was John the Baptist, or Elijah, or one of the prophets is not easy to define. It must be remembered that the Messianic king, the remote descendant of David, is, as in Jer. xxx 9, Ezek. xxxiv 24, Is. lv 4, called simply David; in like manner a successor of John the Baptist or of Elijah might be called simply by his name. People might say—Here we have John the Baptist, or—Here we have Elijah, over again.

1

expected of the disciples.   The question is again
pressed home :   " Who do ye say that I am ? "
And Peter commits himself to the great confession :
" Thou art the Christ."

Once again on the eve of the Passion Jesus is
represented as asking—not the disciples, but the
Pharisees [1]—" What think ye of the Christ ?   Whose
son is He ? "   It was a question not directly about
His own person, but about their idea of " Him who
was to come."   But in the minds of the disciples,
who believed Him to be the Christ, it must have
sounded as a question about Himself.   And both
these questions asked by our Lord imply that His
person presented a problem which must be raised
and solved.   And it is characteristic of our Lord's
generally undogmatic method as a teacher that He
insists that the answer should be found as a judgment
of men's own minds under the teaching of God,
rather than by any explicit pronouncement from His
own lips.

As we know in history, the answer of the first
disciples, who became the Church of Jesus Christ,
was given gradually or in stages.   First it was that
Jesus is the Christ.   Then that Jesus is Lord.
Finally that Jesus, the Christ, is the pre-existent
Son of God, Himself very God, who for us men
and for our salvation was made flesh.   This final
answer was formulated in Creeds and protected by
dogmatic decisions, and became the central point
of the Christian faith.

To-day when the questions of our Lord are quoted
—" Who do ye say that I am ? "   " What think
ye of Christ ? "—what is generally intended is to
ask whether the familiar doctrine of the Church

---

[1] As represented in Matt. xxii 41.   In Mark xii 35 the question is asked of the people, in view of the teaching of the scribes,
" How say the scribes that Christ is the Son of David ? "   So in
Luke xx 41.   I have retained the more familiar form of the question
as the difference is irrelevant.

concerning the person of Jesus gives the true answer to these questions. In our day it is widely questioned and sometimes scornfully repudiated ; or it is suggested that the precise answer to be given to these questions does not seriously matter, if only we are agreed in following the example of the life of Jesus. But the world cannot settle down to regard Jesus as nothing more than the best of men or the greatest of spiritual teachers. Most men feel that there is something mysterious and unique about His person. Nor does it seem possible to leave the great question unanswered. It obtrudes itself upon us and demands an answer. And if we cannot be content to receive passively the dogmatic teaching of the Church, but feel the necessity of opening afresh the question for ourselves, certainly it is not our Lord who will condemn us. He certainly would have men think for themselves, and reach a personal conviction which they can feel to be wrought into their souls by God's own Spirit.

The purpose of this volume, then, is to make the enquiry about Christ's person afresh, with a mind as open as possible to all sources of evidence, and with a resolute determination to go " whither the argument leads." But I shall take for granted the conclusions reached in the volume which preceded this on Belief in God. That is to say that I shall take for granted not only that there is a God in some sense, but that He has really disclosed Himself to men, especially in a historical process through the prophets of Israel and through Jesus of Nazareth, who, whatever else He was, was " a prophet mighty in word and in deed " in the succession of the prophets of Israel. Thus the God in whom we start by believing is indeed the one supreme Spirit who is present and active everywhere in the world, but He is also beyond the world and above it, subsisting in the fulness of personal consciousness and will before

the world was: awful in holiness and perfect in goodness, power, and wisdom : the absolute Creator of
all that is, and the Father and Judge of all rational
spirits. For the justification of this faith I must
refer back to the reasonings of my first volume.
When I say that it will here be taken for granted,
I mean that anyone who is to read this volume
sympathetically and judge of it fairly, must be prepared at least to accept it as a provisional hypothesis
with the consequences which the preceding volume
indicated. He must not have his mind closed by
a dogmatic prejudice against that kind of redemptive action of a personal God to which the Bible
witnesses, or against such special acts of God as we
call miraculous. He must be prepared to follow along
the lines of the growth of the apostolic faith and to
seek with an open mind to appreciate its grounds.

In standing upon this platform to start with, we
have this advantage, that we start where the first
disciples—we may say with all reverence where
Jesus Himself—started. For the Gospels make it
quite evident that Jesus took for granted the God
of Israel and the religion of Israel,[1] even while He
deepened the thought of God and emancipated the
religion from its Pharisaic fetters. Professor Bethune
Baker has recently said " I know almost nothing
about God's character apart from Jesus." [2] This is
a not unfamiliar position, but it is to me amazing.
Something surely of an important kind about the
character of God had become apparent to deep-
thinking men, like Zoroaster and Aeschylus and
Plato, all the world over, and Dr. Bethune Baker
is surely the last man to wish to ignore these verdicts
of the natural conscience. We owe a great debt of
gratitude to Baron Friedrich von Hügel, who is
always bidding us keep in mind that it was not

[1] See *Belief in God*, pp. 94–5.
[2] *The Modern Churchman,* Sept. 1921, p. 301.

only along the line of Israel that mankind had gained real knowledge of God. But what is from our present point of view much more important is that " the Jesus of history " would assuredly have utterly repudiated the supposition that He was to teach men their first serious lessons about God's character. He certainly assumed that His hearers knew a great deal about it—all, in fact, that the prophets had told men, for whom the character of God was the main theme of their mission.

I will counter Dr. Bethune Baker's statement with another,[1] which, if somewhat exaggerated in the other direction, is far nearer the truth than his : " In what way did the teaching of Jesus differ from that of His contemporaries ? Not—and the nature of much modern writing renders it desirable to emphasize the negative—not by teaching anything about God essentially new to Jewish ears. The God of Jesus is the God of the Jews, about whom He says nothing which cannot be paralleled in Jewish literature." I think this is an exaggeration. The teaching of Jesus about the character of God, as the Father of each individual soul whose love goes out to seek and save the lost—the God in whose eyes each individual soul is of identical and absolute value—the Father represented in the Parable of the Prodigal Son—is surely fresh teaching. Certainly our Lord set the character of God in a quite new light in manifold ways. Certainly also His teaching was no borrowed or merely traditional teaching. He said "No man knoweth the Father save the Son, and he to whomsoever the Son willeth to reveal him." But the God and Father of whom He constantly spoke was the Jehovah of the Jewish prophets and Psalmists.[2]

---

[1] From Drs. Foakes Jackson and Kirsopp Lake, *The Beginnings of Christianity* (Macmillan, 1920), vol. i. p. 288.

[2] The only word ascribed to our Lord which appears at first sight to be a repudiation of His Jewish forerunners is John x 8 : " All

2

There was, in fact, no wavering in the early Church as to the continuity and identity of their faith with the old Jewish faith about God. When St. Paul quotes "the Scriptures," though it be a predominantly Gentile Church to which he is writing, he means the books of the Hebrew canon. When he says "Whatsoever things were written beforehand were written for our learning, that through patience and comfort of the Scriptures we might have hope," or that "every Scripture, inspired of God, is also profitable for teaching, for reproof, for correction, for instruction in righteousness, that the man of God may be complete, furnished completely unto every good work,"[1] it is the Hebrew scriptures exclusively that he is thinking of. Indeed, both in St. Paul's and St. Peter's Epistles and in St. James and in the Acts and in the Epistle to the Hebrews the constant assumption is that the Christian Church was the old Jewish Church, the Church of the prophets, reformed and reinspired. This alone accounts for the fact that the earliest Church put in the foremost place among its appeals the argument from prophecy.

Thus it came about that the Bible of the Jews became the Bible of the Christian Church before the New Testament books were written. It is indeed astonishing how wholeheartedly the Gentile world,

that came before me are thieves and robbers : but the sheep did not hear them." But to interpret this single word as a repudiation of Moses and the prophets and John the Baptist would be in glaring contradiction to the Gospels generally and to the Fourth Gospel in particular. See i 7–8, 17, 31, 45, ii 16, iii 10, iv 22, v 46–7, vii 22–3, viii 56, xii 14–16, 39–41, xix 28, 36, 37. The mind of the writer of the Gospel is such that he could not have ascribed to our Lord any repudiation of the ancient prophets. To interpret this startling saying we must refer back to Jer. xxiii 1–4, and Ezek. xxxiv 1–16, concerning the shepherds (rulers) of Israel who maltreat and neglect the flock, with whom our Lord associates the present rulers of Israel, the Pharisees and Sadducees who are set to harass and persecute His disciples, the sheep who hear His voice.

[1] Rom. xv 4, 2 Tim. iii 16–17.

which came very speedily to constitute the vast majority of the Christian society, accepted the Old Testament. There were, no doubt, rebels against such acceptance in the second century, of whom the famous heresiarch Marcion was the most important. He would have discarded the Old Testament and all that belonged to it as the work not of the Supreme Being, but of another lower God, the creator (demiurge) of the material world. He would have had the Church preach a Jesus who revealed a supreme and hitherto unknown God, and a Jesus who had not even a real body of material flesh, such as must have been a creation of the dishonoured demiurge of the Old Testament. There are moderns, amongst whom is Dr. Harnack,[1] who have very deep sympathy with Marcion, at least in his attempt to discard the Old Testament out of the Canon. But the Church teachers would have nothing to do with his revolutionary proposal. They clung to the Old Testament. They saw clearly enough that to reject the Old Testament would be to reject the Jesus of history who stood without hesitation upon that platform.

This is all the more noticeable because some at least of the teachers of the early Church did not, like those of the mediaeval Church or the Churches of the Reformation, rate the Old Testament too high. These Fathers acknowledged frankly that its institutions of worship were of heathen origin and its morals to start with on a barbaric level.[2] But they were full of the principle of God's gradual working in the education of mankind. He justifies Himself, they said, by the results. Only by a large toleration of what was unworthy in a half-barbarous

---

[1] See Harnack, *Das Evangelium vom fremden Gott* (Leipzig, 1921), pp. 248 ff. See also an interesting review of the book by Lowther Clark in *Theology*, vol. iii. no. 17.

[2] Cf. *Lux Mundi*, pp. 240–2 and Pref. p. xxii.

group of tribes, only by a divine patience and
gradualness, could He have educated them up to
the level of the teaching first of the prophets
and then of Jesus. Even St. Augustine, who is
in a measure responsible for the over-estimate of
the Old Testament, says that we wrong the New
Testament if we put the Old on a level with it.[1]
Nevertheless all the Fathers saw that the religion
of Jesus Christ is the outcome of a historical process,
and its roots are fixed in Israel. The Old Testament
and the New cohere inseparably. St. Paul is quite
right in saying that as an apostle of Jesus Christ
there has been no change in the object of his worship.
It is still " the God of our fathers " whom he serves
with a pure conscience,[2] and the whole Christian
Church, though in the main Gentile in origin, in believing in Jesus, knew they were accepting as the true
God the God of Abraham, Moses, and the prophets.

It was the conviction that the self-revelation of
God given through the Hebrew prophets was true and
real that made the Christian Church, when it went
out into the world of the Roman empire, intensely
and deliberately combative not merely for *some* belief
in God, but for the specific belief inherited from Israel
and consummated in Christ.[3]   And this had two very
important results—first, that it made impossible for
the teachers of the Christian Church the " deification " of their Master.

I

As we have seen, the question for the Christian
Church became very soon—Is this Jesus, who is
clearly divine in some sense, really God ?   And that
is the question which interests us to-day.   And the
answer we give depends for its meaning on what we

[1] Aug. *de Gest. Pelag.* 15.
[2] Acts xxii 14, xxiv 14 ; 2 Tim. i 3.
[3] See *Belief in God*, pp. 108 f., 129 ff., 150 ff.

understand by God. The world into which the
Church went out used the term God in a very loose
and comprehensive sense. There were Gods many.
The heavenly bodies were unanimously believed
to be Gods, and very formidable Gods too, for
they dominated the world, like remorseless fates.[1]
Further, there were deified men in abundance—
such as the old hero Heracles, or ancient founders,
like Romulus, or the recent founders of the Empire,
Julius and Augustus, or philosophers who had
brought men the truth. Even the Epicureans
regularly called their founder Epicurus a God. And
the philosophers who believed in a sense in the unity
of God found no difficulty in this wide use of the
term God. For to them, according to the current
Stoicism, God was reason, and reason was God—the
reason in all things and the reason in men. Men,
therefore, were portions of God in respect of their
reason. God and man were of one substance. The
more rational a person was the more he became god.[2]

There is a curious passage quoted by Origen from
some contemporary writer on the Stoic use of words
who defines a " god " in its most general sense as
" an immortal, rational being ; in which sense every
rational soul is a god." Others, he says, add to
the definition that a god must be pure spirit, in
which case human souls will only become gods when
their souls leave their bodies. Others only make
the requirement of moral goodness. " So that every
seemly soul is already a god," even while it is still

[1] See Edwyn Bevan, *Hellenism and Christianity* (George Allen
& Unwin, 1921), p. 78 : " It was from Babylon that the fear of
the stars and especially of the seven [the Sun and Moon and the
Five Planets] had spread through the Roman Empire. It became
an obsession. This earth, the sphere of their tyranny, took on a
sinister and dreadful aspect."

[2] See Bevan, *Stoics and Sceptics*, p. 41. The Stoic poet Manilius
is quoted as saying " Quis possit . . . Et reperire deum, nisi
qui pars ipse deorum est ? " Cf. Arnou, *Le désir de Dieu dans la
philosophie de Plotin* (Paris, 1921), p. 145, note 4.

in the body.   Others confine the term god to beings
" who have some control in the world in respect of
its administration, like the sun and the moon.   In
a different sense the word is applied to the supreme
administrator.   And above all they call god the being
immortal and uncreated, the supreme king, which
is the universe." [1]   The great philosopher Plotinus
in the third century insisted that the root and source
of all things is in unity—in the One.   But this did
not hinder him from recognizing gods in the sun
and the stars and the gods of popular tradition.
With him also the term God " n'est pas du tout un
terme réservé," [2] and this because reason and God
are the same thing.   And thus, because godhead
was comparatively a vulgar thing, Plotinus very
seldom calls his Supreme Being, the One, by the
name God.   Rather, as he is above reason, so he
is something above God.

Obviously from this—the Hellenic—point of view,
it would have been easy and inevitable to deify
Jesus or to call Him a god.   How should one
so excellent in power and goodness not be a god ?
I shall have occasion shortly to discuss the position
of the German, Wilhelm Bousset, and his school,
who contend that in the early Hellenistic churches
it was in fact this pagan spirit which came to be
dominant and led to the conception of Jesus as God.

---

[1] This passage is in the Prologue to Origen on the Psalms ; see
Lommatzsch, tom. xi. 351 ; cf. Harnack, *Hist. of Dogma* (Engl.
trans.), vol. i. p. 119 n., and Inge, *Christian Mysticism*, App. III.
There is no doubt that this Hellenic use of the term God in a very
wide sense affected some Christian writers, as, e.g., when Clement
of Alexandria speaks of the soul of man by a true knowledge
and righteousness "practising to be god" ($\mu\epsilon\lambda\epsilon\tau\hat{a}$ $\epsilon\hat{i}\nu\alpha\iota$ $\theta\epsilon\grave{o}s$,
Strom. vi. chap. xiv. sect. 113) ; and Greek Fathers sometimes
speak of Christians, in Christ, "being made god" ($\theta\epsilon o\pi o\iota\epsilon\hat{\iota}\sigma\theta\alpha\iota$).
Such language is derived from the common Hellenic use, but it is
not properly Christian.   On the whole matter of Hellenic beliefs,
Jules Lebreton's *Les Origines du Dogme de la Trinité* (Paris, 1919),
chap. i., may be very profitably consulted.

[2] Arnou, *op. cit.* pp. 108, 124 f.

But, even according to this school of critics, this
supposed assimilation of the beliefs and worship of
the Church to the model of the religions about them
was not possible on the soil of Palestine or in the
first Jewish circles of the Church. For these first
disciples the idea of a man being raised to divine
honours was something impossible to entertain. No
doubt the religion of Israel had grown upon the
common soil of Semitic religions, and the terminology
of polytheism slightly taints the Old Testament at
its earliest levels.[1] But this taint had long centuries ago been scrupulously purged away. Only
One could be called God or worshipped by any Jew,
He whom St. Paul in true Jewish spirit calls " the
blessed and only potentate, the King of kings and
Lord of lords, who only hath immortality, dwelling
in the light unapproachable, whom no man hath
seen nor can see." [2] Greeks might identify God and
man, but to an Israelite there was no distinction
so deep and impassable as the distinction of the
Creator from all His creatures, even the highest.

Nor was it at all within the compass of the contemporary Jewish imagination that God should manifest Himself in human form. Doubtless there had
been in old days theophanies. God, they read in
the Scriptures, had manifested Himself, as it appeared, even in human form to men. But these
were momentary epiphanies; they had long ceased;
and the later theology had explained them away.
There was no tendency of thought among the Jews
of the time after the Captivity such as would have
led naturally towards an idea of incarnation.

II

The dominant thought of the Greek world, when
Christianity came into it, was <u>pantheistic and</u>

---

[1] See appended note A, p. 28.   [2] 1 Tim. vi 15–16.

polytheistic, but earlier, as in Aristotle, and later, as in Plotinus, there was a philosophical monotheism which believed in the existence of one God absolutely separated from mundane and human affairs, who could take no interest in man, and could influence the world only as an object of desire or intellectual contemplation. Now the religion of the Jews was a monotheism, but totally different from this religion of the philosophers. The one God of the Hebrews, Jehovah, was thought of as intensely concerned in the world and in mankind, as constantly active both in nature and in man. And He had made man in His own image and likeness, so that the activities and emotions of the human mind had their source and counterpart in Him.

That admirable Anglican mystic of the seventeenth century, Thomas Treherne, vividly contrasts the heathen deities who " wanted nothing " with " the Lord God of Israel, the living and true God," who " from all eternity wanted like a God. He wanted the communication of the divine essence, and persons to enjoy it. He wanted worlds, He wanted spectators, He wanted joys, He wanted treasures." [1] It was because of this divine " want " of an enlarging fellowship in the divine life and activity that He had created rational spirits and had appointed men as His vicegerents in the world to "have dominion over the works of His hands." [2] But on the widest scale God had been disappointed in man. Rebellion on his part had baffled God's purpose. Nevertheless, God had not abandoned His good mind towards man, but had proceeded to carry it out by a method of election.

Again and again God is represented as choosing, and making covenant with, some selected group to be the agents of His universal purpose. So it was

[1] See T. Treherne, *Centuries of Meditations* (Dobell, 1908), p. 29.
[2] Gen. i 28, Ps. viii 5-8.

with the family of Noah, with Abraham, with Isaac, with Israel under Moses, with the remnant of Israel who returned, purged and faithful, from the Captivity. And all this selective method of God, choosing a small group out of the whole of mankind to be His instruments, for all its apparent narrowness, had always a universal purpose, as is declared in the call of Abraham : " In thy seed shall all the families of the earth be blessed." This is where Israel stands distinctive among the nations of the earth [1]—in their intense belief in an energetic divine purpose, of which only their own nation is the selected instrument, but which through their nation is to become the heritage of all the world, and which at the last, in spite of all the wilfulness of man, is certainly to take full effect. Because God is God, at the last shall be the Day of the Lord, when God shall come into His own in the whole creation. Thus it is that Israel was the parent of what the Italian philosopher Benedetto Croce proclaims to be the only true history, the history which is also philosophy, which sees the past as alive in the present and pressing on towards a goal and consummation in the future.[2]

The Greeks and Romans never discarded their old legend of a Golden Age in some remote past followed by a gradual decline age after age, so that they are almost totally without the sense of a progressive purpose in the world ; and if their imagination wanders beyond the present world-order they conceive, more after the manner of the Easterns, of innumerable cycles of time, each characterized by gradual deterioration and ending in final catastrophe, without any divine purpose running through the ages

---

[1] See, however, Note B at the end of this chapter on the idea of divine purpose in the teaching of Zoroaster.

[2] See Benedetto Croce, *Teoria e storia della storiographia* (Bari, 1917), pp. 186–92 ; and see *Belief in God*, p. 132, note 1.

as a whole and moving on to its consummation.[1]
Of this conception of divine purpose running through
all things and destined to final effectiveness in spite
of all failures and catastrophes by the way—for
which the rebellion of free spirits is responsible—
a divine purpose with which it is man's highest
joy to co-operate—of this infinitely fruitful belief in
a divine purpose of progress the religion of Israel is
the effective source.

III

This expectation of a kingdom of God [2] to come
is as fully important an element in the Jewish background of Jesus as the belief in the one only God,
the righteous Lord, the Creator of heaven and earth.
And it is necessary for us to get as clear a picture
in our minds as possible of the great expectation,
as it had been formed in earlier days, and as it was
held at the time of our Lord's birth, education, and
ministry. Let us dwell first on some central and
classical expression of the hope from early times.

Here is one which is common to Isaiah and Micah [3]:

" And it shall come to pass in the latter days, that the
mountain of the Lord's house shall be established in

[1] See Bevan, *Hellenism and Christianity*, pp. 180 ff. : " In
some form or other this idea, that the present is vastly inferior
to an ideal past, seems to have been general in classical antiquity.
In the philosophic schools naturally an attempt was made to get
a more far-reaching view of the universe, and here the notion was
elaborated of the process of things being a cyclic movement, in
which history repeated itself over and over again without any end."
. . . " Decline within each period and the periods endlessly repeating themselves in an unvarying round." The whole chapter should
be read.

[2] The actual phrase " the kingdom of God " or " the kingdom of
heaven," as something to be established in the future, does not
appear to occur earlier than the Gospels (see Foakes Jackson and
Lake's *Beginnings of Christianity*, vol. i. pp. 269–70). But the idea
is constant in the prophets and the phrase also, or something like
it, in the sense of the divine sovereignty, *e.g.* Ps. cxlv 12–13.

[3] Is. ii 2–4, Micah iv 1–3.

the top of the mountains, and shall be exalted above
the hills ; and all nations shall flow unto it. And many
peoples shall go and say, Come ye, and let us go up to
the mountain of the Lord, to the house of the God of
Jacob ; and he will teach us of his ways, and we will
walk in his paths ; for out of Zion shall go forth the
law (or ' instruction '), and the word of the Lord from
Jerusalem. And he shall judge between the nations,
and shall reprove many peoples ; and they shall beat
their swords into ploughshares, and their spears into
pruning-hooks : nation shall not lift up sword against
nation, neither shall they learn war any more."

This great vision, and many like it, will be found to
involve certain distinguishable elements.

(1) The idea of the spiritual sovereignty and universality of the religion of Israel—so that all nations
must seek the word of the Lord from Israel as its commissioned dispenser. This idea finds vivid expression
again and again in passages which are amongst the
loftiest in the Old Testament, as when Isaiah sees
Egypt and Assyria linked with one another in one religion through Israel as its medium [1] ; or the Second
Isaiah sees faithful Israel, now purified, reinstated,
and reunited, set " for a covenant of the people,
for a light of the Gentiles " [2] ; or Zechariah sees
" ten men, out of all the languages of the nations,
taking hold of the skirt of him that is a Jew, saying,
We will go with you, for we have heard that God is
with you " [3] ; or Malachi discerns a catholic church
as already in being—" from the rising of the sun
even unto the going down of the same my name
great among the heathen ; and in every place incense
offered unto my name, and a pure offering " [4] ; or
a late prophet sees Jerusalem as the scene of a
divine banquet for all nations " of fat things full
of marrow, of wines on the lees well refined," and of

[1] Is. xix 23–5.   [2] Is. xlii 6.
[3] Zech. viii 23.   [4] Malachi i 11.

a radiant life of knowledge, immortality and joy [1];
or finally where the Psalmist sees the men of all
nations calling Zion their mother.[2] It is a fall
from this high level when the final vindication
of Israel appears as merely their victory over the
heathen.

(2) But, secondly, this glorious vision is only
possible if all the horrible tyrannies, the monstrous
fabrics of pride, insolence, cruelty and lust, which
vex the groaning earth, have been crushed and
annihilated, either by the manifest hand of God
working through whatever external agency He may
choose, or by the strengthening of Israel and its
king. Thus a great part of the writings of the
prophets is occupied with the " dooms " upon
Assyria, Babylon, Egypt, Tyre, and the rest. But
so corrupt and false to its trust is Israel itself,
God's chosen instrument, that it too must fall under
scathing judgment, only never, like the other world
powers,[3] to the point of its utter destruction. Israel
suffers only thereby to be purged, and, though it
be but as a faithful remnant, to pursue its course.
People sometimes ask what element of inspiration
there is in the Book of Esther, and why it is in the
Canon. I should be disposed to answer that nowhere
is the sense of the indestructibility of Israel, even
under circumstances of extremest peril, coupled with
the responsibility of all individual Israelites for the
maintenance of their faith and loyalty, expressed
more vividly than in the words of Mordecai to Esther,
the Jewish wife of a Persian king—" Think not with
thyself that thou shalt escape in the king's house,
more than all the Jews. For if thou altogether

---

[1] Is. xxv 6–8.
[2] Ps. lxxxvii 5. So the Greek Bible rendered it : " Zion is our
mother."
[3] Only in Jeremiah is the idea of a restoration appended also
to the dooms upon the nations, or some of them : see Jer. xlvi 26,
xlviii 47, xlix 6, 39. But see also xxx 11.

holdest thy peace at this time, then shall relief and
deliverance arise to the Jews from another place ;
but thou and thy father's house shall perish ; and who
knoweth whether thou art not come to the kingdom
for such a time as this ? " [1]

(3) In the prophecies which secured the strongest
hold on the imagination of the people, the divine
instrument of the sovereignty of Israel is to be
an anointed king of the house of David, " the
Christ " (anointed one) as he alone came in later
days to be called. This became the national hope
—the raising up by the hand of God of the righteous
king of David's line, who is to administer the divine
righteousness on earth with a resistless power and
finally in perfect peace—to whom God stands so
close that he is to be called His Son [2] and to bear
His name upon him, " Immanuel, God with us,"
" Mighty God, Everlasting Father." [3]

The prophets generally see the glorious Messianic
day looming in the immediate future just behind their
present troubles and sufferings, [4] just as they see the
purging judgment over the whole world behind each
particular judgment on each nation which sets itself in
turn against God and His people. [5] These immediate
expectations are never realized. Nevertheless, their
failure does not destroy the confident expectation.
As God is God, so at last it must be. Even when the

---

[1] Esther iv 13–14.   [2] Ps. ii 7 and (?) 12, lxxxix 26–7.
[3] Is. vii 14, ix 6. The Jews seem never to have interpreted
these names as meaning that the King was himself to be God.
It was the name of God that was to be upon him ; cf. Micah v 4.
We must always distinguish the original sense of the prophecies
from that which the Christian teachers saw in them. But it is, of
course, quite credible that the sense later assigned to them may
have lain in the intention of the inspiring Spirit. In some cases
I should find it difficult to doubt this.
[4] See especially Is. vii 10–17 and Micah v 5 ; cf. the expectation
concerning Zerubbabel in Haggai, and the expectation of Jewish
sovereignty in Daniel immediately after the downfall of Antiochus
Epiphanes.
[5] See later, pp. 139 ff.

figure of the sovereign king of David's line is absent,
the vision of the kingdom remains. And before our
Lord's time, though the hope of the world-sovereignty
of Israel never looked so remote as under Roman
supremacy, the figure of the victorious king of David's
line is again brought into prominence. In the
" Psalms of Solomon "—a Pharisaic work of some
fifty years before our Lord's day—the expected
kingdom has again its centre in the wonderful and
all-powerful king, who is there first apparently called
" the Lord Christ." [1]

(4) The vision of the days of the Messiah, or of
the good time to come, which formed so large a part
of the prophetic message, vague as it remained in
its details, had some other definite features which
must be noted as forming part of the Jewish background of the New Testament. Israel, restored,
converted and supreme, is to be granted by God
a new and everlasting Covenant which shall renew
the old covenant made with David and augment its
spiritual richness.[2] It is to be accompanied by an
outpouring of the divine Spirit " upon all flesh," [3] and
by *a resurrection* of righteous Israelites, who have
died before the dawning of the great day, to participate in its blessings.[4] We cannot understand the
New Testament unless we remember that the coming
of the glorious kingdom, or reign of God and His
Anointed, was to be accompanied by the inauguration

[1] Ps. Sol. xvii 36 : " They are all holy and their king is Christ
the Lord " ($X\rho\iota\sigma\tau\grave{o}s$ $K\acute{u}\rho\iota os$), or it may be translated " an anointed
Lord." But in Lam. iv 20 the Hebrew text " The Lord's anointed "
appears in the Greek Bible as $X\rho\iota\sigma\tau\grave{o}s$ $K\acute{u}\rho\iota os$.

[2] Jer. xxxii 40, 1 5, Ezech. xvi 60, Is. lv 3, lix 21.

[3] See Ezech. xi 19, xxxvi 24 ff., xxxvii 14, xxxix 29, Is.
xxxii 15, xliv 3, lix 21, Zech. xii 10, Joel ii 28–29. The centre
of this effusion of the Holy Spirit of God is the Messiah himself
(Is. xi 1, 2), or " the Servant of Jehovah " (xlii 1, lxi 1). But
the Messiah does not appear in O.T. prophecy as himself destined
to give the Spirit to his new people.

[4] Is. xxvi 19, Dan. xii 2. (Here also is the resurrection of the
unfaithful to shame and contempt.)

of a New Covenant, the effusion of the divine Spirit,
and the Resurrection of the Dead.[1]

(5) This was the hope of Israel, vague in detail,
but fairly definite in general outline, which we find
in possession as soon as we approach the Gospels,
in its more spiritual form in the hopes of the humble
and pious folk among whom our Lord was born,
and in a fiercer secular form in the zealous nationalism
of the popular heart. How Jesus both accepted and
transmuted this hope it will be in part our business
to consider.

But there is one feature of this hope, to which
we shall have to give more detailed consideration
when we come to speak of the much discussed subject of our Lord's apocalyptic teaching,[2] but which
we must not omit now. We shall find our Lord
speaking of Himself as "the Son of Man" who is
to come at the last on the clouds of heaven, with
the holy angels, in great power and glory, to judge
the world and gather together His elect.[3]   Now
there is one only passage in the Old Testament—
a passage which had clearly been given great importance—to which this language refers. It is the vision
of Daniel.[4]

And behold there came with the clouds of heaven
one like unto a son of man, and he came even to the
Ancient of Days, and they brought him near before him.
And there was given him dominion and glory and a
kingdom, that all peoples, nations, and languages should
serve him : his dominion is an everlasting dominion
which shall not pass away, and his kingdom that which
shall not be destroyed.

---

[1] I say nothing here of the figure of the Servant of Jehovah, who
redeems Israel by the sacrifice of his life, in Is. lii, liii, which seems
to have taken no hold on the imagination of Israel before our Lord's
time.

[2] Cap. V. p. 137.

[3] See Mark xiii 26–27 and xiv 62.

[4] Dan. vii. 13–27.

In this vision the being in the form of a son of man stands not for the Christ but for the people of Israel—the "people of the saints of the most high," just as the four animal forms who come out of the sea [1] represent the empires of Babylon, Media, Persia and Greece. They are all merely symbolic figures. What the writer is contemplating under these figures is the establishment, in the place of the Empire of the Seleucid successors of Alexander the Great, now represented by the persecutor Antiochus Epiphanes, of the people of Israel in triumph upon the earth. It is the old Messianic hope without mention of the Messiah.

In the past it was thought that our Lord was simply referring back to this vision, interpreting the figure like to a son of man of the Christ, instead of the whole people of Israel; just as He interpreted the Suffering Servant of Jehovah as the Christ, whereas originally he had stood for the whole people, or the whole of the faithful remnant. But recent study has brought into much prominence the later Jewish Apocalypses, and amongst them, most conspicuously, the Book of Enoch and the part of that composite book which is called the Similitudes, which is held to date from the first century before Christ. And in these Similitudes a unique representation is found. The imagery of the Book of Daniel is revived in a new sense. A celestial being, called the Elect One, in the form of a son of man, and called also "the Son of Man," [2] who has existed in heaven from the beginning, is summoned forth by "the Lord of Spirits" (that is the name of God in these Similitudes) to sit upon His throne and execute His judgment upon the sinful world. He is twice

[1] Verse 3.
[2] The passages, however, which call him the Elect One and those which call him the Son of Man are held by the experts to have belonged originally to different documents.

called " the Anointed," [1] but otherwise suggests in
no respect the Christ of Jewish tradition, the anointed
King of David's line. He is a heavenly being,
neither God nor properly man, but man-like. But
the language used by our Lord about the coming of
the Son of Man in judgment so much more closely
represents the idea of these Similitudes than the
idea of Daniel that it is difficult to doubt that our
Lord had it in mind. We remember that the Epistle
of Jude, one of " the brethren of the Lord," is full
of reminiscences of the Book of Enoch, and there
is no reason why our Lord should not have been
acquainted with it.[2] Only if so, as we shall see, He
sets its imagery on a wholly new background in
applying it to Himself.

We shall have to return to this subject when we
are examining our Lord's language. But it is necessary, in describing the Jewish hope, to say something
about these Jewish Apocalypses which have lately
been engaging so much attention.[3]

[1] In c. xlviii 10 and lii 4. But see *Beginnings of Christianity*,
p. 371. Note also that in lxxi 14, as it stands, Enoch himself is
said to be constituted the Son of Man. Dr. Charles, however,
would alter the text. On the very ambiguous nature of the
document see appended note, p. 30.

[2] I am assuming what I see no good reason to doubt, that the
author of the Epistle of Jude was really one of our Lord's family,
probably a half-brother.

[3] For a general account of the Apocalyptic literature we may
go to Dr. Charles, *Between the Old and New Testaments* (Williams
& Norgate, " Home University Library "), or to Lagrange, *op. cit.*,
or to Drs. Foakes Jackson and Lake, *op. cit.*, pp. 126 following.

Dr. Charles is an expert and, like most experts, is over-enthu-
siastic on his special subject and, I think, greatly exaggerates
its importance. And an American writer, Dr. Simkhovitch, not
a theologian by profession but an economist, who has published
an exceedingly interesting essay, *Towards the Understanding of
Jesus* (Macmillan, New York, 1921), expresses feelings about these
apocalypses which many of us will be found to share : " In the
apocalyptic and eschatological literature of the time the world
was to come to an end. But what really did come to an end in
that literature was the last shred of thinking capacity and common
sense." He would perhaps admit that 2 Esdras is a partial
exception.

This not very attractive type of literature was quite unknown to our learned men of old, except in the case of the Apocalypse of Ezra, which we find in our " Apocrypha " as the Second Book of Esdras. These apocalypses belong to the centuries immediately before or after the birth of our Lord. They were soon discarded by Jews and Christians alike, but found favour for a time in some quarters, and many of them survive in translations into many languages, indicating their former popularity. They are written as in the persons of ancient seers—Adam, Enoch, Noah, the sons of Jacob, Moses, Ezra— recording visions of the mysteries of nature and creation, and of the angels and of the future destinies of the world, the day of judgment, and heaven and hell.[1] And one of their chief characteristics may be said to be that, instead of this world being the scene of the kingdom of God (as in the Old Testament), this world is represented, at least in many of them, as wholly passing away and another world, the world of heaven and hell, as taking its place.

In the prophets and psalms we have a great deal of language about nature, which represents it as violently moved in sympathy with God's acts of judgment and mercy, and in terror at His coming. " The hills melted like wax at the presence of the Lord." " All the host of heaven shall be dissolved and the heavens shall be rolled together as a scroll." " The sun shall be darkened in his going forth, and the moon shall not cause her light to shine." " The mountains and the hills shall break forth before you into singing, and all the trees of the field shall clap their hands." We shall have to come back upon this sort of language, where we find the like to it being

[1] They seem, in their speculative interest in the mysteries of nature and the unseen world, and their elaborate doctrine of angels and in their " other world " hopes, to exhibit an influence alien to Israel. We may perhaps find in Persia the source of this influence.

used by our Lord and His disciples. It is difficult
to say how far it is consciously metaphorical. Certainly in the later days of prophecy the prophets
contemplated a physical catastrophe on the vastest
scale accompanying the divine judgments on the
world and the ushering in of the divine kingdom.
The old heaven and the old earth yield to a new
heaven and a new earth. But the new heaven and
the new earth always, on examination, appear to
be the old heaven and the old earth purified and
renewed, with Jerusalem still at the centre and the
nations of the world doing her homage.[1]

But this was not the case in the later Apocalypses.
There, says Dr. Harnack,[2] " the expectations for the
future become more and more transcendent ; they
are shifted increasingly to the realm of the supernatural and the supramundane ; something quite
new comes down from heaven to earth, and the new
course on which the world enters severs it from the
old ; *nay this earth,* transfigured as it will be, *is no
longer the final goal ; the idea of an absolute bliss
arises whose abode can only be heaven itself.*" So
also Dr. Charles writes : " The hope of an eternal
Messianic kingdom on the present earth, which had
been taught by the Old Testament prophets and
cherished by every Israelite, was then abandoned.
The earth had come to be regarded as wholly unfit
for the manifestation of the kingdom."[3]

I cannot but think that in recent literature the
importance of these Apocalypses has been immensely

---

[1] See Is. xxiv 23 (apparently a late prophecy incorporated in
Isaiah), and Is. lxvi 19–24 and Joel ii 32, iii 16. So it is, as we
shall see, in the New Testament.

[2] *What is Christianity ?* (Eng. Trans., Williams & Norgate), p. 137.

[3] *Between the Old World and the New,* p. 119. If Dr. Charles
means by " then," at the date *c.* 100 B.C., when the new style of
apocalypse begins, then the statement is not, I think, true. The
old hope survived in full operation into N.T. times—see *The Psalms
of Solomon* and the N.T. But it is true within a certain range of
feeling or thought represented in these apocalypses.

exaggerated. For example, we are constantly told that the established belief of the Jews and of the Pharisees in particular, and therefore of St. Paul in his Pharisaic days, included the belief in a Messiah pre-existing in the heavens, after the manner of the " elect one " of the Book of Enoch. This I believe to be so exaggerated an estimate as to be positively untrue, and I have dealt with this at some length in a note appended to this chapter. What I would seek to do here is to point out that the heavenly being of *Enoch*, though he may be called the anointed one, is a substitute for the Christ of Jewish tradition and quite different in idea. When the Jewish idea of a Messianic kingdom of perfection in this world was abandoned by the apocalyptic writers in favour of another world wholly different from this, the tradition of the Messianic kingdom to come became an awkward encumbrance which could not be fitted into their scheme. They either left it out altogether (like the author of our Similitudes of Enoch) and let the day of judgment and the other world succeed at once to the confusions of this world, or they interposed the Messianic kingdom, with or without the personal Messiah, as a temporary preparation for, or foretaste of, the real heaven to come,[1] to be succeeded in its turn by conflict and confusion. From their point of view the Messiah and his kingdom upon earth were not wanted. What they wanted was the other world. And the so-called Messiah of the Book of Enoch, who is the divine instrument of judgment and the harbinger of the world to come, is a substitute for the human king of the family of David who was to inaugurate the kingdom of God in this world. The two ideas belong to different orders of thought. Now, no doubt, the Messianic hope when

[1] This is the first form of the idea of the millennium, which we find in the Revelation of St. John.

our Lord came into the world was full of confusions. Nevertheless nothing is more certain than that what was in possession, and remained in possession, was the old orthodox Jewish tradition of a king of David's line who was to restore the kingdom to Israel and to make Israel the centre of a world-wide kingdom of God. How our Lord dealt with this expectation, and what use He made of the apocalyptic idea on a new basis, we shall see in due course. But all the evidence shows that the old Jewish tradition, as it appears in the " Psalms of Solomon," and not the apocalyptic vision, possessed the ground in the New Testament times. This is the Messianic hope of the circle of humble, pious folk among whom our Lord was born. This is the basis of the preaching of John the Baptist, as it is represented in the Gospels, who expects and finds the Christ as a man among men on earth. All the anxious questioning of the Jews expressed in the Gospels concerning the origin of the Christ, and what is to be expected of Him, is on the same basis. God was " to restore again the kingdom to Israel " through an anointed king of David's line. Like the influence of the Essenes, which hardly appears in the New Testament, so the influence of the apocalypses doubtless existed in a certain circle—a circle, we suspect, from which our Lord was not wholly alien—but it was by no means dominant or common. This the evidence seems to indicate quite unmistakably.[1]

On this basis I may quite briefly indicate the stand-points of the different parties among the Jews with whose names the Gospels make us familiar—the Sadducees, the Herodians, the Pharisees ; and I must

[1] See Matt. ii 4–6, Luke i 32–3, 54–5, 76–9, ii 11, 26, 34, 38. For the preaching of John the Baptist see p. 45. For later indications see Matt. xii 23, xxii 41 ff., xxiv 5, 24, xxvii 42, Mark x 47, xi 10, Luke iv 41 ff., ix 20, Acts i 6 ; cf. John i 41, 45–9, iv 25, vi 15, vii 41–2.

add, though the name is only once mentioned, the Zealots.[1]

The Sadducees are most favourably represented in the Book of Ecclesiasticus, which appears to belong to their tradition. In the New Testament their chief representatives are the high priestly family of Annas, a thoroughly worldly group, occupied with the interests of their position, and determined, above all things, to keep on good terms with Rome, so as to retain whatever relative independence and governing authority were still allowed to them. They probably were totally without the Messianic expectation, and, indeed, it is not anywhere suggested in Ecclesiasticus.

The Herodians were no doubt equally alien to it. They were the adherents of a semi-Jewish dynasty whose consistent policy had been, while maintaining the Jewish religion, at least in form, and giving it a magnificent shrine in the new temple at Jerusalem, to favour the absorption of Israel in the general world of the Roman Empire.[2]

But the Pharisees, as Josephus says, " had the multitude on their side." They were the real leaders of religion. Not that they were advocates of armed resistance to Rome. They saw the hopelessness of this, and in fact they had apparently joined in the petition, offered to Augustus soon after our Lord's birth, that Judaea might be made a Roman province. They anticipated, no doubt, less interference with true religion under a religiously indifferent Roman

---

[1] The point of view of these parties, in relation to our Lord's teaching, is admirably characterized in Professor Vladimir Simkhovitch's *Towards the Understanding of Jesus* (Macmillan, New York, 1921)—a most interesting study ; also in Stephen Liberty's *Political Relations of Christ's Ministry* (Milford, 1916).

That one of the apostles is called the Zealot indicates, what other evidence indicates, that the party was already in existence, as assuredly its spirit was. Of the Essenes, as they do not cross our path in the N.T., I say nothing.

[2] Simkhovitch, *op. cit.* pp. 15–17.

governor than under an Herodian prince bent on
secularizing Judaism.   But they held passionately to
the hope of the Messiah. We probably interpret
them best if we represent them as believing that the
chosen people, by the strict observance of the law
and the tradition of the elders, would merit and
obtain such favour of God as that He would bare
His arm and work the great redemption by His own
omnipotence.

But this acquiescence in foreign sovereignty did
not satisfy the people as a whole. Since the days
of the Maccabean revolt, under the Greek and the
Roman yoke alike, Judaea seethed with nationalism,
and the Zealots were the extremists in this movement. For them the hope of the Messiah meant the
hope of a king who would lead them in revolt against
the Roman supremacy, and, by the power of God
assisting him, do as the Maccabees had done of old,
only on a very much grander scale—that is, win
liberty for Israel, and even world sovereignty. It is
impossible to read the pages of the Jewish historian
Josephus, without seeing what a seething mass of
nationalism Judaea was in our Lord's lifetime, and
how the Messianic hope presented itself to the heart
of the people.[1]

*   *   *   *   *   *

I hope enough has been said to enable any reader
who has an ordinary acquaintance with the Old
Testament to realize the extreme importance of
beginning the study of Christ on the background

[1] See Simkhovitch, *op. cit.*, pp. 27 f.: " The religion of their fore-
fathers became [to the Jewish people at large] the unfurled banner
of a nation at bay. . . . From now on, whether in passive resistance or in open rebellion, the only Lord and Master they recognised
was the Lord of Hosts . . . with whom they were in covenant,
and who must send the great Deliverer to save His people in their
hour of need." Cf. p. 30 and p. 48 : " The loud nationalist call
to rebellion, the fervid hope for a Messiah, God's anointed leader
and the redeemer of Israel, stirred the deepest emotions."

of the traditional Jewish faith and hope. This
is equally important for what it excludes—that is,
the possibility of our Lord's first disciples " deifying "
their honoured Master in the way Greeks would have
done, because their minds were full of the " jealousy "
of the One God the Creator ; and for what it involves—that is the eager expectation of divine redemption, which, at the period when Jesus was born,
was especially acute and which ran upon the traditional lines of the prophetic forecast of the Messiah
and his kingdom on earth.

NOTE A

Traces of Polytheism in the Old Testament

As is well known, the common Hebrew word for
God is a plural " elohim." But this is interpreted by
A. B. Davidson (*The Theol. of the O.T.*, p. 100) and
Driver (*Genesis*, pp. 402 ff.) as a plural of majesty rather
than as a relic of polytheism. Nevertheless, we find
phrases in the O.T. which suggest that there were other
Gods besides Jehovah—phrases which would not have
been used in the later days of Israel : and the same
must be said of the use of *elohim* for judges and rulers
(Psalm lxxxii 6), or for the dead (1 Sam. xxviii 13),
or perhaps for angels (Psalm viii 5). Such uses are
probably derived from a tradition older than strict
monotheism. But all this laxer use of the title God
had been rendered impossible by the teaching of the
Prophets. Only One could be called God or worshipped.

Of course the use of Psalm lxxxii (" I have said ye
are Gods ") ascribed to Jesus in John x 34 is interesting.
It might suggest that our Lord wished to encourage
something like the extended Hellenic use of the term
God. But a single phrase in a single Gospel must not be
interpreted so as to be quite out of harmony with the
general teaching of our Lord. This particular passage
is, I think, one of those in which (granted its genuineness)
our Lord asks questions solely to force men to think out
their own meaning without conveying any positive

teaching at all. He means "How can you object to my calling myself the Son of God, when you yourselves are bound to recognize that in the Psalms judges are even called Gods in some sense ? There is here plainly some sort of communication of divine authority to men such as you should recognize also in me." I shall have occasion later (pp. 186 f.) to point out that it was part of the method of our Lord to test men's sincerity and consistency by questions which cannot be taken as suggesting any positive teaching on His part, *e.g.* Mark x 18 and xii 35–37.

NOTE B

The Idea of Divine Purpose in the Teaching of Zoroaster

Quite independently of Israel, the Persian or Iranian race, under the prophetic guidance of Zoroaster, whose date is quite uncertain but who was assuredly a real man and a great prophetic soul, was taught to see this world as the scene of a divine purpose one day to triumph. Whether Zoroaster was an ultimate dualist appears to be uncertain. But certainly he saw this world, and the larger universe, as the scene of a conflict between a good spirit and a bad. But the good spirit is to triumph. "Deliverers" or "saviours" are sent to help forward his victory. And the call to all men is to exercise their free will by co-operating with the good god and His instruments, and so "make the world advance." The end—"the last turning of the creation in its course "— is certain. The scene of history is to close in a day of judgment, beyond which is a perpetual heaven for the righteous ("the best mental state"), a perpetual hell ("the worst life ") for "the liars " or those who have followed the false spirit, and perhaps a middle region for "those whose false things and good things balance." This primitive ethical gospel of Zoroaster became much overlaid and buried in rubbish ; and thus it contrasts with the Jewish faith in having been on the whole in-effectual over any wide area : see Dr. Sydney Cave's *Introd. to the Study of some Living Religions of the East* (Duckworth, 1921—a very useful study), pp. 64 ff. ;

cf. Höffding's *Philosophy of Religion* (Eng. trans.,
Macmillan, 1906), p. 53, and Bevan's *Hellenism and
Christianity*, p. 187, where, however, the statement that
Zoroaster looked for one Saviour in the fulness of time
to destroy evil does not seem to be borne out by the
earliest authorities. It is certainly not to be found in
the deeply interesting Gathas (*Sacred Books of the East*,
vol. xxxi.).

In the recent work of Eduard Meyer, *Ursprung und
Anfänge des Christenthums*, vol. ii., a very important place
is assigned to Persian beliefs—the beliefs emanating from
Zoroaster—in influencing the later religion of Israel.
In particular the whole idea of the " world to come "
as a world quite different from the present world—a
world of heaven and hell which begins when this world has
vanished—such as appears in many of the later Jewish
Apocalypses, is supposed to be due to Persian influences, and also the developed angelology and doctrine of
Satan.

NOTE C

The Belief in the Pre-existing Son of Man

It is the fashion to-day to speak as if the Jews, and
especially the Pharisees, of our Lord's day believed in
the Messiah as the Son of Man, already existing in the
heaven from the beginning of time and destined to be
manifested in God's good time. So Dr. Rashdall [1] (quoting
Weiss) : " Wrede and Brüchner have conclusively shown
that Paul before his conversion held the belief, as a
Pharisee, that the Messiah existed from all eternity with
God in heaven." Thus, " as an apostle of Christ, he
thought of Jesus as the Messiah and therefore . . . a
heavenly being who existed with the Father before His
manifestation on earth." So Dr. Stanton [2] : The pre-
existence of Jesus " was inevitably suggested by the
identification of Jesus with the heavenly Son of Man."
So also Dr. Harris, *Creeds or No Creeds* (Murray,
1922) : " It is one of the most assured results of recent

[1] *Idea of Atonement*, pp. 127–9.
[2] *The Gospels as Historical Documents*, vol. iii.

Synoptic criticism (liberal as well as orthodox) that the title Son of Man implies pre-existence, and that not merely impersonal or ideal pre-existence, but actual and personal pre-existence in a state of divine glory and majesty with the Father in heaven " (see pp. 220, 264, 367). But we must confront these scholars with Dalman,[1] than whom, I suppose, there is no greater authority on Jewish matters : " Judaism has never known anything of a pre-existence peculiar to the Messiah, *antecedent to his birth as a human being*." " The dominance of the idea in any Jewish circle whatever cannot seriously be upheld." " The common opinion that Paul simply adopted his designation of Christ as 'the last Adam' and ' the second man ' from the Rabbinic theology is erroneous, for their theology knew nothing of such a comparison between Adam and the Messiah." Nor did it know anything of a *pre-existent* ideal man. Dalman seems to me to prove his case.

(1) In documents which can reasonably be held to be pre-Christian there is nothing to suggest a pre-existing Son of Man or pre-existing Messiah except the Similitudes of Enoch, of which we are just going to speak, and in post-Christian Judaism only the " Ezra Apocalypse " (see 2 Esdras vii 28, xii 32, xiii 26–52, xiv 9),[2] and nothing else till we come to a seventh- or eighth-century document, and later to mediaeval mysticism. The only pre-Christian ground of the idea, then, appears to be the Similitudes of Enoch.

(2) But we must be very careful in quoting this document. What we have to do with is a translation in Ethiopic from a Greek translation of the original. Our existing version is confessedly greatly interpolated. Moreover, it has passed through Christian hands. Again, the critics rightly discern, underlying our existing Ethiopic text, *two documents*, from which the relevant passages are quoted—one of which (A) speaks of a celestial figure which is called " the Elect One," and another different document (B) which speaks of " another

---

[1] *Words of Jesus*, pp. 128–32, 248, 252.
[2] See Dr. Box's *The Ezra Apocalypse* (Pitman, 1912). The date of the whole book is *c.* A.D. 120. Some of the passages referred to belong to an older document, *c.* A.D. 90.

being whose countenance had the appearance of a man,"
and who is afterwards called "that Son of Man" or
"the Son of Man."[1] Both documents appear to have
assigned to the celestial figure the same functions, though
pre-existence is only asserted of "the Son of Man."[2]
Now it seems to be probable that the document (A) is
original and the document (B) interpolated either by a
Jew who sought to divert the title Son of Man, derived
from the Book of Daniel, from the Christian human-born
Christ, or (less probably) by a Christian from a somewhat
different motive. See Lagrange *Le Messianisme chez
les Juifs* (Paris: Lecoffre, 1909)—a careful and ex-
haustive examination. On the general idea of pre-
existence see pp. 43 ff.; on *the Similitudes*, pp. 87 f.

Further, we must notice that the Similitudes as they
stand give a confused impression. The "Son of Man,"
or Elect One, is a celestial quasi-angelic being who is
properly neither God nor man and is never destined for
human birth and life. He is rather a substitute for the
Messiah than the Messiah (see *Beginnings of Christianity*, by Foakes Jackson and Kirsopp Lake, p. 371).
But in one passage (lxxi 14), which is supported by
another interpolated passage (lx 10) and by the "Book
of the Secrets of Enoch" (see Lagrange, p. 97) Enoch himself is represented as that Son of Man. (See *Beginnings*,
p. 371. Dr. Charles would alter the text.)

(3) Dr. Charles' theory that the wicked 'Kings' and
'mighty men' of the Similitudes, whom the Elect is to
overthrow, are the later Maccabean princes is surely con-
tradicted by the plain statement that they are idolaters.
"Their faith is in the gods which they have made with
their hands" (xlvi 7). His suggested parallels from the
Psalms of Solomon are not parallels. There the
Maccabean rulers are described as worse than the heathen
(*Ps. Sol.* i 8, viii 14, xvii 16) but not as idolaters. The
fact that in the Similitudes the adversaries are described
as heathen seems to leave us without any certain evidence
of date except what is found in the traces of the
Similitudes in the Gospels.

---

[1] See Charles, *Book of Enoch*, pp. 64–5.
[2] Charles, *op. cit.* p. 65.

(4) All, then, that I think it is at all safe to assume is that the pre-Christian author of the Similitudes of the Book of Enoch borrowed from Daniel the idea of a celestial figure " like unto a Son of Man "—regarded it as an individual and not a mere image of the sacred nation—called the individual " the elect one," and represented him (still with Daniel) as coming on the clouds of heaven to " the Lord of Spirits " (as he calls God) and being appointed by God to sit on His throne and judge the world and usher in the world to come. This celestial being was, of course, conceived as pre-existing, and the idea would have been known to whatever circle of persons was familiar with the Similitudes. But the circle does not appear to have been a large one. As I have shown, it was the old-fashioned idea of the Messiah, who was to be the Son of David and to restore the kingdom to Israel on earth, which is assumed to prevail in the Gospels and early chapters of Acts, and none other. And it is (I think) quite certain that in our Lord's day " the Son of Man " was not recognized (before He adopted the name) as a title of the Messiah. Also there does not appear to be in the New Testament any recognition whatever of a pre-existing *Man* or celestial being in human form (see below, pp. 76 n. 2, 87 f., 115, 313).

CHAPTER II

THE BELIEF OF THE FIRST DISCIPLES

Upon the basis of the Jew's belief in God, and his vivid, though confused, expectation of His coming and His kingdom, our task lies now with a certain group of Jews, the first disciples of Jesus. We have to examine the gradual growth of their faith in their Master, first as the promised Messiah, then as the Lord of all, then as the incarnate Son of God ; and our object will be to enquire whether this faith, as it reaches expression in St. Paul and the Epistle to the Hebrews and St. John, was in such sense inevitable, or required by the facts of the case, as that it can be pronounced the only legitimate interpretation of the person of Jesus, valid for us to-day as for them of old.

I

This is a profoundly interesting study of the growth of a conviction in a gradually expanding group : but it is also a difficult study because every step of our progress will be over ground which has been the subject of acute controversy—controversy which is still as far as possible from any general settlement in the world of Biblical criticism ; and my readers must be patient with me if I proceed very carefully.

As has been explained [1] in the volume which preceded this, the mass of the critical work which has

---

[1] *Belief in God*, pp. 215 ff.

been poured from the European press, and the most famous of the attempted reconstructions of " the Jesus of history," have been produced upon the basis of an assumption that the miraculous and generally the supernatural—that is the coming of God into the world of man and nature in a new sense with a directly redemptive purpose, accompanied with special acts calculated to mark that purpose—cannot really have occurred, or, at any rate, is not rationally credible. As has been shown, to start from such an intellectual assumption involves very violent treatment of our documents, the Gospels, which are full of the miraculous and of the faith in a special activity of God for the redemption of mankind. Thus it leaves the fabric of the evangelical narrative in so shattered and precarious a condition (as anyone can see for himself) that each critic who aims at reconstruction can select and reject amongst the materials that remain almost at will. This is what accounts for the amazing differences in the resultant " Jesus of History " which is offered us by different schools of critics.

(1) To-day there are three such schools which excite the most interest. There is first the Liberal Protestant School, of which Professor Harnack may be taken as the outstanding representative. In his famous lectures on " The Essence of Christianity " [1] Jesus appears as a simple and gracious figure indeed, preaching an ethical gospel, inspired by the conviction of the Fatherhood of God, the infinite and equal worth of every human soul, the duty and joy of self-sacrifice and brotherliness, and the inwardness of true religion or the kingdom of God. " In the combination of these ideas—God the Father, providence, the position of men as God's children,

[1] In the English translation, *What is Christianity ?* (Williams and Norgate) ; in the original, *Das Wesen des Christenthums.*

the infinite value of the human soul—the whole gospel is expressed." [1] The work of the gracious teacher was accompanied by a marvellous power of healing (" by suggestion " as we should now say), which is represented in an exaggerated form in the Gospels as they stand, mixed with nature miracles which, of course, it is taken for granted cannot really have occurred.[2] But the " miracles," of whatever sort they were, and the claim of Jesus to be the Christ (which in some sense is admitted), with everything that would involve superhuman quality in Him, are passed over by Harnack very lightly. His ethical teaching and influence was the thing that mattered. The subsequent belief of the disciples in His corporal resurrection from the dead, and their expectation of His coming in glory, and the later introduction of a doctrine of Incarnation, with a metaphysic of Christ's person and of the Trinity in God, and the theory of a visible church with sacraments and priesthood—all these elements of Christianity are treated as regrettable necessities, due in part to the pressure first of the Jewish and then of the Hellenic environment, and in part to the exigences of an elementary organization struggling to maintain itself. They were the husk necessary for the time to the preservation of the kernel. They are for the most part quite alien to the spirit and intention of Jesus, and their sole justification lies in the extent to which they enabled the one thing necessary—the essential ethical spirit of Jesus—to maintain itself and again and again to be revived. But the Christ of Pauline and Johannine theology, and even the Christ of the Acts, stands already at a great distance from the Jesus of history.

[1] *Op. cit.* p. 70 ; cf. p. 79: " The thought that he who loses his life shall save it . . . effects a transmutation of values."
[2] See pp. 27–31.

(2) In violent contrast to the Jesus of the Liberal Protestant School, which has many representatives in this country, stands the Jesus of the Apocalyptic school represented by Schweitzer and Loisy, which also has had great influence on not a few English writers.[1]

All the startling " apocalyptic " features of the Gospels which Harnack sought to eliminate or reduce in significance, are by these writers brought to the front in their reconstruction of the original history, and made to occupy almost the whole ground. Jesus is represented as what we cannot but call an enthusiastic fanatic, who believed himself to be destined to be manifested immediately from heaven as the Christ or the Son of Man (of the Book of Enoch) to judge the present world and inaugurate the next world.

Schweitzer and his school make it a chief point of their contention that " the Christ " of the Gospels is not an earthly person, but one to be manifested in glory from heaven, according to the picture in the Similitudes of Enoch. Therefore our Lord on earth was not the Christ, but only believed Himself to be destined to become the Christ on the Day of Judgment. Incidentally I would note [2] that this is flatly contrary to the evidence of the Gospels. There, whatever the Christ is afterwards to become, He is represented as first of all an earthly person, born of the seed of David.

When Jesus first sent out the Twelve, He expected

---

[1] The best book by which to judge of Schweitzer's view is the second part of his treatise on " The Lord's Supper " (*Das Abendmahl*). This second part has been translated as *The Mystery of the Kingdom of God : The Secret of Jesus' Messiahship and Passion*, by Walter Lowrie, and published in New York (Dodd, Mead & Co., 1914). It is most illuminating. In his larger and later work, published in English as *The Quest of the Historical Jesus* (Black, 1910), his theory is constantly referred to and assumed. But its grounds are not continuously given as in the earlier book.

[2] See below, p. 76 n. 1.

4

His coming as Christ to occur before their mission
to the cities of Israel was completed, that is within
a few weeks.[1] As a result of His disappointment
in this expectation, and by reflecting on the death
of John the Baptist and on the figure of the Servant
of Jehovah in Isaiah liii, He came to the conviction
that His own sacrificial death was necessary to
bring the day of Resurrection and the coming of
the Christ in glory, and so gave Himself to death.
He died upon the cross with the cry of desolation
on His lips, and left His disciples overwhelmed with
the consciousness of failure. But their reviving
faith, feeding upon " visions " of Jesus as risen and
glorified, built the fabric of the belief of the earliest
Church in the heavenly Christ immediately to appear
in glory, which again was gradually transmuted
into the Christ of later Christian belief. By this
apocalyptic school of interpreters Christ's ethical
teaching is even ludicrously minimized. He had,
according to them, no thought of founding or re-
founding a Church to live a new kind of ethical
life in this world. He was a man possessed with
one idea, the idea of the immediate end of the world
and of Himself as the instrument of the divine
judgment; and this idea rendered all this world and
its concerns a matter of little moment, as indeed
the life of the world was almost over. All that is to
be done is to repent and to detach oneself absolutely
from all worldly ties, so as to be free to be admitted
into the world to come which is immediately
imminent.[2]

From this Jesus the Christ of the Church is indeed
very far removed. It was only in fact by His ceasing
to be remembered as historically He was, that He
could be serviceable for the generations to come.

---

[1] This is based on Matt. x 23, on which see below, p. 152 n.
[2] This is what is meant by describing Christ's moral teaching as
merely " interims-ethik."

(3) There is a third school, for so it must be ranked, which is best represented by Bousset in Germany and Kirsopp Lake in England.[1] In this school the Jesus of history is a very dim figure indeed. Little or no originality of preaching about God or human life is ascribed to Him. He preached a "message of the kingdom of God and the duty of fellowship in righteousness and love and mercy and forgiveness," [2] a message also of obedience to God and the pre-eminence of spiritual values, largely presented in parables. He died a loyal martyr to his witness for real righteousness against the selfish conservatism and religiosity of the Pharisees, the worldly hostility of the Sadducees, and the violent ideals of popular leaders of nationalism. But all the supernatural features of the Gospels, and almost all the apocalyptic claim, is to be ascribed to the first Jerusalem community of disciples, and not to Christ.[3]

The account which Bousset gives of the belief of this community is very similar to that given by Schweitzer, but it is ascribed, as I say, to the community and not to Jesus. This is the first transformation—that by which the historical Jesus becomes the apocalyptic Christ. The second transformation is still more important. It occurred in the Hellenistic churches such as Antioch, Tarsus and Damascus. There the Pagan religious world was largely occupied with " mystery cults "—that is religious societies, which worshipped hero-gods— Dionysus or Hermes or Serapis, or Cybele and Attis, or Osiris and Isis—by whose patronage they believed

[1] The central work of this school is *Kyrios Christos* (a history of the faith in Christ from the beginnings of Christianity to Irenaeus), by Wilhelm Bousset, Göttingen, 1921. The school is best represented in England by Dr. Kirsopp Lake, *Landmarks of Early Christianity*, and the larger work, *The Beginnings of Christianity*, in which he collaborates with Dr. Foakes Jackson.

[2] Bousset, *op. cit.* p. 74.

[3] P. 37 : " Hier nicht der historische Jesus spricht, sondern die Gemeinde, die ihren Glauben an den Menschensohn verkündet."

themselves to be about to be translated from the miseries and bondage of material life and death into immortality and bliss. These mystery religions, about which I shall have more to say, were " sacramental "—that is to say, participation in the blessings of the redemption offered by them was to be secured by undergoing certain ceremonies of initiation and subsequent fellowship in a community of initiated persons, who held some secrets of mystical knowledge not communicated to the outer world. And they had emancipated themselves from their original national or local boundaries, and become, as we may say, world religions. In these mystery religions the hero-God, who was the object of worship, was called " Lord." In the Christian communities, then, of the Hellenistic world Jesus also began to be called " Lord "; and this title, for the majority of the Gentile converts, carried with it all the associations of their former cults. Even before St. Paul came to the front in these Gentile churches, they were already in part assimilated to these Pagan societies. But it was St. Paul's genius which, on a basis of the old Jewish monotheism and apocalyptic beliefs, developed a doctrine of Jesus the Lord, the author of individual and present salvation " in Christ " or " in the Spirit," mediated by sacramental actions and in a sacramental fellowship, for any man of any race, whereby the old Jewish and the new Hellenic ideas of religion were brought together in one system; and this was the basis on which what we know as the theology and sacramental system of the Catholic church was founded. Substantially the same principles later found similar expression in the theology of the unknown thinker whom the Church called St. John. This was the second great transformation by which the Christ of St. Paul and of " St. John," which is almost the Christ of the Catholic Church, takes the place of the apocalyptic Christ, and becomes still further removed from the Jesus of history.

The educated Englishman to-day who is interested in religion is fairly familiar with the Liberal Protestant conception of Jesus, and with the conception of the Apocalyptic school. But the theory of the school of Bousset is still strange to him. However we shall hear more of it. We are being frequently warned by grave voices that this is the most important of the theories with which orthodoxy or traditional Christianity is confronted. I shall, of course, have to return to it, and to the others just described. But for the present I leave them. The method which I propose to follow is first of all positive not negative. Confessedly all these theories involve leaving out and repudiating as unhistorical large elements in the Synoptic Gospels and Acts as they stand. Now I am making no claim for complete freedom from error in the Gospels. But I have sought to establish [1] their claim to be regarded as serious history compiled by competent men, which must not be violently dealt with ; and I have given my reasons at some length for refusing to regard the strictly miraculous and supernatural elements in the Gospel narratives as incredible on *a priori* grounds.[2]

I do not propose to go over this ground again ; but perhaps I had better briefly restate the position with regard to the Gospels and Acts which it was sought to establish in the first volume and which is to be taken for granted in this.

The position is (1) that the second of our Gospels was really written by John Mark, who from his youth up had lived in his mother's house at Jerusalem, at the very centre of the apostolic fellowship, and had been afterwards the companion of his cousin Barnabas and of St. Paul, and more particularly,

---

[1] See *Belief in God*, chaps. viii. and xi.
[2] *Belief in God*, chaps. ix. and x.

according to an early and trustworthy tradition, of St. Peter, whose customary teaching about the things said and done by Christ he set himself to reproduce as faithfully as possible ; (2) that the third Gospel, which is based upon Mark's material, and also upon another document containing matter common to the third Gospel with the first, which is commonly called Q, as well as upon information from other " first-hand " sources, was really written by the physician Luke, the companion of St. Paul, who has explained his motive and his method in a luminous preface to his Gospel, which its contents amply vindicate ; and (3) that the Acts is part of the same work as the Gospel, by the same author, who had the fullest opportunities of obtaining trustworthy information about the beginnings of the Christian Church. It follows that these books ought to be taken, provisionally but in all seriousness, as credible historical documents, unless indeed they should prove themselves otherwise.

I propose then that we should build the structure of our argument in the main upon the Gospels of St. Mark and St. Luke and upon the Acts, and upon the other books of the New Testament which are not involved in serious controversy, letting nothing of importance rest upon the unsupported testimony of the first Gospel and using the fourth only as subsidiary.[1]

But I would call my readers' attention to the fact that to-day controversy is not so much concerned as formerly with the authenticity and date of documents. Thus perhaps the most important recent German work on " Christian origins " is that of Eduard Meyer, the distinguished author of the immense *History of Antiquity* (*Geschichte des Alterthums*). He comes to his task [2] therefore on the basis

---

[1] But see below, Chapter IV., pp. 107 f.
[2] The *Ursprung und Anfänge des Christenthums*, 1921, in two volumes, awaiting a third.

of very wide knowledge and a high general authority as a historian. He talks with some impatience of modern criticism as unreasonable, meaning, I suppose, specially modern New Testament criticism.[1] He ascribes the third Gospel and the Acts to Luke [2] and the second Gospel to Mark, the " interpreter " (Dolmetscher) of Peter, according to the tradition,[3] and recognizes the work of Matthew behind our first Gospel. If he has in fact to give his readers a conception of Jesus widely different from that of the Evangelists, it is not because they were not in a position to know the facts, but because he cannot apparently conceive of the supernatural as being really historical.[4] It is just this assumption that I desire we should not take with us to our study of the Evangelists, but should approach them with an open mind and give them a chance to tell their story as to those who have ears to hear.

II

All the Gospels put the activity of Jesus upon the immediate background of the preaching of the great prophet who deeply stirred Jewish society, John the Baptist. Josephus, the Jewish historian, gives some account of him as a good man and a preacher of righteousness, who used baptism as his instrument for gathering the followers of righteousness together ; and tells us that because of the great excitement which he caused among the

---

[1] E.g. vol. i. p. 314 : " How that (i.e. that the author of the Fourth Gospel intended to represent himself as being John the son of Zebedee) can have been called in question is one of the many things which remain unintelligible to me in the positions of modern criticism."

[2] See p. 51.   [3] P. 159.

[4] See, for example, his account of the Last Supper, pp. 174 ff., and of the saying of Matt. xi 25 ff., p. 291.

people and the persuasive power over them which he showed, Herod put him to death for fear he should cause some rebellion; and he thought it better to act betimes and put him out of the way rather than to repent at leisure for having done nothing.[1] In all the Gospels he is presented to us, not only as a preacher of righteousness, who revived the memories of the old prophets by the tremendous force of his denunciations and encouragements, but also as one who was conscious of a definite mission to proclaim the immediate advent of the Kingdom of God, to herald the Christ who was to come, and " to make ready a people prepared for the Lord." [2]

There are matters of detail concerning the Baptist on which the Gospels appear to disagree, but on the chief points which alone concern our present enquiry we may feel sure.

(1) The spirit of ancient prophecy revived in John in the sense especially that for him the coming of the Kingdom was as far as possible from being something which the nation, as it was, could afford to welcome. Their eager nationalism was not enough. God who was to visit them in the coming of His

---

[1] *Antiq.* xviii. 52. Josephus' particular phrases are obscure, though the general sense is plain. The editors of the *Beginnings of Christianity*, pp. 101 ff., put a definite meaning on Josephus which, I think, Mr. Creed (*J.T.S.*, Oct. 1921, p. 59) has shown to be mistaken.

The motive assigned to Herod for John's imprisonment is not necessarily exclusive of the motive assigned by the Gospels. His motives may well have been mixed. It has been pointed out (*Belief in God*, p. 206) that Josephus, writing always to conciliate Roman opinion, observes a discreet silence about Christianity; and his silence about any relation of John to Jesus should not be allowed to discredit the Gospel account.

[2] The phrase, " the kingdom of heaven is at hand," occurs only in St. Matthew iii 2; but the same message is implied in all the other Gospels. Schweitzer tries to persuade us that he believed himself sent to prepare for—not the Christ, but Elijah, who was to precede Christ. But " the mightier than I, the latchet of whose shoes I am unworthy to stoop down and unloose," who " *shall baptize you with the Holy Ghost* " (Mark i 7, 8), can be none other than the Christ.

Christ would take no account of their descent from
Abraham. He demanded a holy people; and
sinners in Zion, however alert their national zeal,
had as good cause as in the days of Isaiah to tremble
at the approach of the day of God as before devouring
fire and everlasting burnings. A fundamental
change of mind was needed, and John's baptism
was the symbol of admission to a new Israel—a
" people prepared for the Lord."

(2) It is the testimony of all the Gospels that
John not only announced the immediate coming of
the Kingdom and the Christ, but recognized Jesus,
on the occasion of His coming to his baptism, as
" the greater one " who was to come. The meagre-
ness of Mark's narrative, till he reaches (at ver. 14)
the Galilean ministry, suggests that only at that
point did his special information begin. What
precedes is a bare summary of what everyone knew.
But his brief narrative implies that, though the
vision of the opening heaven and the descending
Spirit was for Jesus only, the divine voice was for
John also—whether heard with his outward ear
or only in his inward spirit, like the word of the
Lord by the old prophets, we need not enquire—
and it proclaimed Jesus the Son of God, by which
was then understood, I think, neither more nor less
than the Christ. This information must have been
conveyed, we should suppose, by John himself to
some of the first disciples; and St. Peter in the
Acts represents the companionship of the apostles
with one another and with the Lord Jesus as
" beginning from the baptism of John." [1] There
are differences in detail among the Gospels,[2] but
there is a common witness which we have no reason
for hesitating to accept.

But with the narrative of the Galilean ministry
of Jesus, we get upon the ground of chief importance.

[1] Acts i 21-2.   [2] See appended note p. 68.

III

If we are to do our best to judge of the impression produced by Jesus upon the first group of His disciples, and especially upon those who came closest to Him and whom He chose to be "the Twelve," we should read, at one sitting, with as fresh and free a mind as possible, ignoring difficulties of detail, the Gospel of St. Mark down to the beginning of the Passion narrative, and then, again at one sitting, the Gospel of St. Luke from the beginning of the ministry down to the Passion, and then at least the Sermon on the Mount and the Parables in St. Matthew. What follows represents my often-renewed impression of such readings, of the justice of which my readers must judge.

To speak in the most general terms, I submit that whatever previous ideas may have been in the minds of these disciples concerning the purpose of God for Israel, and concerning His kingdom and the Christ who was to come, were quite overwhelmed by a new influence or impression which threw everything else into the background—the overwhelming impression of the person of Jesus—"the Son of Man," or "the Man," as He called Himself.

I do not think it is possible to doubt (1) that the evangelists intend to convey the impression that Jesus, habitually from the beginning of His ministry, called Himself the Son of Man.[1]

(2) That He really so called Himself. Seeing that, except on one occasion, when Stephen, at the moment of his martyrdom, calls Jesus the Son of Man, with obvious reference to His own words before the Sanhedrin (Mark xiv 62), the first Christians, according

---

[1] See *Beginnings*, pp. 374–7: "The opinion of the writers of the Gospels is thus clear that Jesus used the phrase ; that he used it of Himself." "The writers understand Jesus to refer to Himself." So also Bousset, *Kyrios Christos*, pp. 5 ff.

to the evidence, did not use this title of their Lord
at all, or in addressing Him, it seems the extreme of
perversity to maintain that the attribution of the
title to Jesus is due to the early community,[1] and
that He probably did not in fact use the title as a
designation of Himself.

(3) That, whereas after Peter's confession of His
Messiahship, the title acquires in the mouth of Jesus
a quite distinctive Messianic significance, it was as
first used by Him plainly not intended or understood
in a Messianic sense at all. For we are repeatedly
told that Jesus was refusing to make any public
claim to be the Messiah. The Aramaic word, translated Son of Man, would apparently have meant
simply " the man." Its use by Jesus may be compared to its frequent use in the case of Ezechiel as
the name by which the divine voice called him.
There it signifies that he is a man, and also a man
singled out for a special vocation.[2] So also in Ps.
viii 4 it represents mankind viewed, as we may say,
in the ideal. I suppose when our Lord first so called
Himself, quite without reference to Messianic distinction or glory,[3] He meant His hearers to think of
Him as " the man " in some specially representative
sense, though I should shrink from such a modern-
sounding phrase as " the ideal man."

The Jews were distinguished by profound reverence for their teachers, who were primarily teachers
of religion, and those who heard Jesus came very
speedily to regard Him as a great teacher sent from
God. They were impressed at starting by the novelty
of His teaching. " What is this ? " men cried out.
" A new teaching ! " [4] Already they had heard what
seemed a new teaching from John the Baptist. If in

---

[1] So Bousset and Kirsopp Lake.
[2] See Ezech. ii 1, iii 1, and constantly.
[3] As in Mark ii 10, 28, Luke vii 34, ix 58, xii 10 (all from Q).
[4] Mark i 27.

substance it was the teaching of the ancient prophets
revived, yet, at least by contrast to what many
generations of the people had received from their
official guides, or by comparison with popular ideas
about the Christ who was to come and the kingdom
of God, it was very new teaching which they heard
from John. And doubtless they were prepared for
the like from Jesus. But what they heard—for instance in the sermon given by St. Luke, or the longer
version, the " Sermon on the Mount " in St. Matthew,
or the teaching about the merely relative obligation
of the Sabbath, or about the new wine which could
not be put into old bottles, or about sin having its
seat only in the heart—the great saying of which
St. Mark [1] says that it " cleansed all meats," or again
our Lord's estimate of the absolute worth of every
human soul—all this no doubt struck in their hearts
a profounder and richer note of novelty than anything said by John the Baptist.[2]

Moreover, we are bound to believe that some of
the disciples at least were impressed sufficiently to
be able to treasure the words of Jesus—doubtless in
many cases the often-repeated words—and to reproduce them accurately, with even sharp precision.
This was in the Jewish schools the quite normal
faculty of the pupils of any teacher.[3] We may be
prepared to maintain against all comers that the
reports in the Synoptic Gospels of the words of Jesus
bear, with not much exception, the quite unmistakable stamp of genuineness. This, I think, must be
the verdict of the literary sense. Nevertheless, it
is also quite apparent that the disciples had very

[1] St. Mark vii 19.
[2] There are admirable modern accounts of the ethical teaching
of our Lord, amongst which I still think *Ecce Homo* pre-eminent.
But in this book I am concerned only with the estimate of our
Lord's person and restrain myself from the consideration of His
teaching.
[3] See *Belief in God*, pp. 191-2.

little intelligent perception, during our Lord's human lifetime, of His meaning. They were capable of what we cannot but call stupid misunderstandings. They were even astonishingly dense, unimaginative, and unsympathetic. It would be quite untrue, we feel as we read, to interpret the influence of Jesus upon them as the influence of His teaching upon receptive pupils. It really was not in the main the substance of His teaching that was gradually making them new men. Unmistakably it was the commanding authority of His person and their unbounded faith in Him.[1]

Critics of the orthodox tradition are always reproving the theologians for having overstated the prominence of the person, and the personal claim, of Jesus. "To lay down any 'doctrine' about his person and his dignity, independently of the Gospel, was quite outside his sphere of ideas."[2] "He does not talk about himself."[3] The measure of truth in such statements we shall have to consider later. But let there be no mistake. The dominant influence of Jesus upon the disciples did not lie in anything that He taught them, whether about Himself or about God or about the kingdom of God, but in "The Man" Himself—in the impression of overwhelming authority, certainly supernatural and "of God," resident in Him.

It is this that constrains them at the beginning to leave all and follow Him. It is authority which expresses itself in His works of healing, especially, but not only, the healing of the possessed. The sense of it is vividly presented to us in the case of

---

[1] Simkhovitch, *op. cit.* p. 78, has a very good passage about the difference in powerful movements which stir mankind between faith in ideas and understanding of ideas : " Do not think for the moment that it is understanding of the ideas which moves mankind ; it is their faith in the ideas." With the disciples it was not even yet faith in the ideas of Jesus. It was simply a bewildered confidence in Him.

[2] Harnack, *What is Christianity ?* p. 129.

[3] *Beginnings of Christianity*, p. 288.

one who was neither a disciple nor a Jew—the
Roman centurion who had been paying attention
to Jesus, and had gained the conviction that He
occupied in nature a position comparable to his own
in the army. No doubt, that is to say, He was
" under authority "—the authority of God ; but
within the sphere of His activity He could do as He
willed with nature, as the centurion could with his
subordinates. " With authority He commands," and
it obeys Him. He speaks, and it is done.[1] So again
it is that the ruler of the synagogue falls at His feet—
full of belief in His power.[2] That is the impression.
His authority in working what we call miracles and
what the Gospels call " powers " is paralleled by His
moral authority. He taught as He worked, " as one
having authority " of a divine kind in Himself. So
as " the Man " He claims to forgive the sins of the
paralytic and, to prove His right to do so, He heals
his disease. And in teaching He does not generally,
though He does at times, refer beyond Himself—
" This is the word of the Lord," or " Thus saith
Scripture." Even in revising the divinely-given law
of Sinai, it was enough to say " But I say unto you."

Many moderns seem quite to underestimate or
almost to ignore this overwhelming impression of
authority. The disciples are being led to believe
that in the physical world, though He will do nothing
to help Himself, He can do anything to help those
in need, or themselves, His companions. Such was
doubtless the impression of His feeding of the five
thousand out of so miserably inadequate a supply, or
rescuing the disciples suddenly, when they roused Him
out of sleep in the storm at sea. They were growing
to believe that He would be equal to all the emer-
gencies which might occur. And in the moral sphere
His word was enough. They could not question it.
And though He did not seem to know everything, yet

[1] Matt. viii 5–13, Luke vii 1–10.   [2] Mark v 22.

He had a strange power of reading men's hearts; and at times He spoke as if He were the final judge of men, not only in view of their public acts but of their secret lives. In certain of the parables this assumption that He is the final judge is plain.[1] But it is implied elsewhere. We think of such a saying as " Many shall come to me in that day . . . then will I protest unto them, I never knew you." [2] Here what is implied, both in St. Matthew and St. Luke's version, is that nothing matters to a man at last except the judgment of Jesus on him, and that this judgment goes to the heart of the reality and cannot be misled by appearances or professions. So elsewhere we hear that to deny Him and be ashamed of Him here in this world means to be disowned by Him at last, and that that is the final disaster.[3] He is the ultimate judge.

There are three other kindred features in the impression which our Lord plainly made on His disciples which we shall note. He spoke as being infallible. He was indeed as far as possible from being a dogmatic teacher who loved to teach men a secret lore *ex cathedra*. There was nothing about Him of this tone. And He did not shrink from telling the disciples of something which was not within His knowledge. But whatever He did teach, He taught as if it were certainly true, and (unlike the prophets who delivered a message from God) as if the fountain

[1] So most dramatically in Matt. xxv 19. I know that St. Matthew seems at times to heighten the Messianic colouring of our Lord's sayings. But I agree with Sanday (*The Life of Christ in Recent Research*, p. 128, note 1) that it is " wanton " to doubt this parable. See also the Tares, Matt. xiii 41, and the Talents, Luke xix 11 and Matt. xxv 14. Dr. Rashdall, *Conscience and Christ*, p. 48, seeks to substantiate the doubt whether our Lord ever spoke of Himself as the actual judge. But the witness that He did is not only St. Matthew's.

[2] Matt. vii 22 ; cf. Luke xiii 24 ff., which is vivid and clear in its implication.

[3] Mark viii 38, Luke ix 26, Matt. x 33 ; cf. Luke xxi 36 " To stand before the Son of Man."

of truth was in Himself. "No man knoweth the Father save the Son and he to whomsoever the Son willeth to reveal Him." "Heaven and earth shall pass away, but my words shall not pass away." Secondly, there was not in His language the least trace of a sense of sinfulness, or even possible unworthiness, such as has possessed at all times prophets and seers. Finally, there was an exclusiveness about His claim on men, as if He were not merely one of the representatives of God but in some profound sense the only one. He appears, indeed, to delegate to the Twelve and the Seventy authority to teach and to heal diseases, but this is in His name or in utter dependence on Him. In Himself He seems to brook no rival. "Come unto me," He says, "and I will give you rest. Take my yoke upon you and learn of me." "He that loveth father or mother more than me, is not worthy of me." "Follow me and let the dead bury their own dead." This sort of language seems to breathe nothing less than the divine jealousy over human souls.

Now all this time questions were pending in the minds of the disciples as to who He was. There was some secret, some mystery, about His person.

The report of the divine voice at the baptism, the story of the temptation in the wilderness which Jesus must at some time have communicated to them, the strange cries of the demoniacs "Thou art the Son of God—the holy one of God," and their horror of Him as of some awful power, and also certain solemn and hardly intelligible words of His own, made them conscious of a mystery. There were names, "Son of Man," "Son of God," "Christ," which were in their ears and would have to be explained. But while all this process of questioning was going on, something deeper was happening. Beyond all possibility of question, and seemingly by His own deliberate intention, Jesus, so far as they

yielded their faith to Him, was taking the place of
God, or in modern phrase gaining "the values of
God," for their souls. Not all the values of God.
They did not, I suppose, at that time dream of Him
as the creator of the world and the ruler of the course
of nature. No doubt they thought of Him as wholly
under God. But within the sphere of their personal
lives, He had been growing to have to them the
values of God, as the object of their absolute faith,
their infallible refuge and informer and protector
and guide.

This seems to me quite an irresistible impression.
There is an old saying of unknown origin—either
Jesus Christ was God or He was not a good man—
which critics sometimes treat with great derision. I
do not think it can be so derided. There is more
in it than they seem to recognize. How could men
be in the constant companionship of the Jesus of
the Synoptic Gospels—such as we have been seeking
to describe Him, surely without exaggeration—
without coming to be in the attitude towards Him
which is only legitimate towards God? And was
He not deliberately encouraging, and bringing about
this attitude towards Himself in their souls? Did
He not exhibit the sort of exclusive claim which
suggests nothing else but the "jealousy" of God?
And is it not the supreme sin of pride or arrogance
for any man, even a commissioned prophet, to allow
himself to assume this exclusive position? Must
not every commissioned servant be always crying
"Send, O Lord, by whom thou wilt send! Thou
hast many messengers and all of them subject to
error and weakness, I most of all"? The implication of infallible, exclusive authority which seems
to inhere in the words and tone of Jesus does
seem to me to express, if not the jealousy of God,
then some such quality as lies at the heart of all
spiritual tyranny and false sacerdotalism.

5

IV

We have now to consider the question of the
person of Jesus from another point of view, that is,
of the titles by which He was called or by which He
called Himself. I have argued that if we regard
the Synoptic Gospels as giving us good history, we
must also regard it as certain that John the Baptist
pointed to Jesus as the Christ who was to come, and
did so on the ground, in part at least, of the divine
voice heard by himself at the baptism of Jesus proclaiming Him " the beloved Son in whom God was
well pleased." The record of the baptism as given
in the Gospels would have come, we should suppose,
from John. Whether " the voice," either on this
occasion or at the Transfiguration, was one which
an indifferent by-stander would have heard with
his ears, or whether it came, like " the word of the
Lord " to the prophets, only to the spiritual hearing,
we need not discuss, any more than the question
whether the narrative of the temptation, which I
suppose our Lord related to the Twelve, is
intended as an allegoric expression of events which
happened only in Christ's consciousness or as a
record of outward events.[1] In either case it is
certain that Jesus was believed by Himself and by
John to have been divinely certified at His baptism
as the Son of God and the temptation of Jesus involved His consciousness that He was so.[2] So

[1] Though, for myself, I can feel no doubt (with Origen) that the
former is the true interpretation ; see *Epistles of St. John*, pp. 236–7.

[2] I see no sign whatever in the Gospels of any advance in our
Lord's estimate of His own person. This idea, which is constantly
asserted, as if it were to be taken for granted, may or may not be
open to theological objection, but the question need not be raised.
There is no evidence. And whether the word of God at the
baptism, " In thee I have been well pleased " (εὐδόκησα), refers
to the past of the human life of Jesus or to the " eternal past " or to
the Christ as prefigured in prophecy, it certainly does not support
the idea that the moment of baptism made any difference to His
Sonship. The " Western " reading of St. Luke iii 22, " Thou art

says the only story we have of His childhood—the scene in the Temple when He was twelve years old—" Wist ye not that I must be about my Father's business," or " in my Father's house." It follows that those who received the testimony of John and Jesus believed Him to be truly, in some sense, the Son of God, and when they heard the demoniacs so hailing Him and heard Jesus seeking to silence them, they must have felt that there was mystery attaching to this title; but on the whole, they probably simply identified it in meaning with the Christ, the king of David's line in whom God's promises to Israel were to be fulfilled, neither more nor less. It would not appear that till St. Paul comes on the scene the Church generally realized its true significance.[1] It is true that there is no evidence of the title Son of God being used in the later Jewish literature of the Christ, but it was twice used of the Son of David or of David in the Psalms [2] and of the righteous man in the Book of Wisdom,[3] and the evidence appears to be conclusive that the disciples took it as meaning no more than the Christ.[4]

my beloved son; on this day have I begotten thee," is surely due to a reminiscence of Ps. ii 7.

[1] See later, pp. 78 ff.

[2] Ps. ii (which is treated as Messianic in the Psalms of Solomon) verses 7 and (perhaps) 12, and lxxxix 26–7. See Dalman's *Words of Jesus* (Eng. trans.), pp. 268 ff.

[3] Wisdom ii 16, 18.

[4] So it appears to have been understood when the demoniacs hailed Him by the title " Son of God," in Mark iii 11, v 7; cf. Matt. viii 29, Luke viii 28: " He suffered not the devils to speak because they knew him "—*i.e.* knew Him as Christ; cf. Luke iv 41, where, after the exclamation " Thou art the Son of God," is the explanation " They knew that he was the Christ." So at the trial, Matt. xxvi 63, and parallels in Mark and Luke; and when our Lord is mocked upon the Cross (see Matt. xxvii 40–3; cf. Mark xv 32). St. Matthew seems to represent the disciples as identifying " Son of God " with Christ in the confession of Peter, xvi 15. The same appears to be the representation of John i 49. The " King of Israel " is the synonym for " the Son of God."

This, however, is by no means true of the sense
in which our Lord used it of Himself. The great
passage, " No one knoweth the Son save the Father :
neither doth any know the Father save the Son,"
which occurs in both St. Matthew and St. Luke,
and with its wonderful context is authentic beyond
reasonable dispute, asserts a relationship of mutual
knowledge between Father and Son which suggests
something essential and eternal.[1] So the phrase
" Of that day or that hour knoweth no one, not even
the angels in heaven, neither the Son," [2] which again
must surely be authentic, because no later believer
would have attributed such limitation of knowledge
to the Christ, suggests at least a super-angelic sonship. Once more in the parable of the husbandmen
Jesus distinguishes Himself as the only Son sharply
from all the other messengers of God.[3] As I have
said, it would not appear as if these utterances made
much impression at the time. The thoughts of the

[1] Matt. xi 27, Luke x 22. See Dalman, pp. 283, 285: " But
in this case of mutual understanding, its thoroughness [*i.e.*
the thoroughness of mutual knowledge] and absolute infallibility
are assumed. He who stands in so uniquely close a relation to
God is the only possible mediator of the kind, and also at the same
time the absolutely reliable revealer of the whole wealth of the
divine mysteries." . . . " The passages appear to imply that Jesus
had shown no cognizance of any beginning in this relationship.
It seems to be an innate property of His personality." See also
Harnack, *Sayings of Jesus* (Eng. trans., Williams and Norgate),
p. 302. " A formal likeness of Father and Son, who are distinguished only by the different names, and a relationship of Father
and Son which never had a beginning, but remains ever the same,"
is here expressed. This is unacceptable to Harnack and, quite
arbitrarily, he omits part of the text. Other writers make the whole
passage the work of a later Jewish Christian prophet, basing himself
on Ecclus. li 1, 23, 26, 27. But this sort of criticism can dissolve
any evidence. I shall recur to the passage later (see pp. 89 f, 109 f).

We notice that our Lord never speaks to the disciples of "our
Father," except in giving them for their use the Lord's Prayer.
He speaks of "your Father," or "the Father," and of "my
Father." This appears with express emphasis in John xx 17.
But it is apparent also in the Synoptists.

[2] Matt. xiii 32 and Matt. xxiv 36 (R.V.).

[3] Mark xii 6 ; also Matthew and Luke.

disciples were confined to the question, Is he the
Christ? But they have survived among our Lord's
most indisputable words, and they seem to me to
bear beyond question the sense of a sonship unique,
superhuman and essential. There is not really much
difference between what they involve and what is
taught in the discourses of St. John.

It is profoundly characteristic of what I have
called our Lord's undogmatic method that He should
have uttered these solemn sayings—which seem
to open out such momentous glimpses into the
mystery of His personality—but, as it were, incidentally or by implication only, and left them
as germs to fertilize later in men's minds. So with
regard to His being the Christ, though in that case
there were many suggestions from without, He chose
that the conviction of His messiahship should mature
in their own minds and become a confession of their
own lips, not something dictated to them by Him.
Thus, under circumstances of deepening anxiety,
and in or near a city the very name of which—
Caesarea Philippi—spoke of alien and foreign influences repugnant to the heart of every Jew, He
asked them the question, "Who do men say that
I am?" and then pressed home upon them the more
searching question, "But who do ye say that I
am?" and Peter replied with the great confession,
"Thou art the Christ." It was a decisive moment,
and it strikes us as most natural that our Lord
should have signalized the greatness of the moment
by meeting the confession with the solemn and
rich benediction which Matthew alone records:
"Blessed art thou, Simon Bar-Jona, for this is
not anything thou hast learnt by human influence.
It is a real disclosure made by my heavenly Father
in thy soul. It is a conviction wrought in thee
by God."

Henceforth, though the world is not at present to

know it, the secret that Jesus is the Christ is an open secret in the apostolic company, and Jesus proceeds at once to build upon it in the way most calculated to test them and terrify them. " From that time began Jesus to show unto His disciples, how that he must go unto Jerusalem, and suffer many things of the elders and chief priests and scribes, and be killed and the third day be raised up." This prophecy is made " openly " and repeated again and again.[1] The ideas suggested were profoundly contrary to the vague and elastic, but always glorious and radiant, ideas of the Messianic king which the Jews, and the disciples amongst them, entertained. They had all along had cause for anxiety as to whether the crowds drawn by the " powers " and by the words of their Master were the prelude to His real triumph. It was quite plain that there was a wide interval between welcoming His words and wonderful benefits and really obeying from the heart His searching doctrine. Of the latter there was no sign on any large scale. And the leaders of the nation appeared to be all against Him. Nevertheless there had been something radiant and triumphant about their earlier experiences with Him in Galilee. Nothing less is implied in the description which Jesus gave of His company, in explanation of their having no special fasts of their own, such as the Pharisees had, and John's disciples. He compared them to a happy band of friends round a bridegroom in the moment of his joy and triumph. No doubt He struck the note of loss and sorrow to come—" The days will come when the bridegroom shall be taken away from them "—but the present scenery is painted in radiant colours. It might be a fitting prelude for the glorious days of the Messiah. But anxiety had deepened ; and now, just when they had given full expression to their faith that He verily was the Christ, He let

[1] Mark viii 31, ix 12, 31, x 33–4.

the blow fall upon them in all its weight, and drove it down upon them again and again. The way of the Christ was to be the way of the Cross, the way of failure and death. And Peter's impulsive protest brought upon him the sternest rebuke "Get thee behind me, Satan !"

We cannot doubt that this profound change in the idea of the Christ was effected by our Lord's identifying Himself, the Son of Man, with the Suffering Servant of Jehovah in the later Isaiah. In these wonderful chapters (Is. xl onward) " the servant of Jehovah " is first Israel in general (xli 8 f.), and then apparently the select remnant of the people, who alone are the true Israel (xlix 1–3), through whom alone the purpose of God can realize itself. But though no doubt the prophet begins by using " the Servant " as a personification of the nation or group within the nation, yet he appears to be carried away as he contemplates the Servant to think of him as a real person who is by his obedience and his undeserved sufferings and death to win the redemption of " the many." We feel this already in earlier passages,[1] but the impression becomes overwhelming in the familiar passage (lii 13 and liii), which sounds to us for the most part, as we hear it, as simply the history of the passion of Jesus written beforehand. I will present the passage in Dr. Driver's careful analysis[2]:

The preface in cap. lii 13–15 describes " the ideal servant's exaltation after an antecedent period of humiliation and distress." Then this is developed in cap. liii. The first part (1–9) presents " three several stages in the ideal Servant's humiliation : the persons speaking are the Israelites, represented as at length perceiving the truth to which they had before been blind, and

---

[1] *E.g.* 1 4–10.
[2] *Isaiah, his Life and Times* (Nisbet), pp. 152–5, very slightly abbreviated.

reviewing the period of their incredulity. First, in spite of the prophetic report, or message, pointing to him, few or none, they say, amongst his nation recognized him : he had no outward grace, or beauty of form, attracting attention ; he grew up in their midst like some mean or lowly shrub, struggling to maintain itself in an arid soil : men despised him, and even held aloof from him in aversion. In truth, however," [so they proceed to confess], they themselves were the occasion of his distressed appearance : " he was bearing the consequences of our sins, although we in our blindness imagined him to be stricken, smitten of God, and afflicted "— *i.e.* smitten, as by a divine judgment, for some heinous offence—" whereas, in fact, it was we who had gone astray, and the penalty, instead of recoiling upon us, lighted in its entirety upon him. So far from being guilty himself, he bore the guilt of others and relieved them of its penal consequences. Though he suffered willingly, and made no answer to his accusers, he was still oppressed : first imprisoned by an unjust sentence, he was afterwards led away to execution, not one among his contemporaries considering that he was thus cut off, not for his own sins, but for those of the people. In spite of the innocence of his life, his death was that of a malefactor and his end inglorious."

[The final paragraph, however, reverses the character of the scene and introduces the promise for the future.] " It was Jehovah's pleasure thus to bruise him : but out of death will spring a new life : after his soul has been made a guilt offering, he will live again, enjoy long life, and be rewarded with the satisfaction of seeing God's work, or ' pleasure ' prosper in his hand. Possessed of an intimate ' knowledge ' of the dealings and purposes of God, he will ' justify the many,' whilst his final reward for having submitted to the death of a transgressor will be that he will be ranked as a conqueror and honoured among the great ones of the earth : inasmuch as ' he bore the sins of the many and made intercession for the transgressors.' "

This astonishing vision of the prophet appears to have made little or no permanent impression on the

imagination of Israel.[1] Its idea of kingship quite
escaped them. They never identified the glorious
Messiah with the Suffering Servant. This was the
work of Jesus. Some modern critics have ventured
to doubt whether Jesus shows the influence of this
prophecy. But, I think, quite unreasonably. Two
points seem to prove it :—(1) that our Lord plainly
regards the sufferings of the Christ and His death
as necessary because prefigured in Scripture.[2] " How
is it written of the Son of Man ? " " The Son of
Man goeth as it is written of Him." " How, then,
should the Scriptures be fulfilled, that thus it must
be ? " And the same intense conviction of prophecy
and fulfilment appears in the earliest Church,[3] and
it appears from the beginning associated with the
figure of the " servant of Jehovah." [4] Indeed it
could hardly have been otherwise, for, though the
Old Testament may provide types and suggestions
of the idea of a suffering Christ, it contains nothing
which can be compared with Isaiah liii in vividness
and impressiveness.

(2) Our Lord seems plainly to identify Himself
with " the Servant," when He quotes from the
" Servant " section of Isaiah to interpret His mission
at Nazareth,[5] and St. Luke also represents Him

[1] It left apparent traces on certain psalms and on the books of
Job and Maccabees (see below, pp. 285 f), but it never became recognized for its importance in the Jewish tradition. In the *Targum*
on Is. liii, which has recently been translated by the Rev. R. B.
Aytoun (see *J.T.S.*, Jan. 1922, pp. 179–80), the Servant is interpreted of the Messiah, but, by a violent perversion of the sense of
the passage, all the marks of ignominy and shame are diverted from
him upon his people and his adversaries. This is a most curious
document.

[2] Mark ix 12, cf. Matt. xxvi 24, 54, 56, Luke xviii 31, xxiv
25–7, 46.

[3] 1 Cor. xv 3, Acts ii 23, xvii 2–3, xxvi 22–3, 1 Peter i 10–11.

[4] See Acts iii 13 " His servant Jesus," and 26, and iv 27, 30
" Thy holy servant Jesus." So Philip expounds to the eunuch,
viii 31 ff. So 1 Peter ii 21 ff. and Matt. viii 17.

[5] Luke iv 18, from Is. lxi. Driver is surely right in representing
these words as put in the mouth of the Servant.

as quoting of His own end the words concerning the
Servant, "He was reckoned with transgressors." [1]
But perhaps more convincing in their originality
are the two passages in St. Mark where our
Lord speaks of Himself as to give His life a
"ransom *for many*," and of the cup, at the Last
Supper, as "this is my blood of the covenant which
is shed *for many*." [2] It does not seem to me to be
doubtful that this "for many," twice repeated, is a
reference to Isaiah liii. "My righteous servant shall
justify *many*." "He bare the sin of *many*." [3] This
is all the more noticeable because the significance
of the precise word does not seem to have been
perceived, so that it has vanished from the versions
of St. Luke and St. Paul.

Our Lord then, who was plainly set radically to
revise the conception of the Christ, and who, though
He did not disclaim His Davidic descent, yet was
manifestly anxious not to emphasize it,[4] deeply
involved as it was in ideas of temporal sovereignty,
sought to effect His purpose by identifying the
Christ, as no one had done before Him,[5] with the
Suffering Servant, and that by associating both with
the title He had chosen for Himself—the Son of
Man or the Man. Henceforth the Man, the Christ,
and the Suffering Servant are the same person. And
one more step had to be taken to complete our
Lord's profoundly new doctrine of the Christ, and
that was, as the sequel to suffering and death, to

Luke xxii 37.

[2] Mark x 45, xiv 24 ; so also in St. Matthew, cf. Heb. ix 28, Rom.
v 15.

[3] Is. liii 11, 12.   In the LXX the word πολλοῖς, πολλούς, πολλῶν
recurs three times.   Also as one reads the LXX of Is. liii 12—
παρεδόθη εἰς θάνατον—it is difficult to doubt that this phrase promoted the constant use of this verb in connection with our Lord's
betrayal and surrender to death.

[4] On our Lord's Davidic descent as a real fact, see Dalman,
op. cit. pp. 316 ff.

[5] Unless, indeed, John the Baptist : see John i 29.

introduce in a new form, what was already suggested in Isaiah liii, the idea of resurrection and glory. In a new form—for He identified the Christ with the figure of glorified manhood in the visions of Daniel.

The passage has been already quoted and its original sense explained. It is an image of the people of God, by the side of the world-empires imaged in the four great beasts—" And I saw in the night visions, and behold there came with the clouds of heaven one like unto a son of man, and he came even to the Ancient of Days. . . . And there was given him dominion and glory and a kingdom, that all the people, nations and languages should serve him ; his dominion is an everlasting dominion, which shall not pass away, and his kingdom that which shall not be destroyed." Now, I have already explained how probably before our Lord's time, in the Similitudes of the Book of Enoch, this figure of the chosen people was converted into the figure of a heavenly being, " The Elect One," pre-existing in the heavens, who at the end of the world was to be manifested in glory as the agent of divine judgment, seated on the very throne of God. This being, first described as in countenance like a man and possibly called " The Son of Man," [1] is the " Anointed One," and, as one may say, is a substitute for the old prophetic Messiah. This is a truer expression than to say He is identified with the Messiah, for He has no connection with any earthly son of David in the imagination of the Apocalyptic writer. Now I have insisted that it must be regarded as certain that " The Son of Man " was *not* a term which for the crowd or the disciples carried with it Messianic associations when our Lord first used it. It was our Lord who first for them identified the Son of Man both with the Suffering Servant and with the Christ, the Son of

[1] For doubts on this subject see above, p. 31.

David. But I think it is most probable that the Book of Enoch had already interpreted the human figure in Daniel as being—not an image of the nation, but a mysterious person, who is to be manifested in the clouds as God's vice-gerent in judgment at the end of the world, and had given this interpretation of Daniel such currency that our Lord can use it as a means of extending the meaning of His own title, the Son of Man, and giving to the conception of the Christ its new meaning.[1]

We had better have before us the Pharisee's conception of the Christ to come and the Apocalyptic conception of the Son of Man, that we may see how our Lord both fused and remodelled them.

We take the Psalms of Solomon, dating from a Pharisaic source about a generation before our Lord's birth, and in the 17th Psalm we find this account of the Christ :

" Behold, O Lord, and raise up unto them their king, the Son of David, at the time which thou sawest, O God, that he may reign over Israel, thy servant, and gird him with strength that he may shatter unrighteous rulers. Purge Jerusalem from nations that trample her down to destruction. . . . He will not suffer unrighteousness to lodge any more in the midst of his people ; nor shall there dwell with them any man that knoweth wickedness ; for he shall know them, that they are all sons of their God, and he shall distribute them in their tribes upon the earth, and no sojourner or foreigner shall sojourn any more among them." [2]

This is the old prophetic vision, only without any of the wide hope which is found in many of the old prophets for all the nations of the earth. There is in this Psalm nothing but destruction for the heathen.

[1] It must be remembered that on all showing the Jewish Messianic ideas were confused and vague. Our Lord seems first to have given them spiritual coherence.
[2] Psalms of Solomon, xvii 23–5, 29–31.

And the method of the Christ-King is to be the method of the ruthless conqueror. We have seen already how utterly our Lord repudiated any such conception of the office of the Christ, and both profoundly spiritualized and universalized the conception of the Kingdom. He went back to the noblest form of the ancient vision, and far beyond it.

Then let us take the Apocalyptic conception of the Elect One from the Similitudes of Enoch, based manifestly on the vision of the Book of Daniel.

" And there I saw one who had a head of days, and His head was white like wool, and with Him was another being whose countenance had the appearance of a man, and his face was full of graciousness like one of the holy angels. And I asked the angel who went with me and showed me all the hidden things, concerning that Son of Man, who he was, and whence he wai, and why he went with the Head of Days. And he answered and said unto me : This is the Son of Man who hath righteousness, with whom dwelleth righteousness, and who revealeth all the treasures of that which is hidden. . . . And this Son of Man whom thou hast seen . . . shall loosen the loins of the strong and break the teeth of the sinners . . . and darkness shall be their dwelling, and worms shall be their bed . . . because they do not extol the name of the Lord of spirits." " At that hour the Son of Man was named in the presence of the Lord of Spirits, and his name before the Head of Days. . . . He shall be the staff to the righteous whereon to stay themselves and not fall, and he shall be the light of the Gentiles, and the hope of those who are troubled in heart. . . . And he hath been chosen and hidden before Him, before the creation of the world and for evermore." " And he sat on the throne of his glory, and the sum of judgment was given unto the Son of Man, and he caused the sinners to pass away and be destroyed from off the face of the earth, and those who have led the world astray." [1]

[1] The Book of Enoch (Dr. Charles's translation), xlvi, xlviii 2, 4, 6, lxix 27.

If this, as seems probable, is really a writing which dates before the time of our Lord, and the passages just quoted are not, as a whole, Christian interpolations,[1] which again seems probable, we need not doubt that this interpretation of Daniel's, " one like unto a son of man," who came with the clouds of heaven and was brought near to the Ancient of Days and given universal and everlasting dominion and glory and a kingdom,[2] was known to our Lord and used by Him.   But He transformed completely the whole basis of the conception of the " Elect One," who in Enoch is a purely celestial figure, angelic rather than human.   In our Lord's use of the figure, he is first of all the man born of a woman and living the human life among His fellows ; then the suffering " Servant of Jehovah," who wins redemption for the many by the sacrifice of His life ; and so only passes to resurrection and glory and the awful dignity of the judge of the world.   It is on this basis that the note of resurrection and glory and power is sounded in the ears of the disciples, side by side with the note of suffering.   " The third day he shall rise again."   And they are to " see the Son of Man coming in the glory of His Father with the holy angels." [3]

This, then, is the conclusion of our enquiry.   The conception of the Messiah which Jesus caused to grow in the minds of the disciples was profoundly original in the sense that it took up all the elements of ancient prophecy and recent interpretation, and

[1] See Dalman, *op. cit.* p. 243 : " A Christian interpolator should above all things have made it clear in some way that the Son of Man coming in judgment was Jesus of Nazareth.   But the Son of Man in this case appears never to have been upon earth, far less to have passed through the state of death."   See, however, above p. 31, for the title Son of Man.

[2] Dan. vii 13–14.

[3] Mark viii 31, 38, xiv 62.   On the eschatological teaching of our Lord and the question of its relation to reality see at length pp. 135 ff.

combined them in a whole in His own person—in a whole which, while it realized their best spirit, was quite remote from the expectations of His contemporaries. According to Jesus' teaching, the Messiahship had its basis in His humble and patient manhood, and it was to have its centre in His rejection and suffering and crucifixion, and its vindication in His resurrection and in the mission of His Spirit (for the resurrection of the dead and the effusion of the Spirit were, as we have seen, elements in the ancient prophecies of the Messianic days), and it was to find its consummation in His Lordship in heaven and in His coming to judge the quick and dead.

But in spite of the special help given to them in the vision of the Transfiguration, the disciples had at present no ears for the note of glory beyond humiliation and through it. They could only attend to the announcements of utter shame and rejection and death. Not only did He speak to them of His own death, but of the death of their national hopes. He told them quite plainly that Jerusalem was doomed,[1] and that their city and temple would be destroyed ; and He bade them accept this utter seeming failure, both of Him, their Master, and of all that their patriotic hearts held dear, as something inevitable and necessary for the kingdom to come.[2] It was too much for them. It stirred in their minds a despondency and repulsion which overcame even their loyalty and their faith in Him.

There is hardly any tragedy in history which moves us more than the failure of the disciples. But it was a temporary tragedy. Their failure became an element in their strength and power. Their faith in Jesus lived again, and took form and glory after their recovery, and in the next chapter

---

[1] On this see below, pp. 146 ff.
[2] Luke xxi 28.

we shall trace its course. What we have done so far is to recognize that, quite apart from their ideas about the person of Jesus their Master, which were no doubt vague and uncertain, quite apart even from the new conception of the Christ which Jesus had planted in their reluctant souls to bear fruit after their temporary failure, there was another and deeper impression which they could not shake off. They had been keeping company with one who, deliberately as it seemed, had come to occupy towards their souls a place of authority which is practically God's place. He had come to have for them the values of God. We can conceive nothing further from the method of Jesus than that He should have startled and shocked their consciences by proclaiming Himself as God. But He had done something which in the long run would make any other estimate of Him hardly possible.

NOTE (to p. 45)

On the Relation of John the Baptist to Jesus

We need not dwell upon the small differences of detail between the first three evangelists in their accounts of the circumstances of the baptism of Jesus and His recognition by John as the Christ. But the Fourth Gospel makes a great deal of John's testimony to Jesus as the Son of God, by which he appears to mean simply the Christ (see i 8, 26, 32–5, iii 22–30, v 33, x 41). John is also there represented as calling Him " the Lamb of God which taketh away the sins of the world," thus identifying Him with the Suffering Servant of Jehovah of Is. liii; and it alone records, what is very interesting, that some five of the apostles had been previously disciples of John and had been directed by John to Jesus, and had in some sense become His disciples then and there, and had acknowledged Him for the Christ (John i 35–51), and had had some profound experiences of Him before the end of John's ministry and their call

to be " fishers of men " (John ii and iii 22). I do not
think all this is at all impossible. As Dr. Holland points
out,[1] their early confession that Jesus was the Christ,
or " the Son of God, the King of Israel," was an echo of
the popular Jewish hope which their subsequent experience obliterated, so that they had to rediscover His
Messiahship in a quite new sense. Nor do I see anything improbable in John having, perhaps first among
the Jews, identified the Suffering Servant with the Christ.
I think we have in these additions to the story of the
Synoptists genuine memories. See Burney, *Aramaic
Origin of the Fourth Gospel*, pp. 104 ff.

It is worth noticing that the record of the divine voice
at the baptism is given by all the Synoptists as " This is
my beloved son in whom I *was* " or " I *have been* well
pleased." This makes it plain that none of them regard
the Sonship as dating from the baptism, though I think
that to the consciousness of John (but not to that of
Jesus), as to the rest of the Jews, the term at that time
meant no more and no less than the Christ. This idea
of the Christ must have come from Ps. ii 7 and
lxxxix 26.

As a result of his preaching and baptism " the disciples
of John " appear to have constituted a distinctive
fraternity, whom John bound together by special rules.
He taught them to pray and to observe special fasts,
and " on some points of ceremonial he may have had
tenets of his own " (see Luke xi 1, v 33, John iii 15 ;
cf. Acts xviii 25, xix 3–4; and see Latham's *Pastor
Pastorum*, p. 155). But it does not appear clearly in the
Acts how much they understood " concerning Jesus."

---

[1] In *The Philosophy of Faith and the Fourth Gospel* (Murray, 1921),
pp. 172 f.

CHAPTER III

THE FAITH OF THE FIRST CHURCH AND OF ST. PAUL

IT would seem that all the effort of Jesus was directed, in the latter part of His ministry, to the training of the Twelve, and especially to the preparation of their minds to welcome the principle of sacrifice, and withstand the shock of the Cross.[1] Crucifixion in the Roman provinces was an exceedingly common punishment. The spectacle of men bearing the cross-beam to their place of punishment would have been familiar enough. But to the heart of the Jewish nation it must have been the symbol of subjection and ignominy. And to the natural heart of the disciples the course which Jesus, whom they had confessed to be the Christ, had, as it appeared, so deliberately chosen, seemed doubtless an intolerable betrayal. There was, indeed, at the last hour one moment of seeming triumph; for Jesus, who was so reluctant to figure as the Son of David, because of the false associations of royalty implied in the title, accepted it from the blind beggar Bartimaeus on His way to Jerusalem, and later consented to be hailed as King by a mixed crowd, in a momentary fit of

[1] Crucifixion was the ordinary Roman punishment for persons supposed to be dangerous to the Empire, see Hastings' *Dict. of the Bible*, i, p. 528. After the death of Herod the Great Josephus (*B.J.* ii v 3) tells us that Varus crucified 2000 rioters at one time, cf. ii xii 6, xiii 2, xiv 9; also (v xi 1) that, at the destruction of Jerusalem, the crucifixions inflicted by Titus were so constant and numerous that there was neither room for the crosses nor wood to make them.

enthusiasm, at His entry into Jerusalem.[1] And if
the cleansing of the temple occurred immediately
afterwards,[2] that was another triumph, which would
have raised the spirits of the disciples. It would have
seemed for the moment as if He was now going to
assert His power. But this brief elevation of spirits
was followed by the warnings of immediate betrayal
and death, and it became plain that not all that
Jesus could do had availed at all to inspire into the
disciples' minds the acceptance of the Cross.

There is no tragedy in history more moving than
the rejection of Christ—all the more that it was not
due to any extraordinary wickedness in the Jews
or the Romans, but to the ordinary motives of men.
In the Sadducean family of Annas it was due to
the selfish determination to uphold by all means
their own precarious position of authority, dignity
and wealth, under the Roman sovereignty, and to
suppress every movement that might make the
Romans jealous ; in the Pharisees, to their refusal,
at the bidding of one who was in their eyes the merest
layman, to acknowledge profound mistakes, and to
think over again from the beginning what was the
meaning of the religion of which they were the
orthodox representatives ; in the mass of the people
to their worldly preoccupation of mind and their
stubborn nationalism, which made them entertain
wild hopes, and blinded them to the spiritual " way "
of redemption which Jesus presented to them ; in
Pilate, to the refusal to do what very few Roman
governors would have dreamed of doing—to prefer
abstract justice, in the case of an impotent individual,
to the apparent interests of the Empire and himself.

[1] I cannot but think that St. John's explanation of the fit of
enthusiasm by the excitement due to the raising of Lazarus (xii
9–19) is the only explanation of it which makes it at the moment
intelligible. In the Synoptists taken alone it appears unaccountable.

[2] St. John, however, puts it at the beginning of the ministry.
I think it is not improbable that it occurred twice.

Such refusals and obsessions are all around us every day. They constitute the common atmosphere of society, certainly in our own time as much as of old. The mind of the ecclesiastical authorities, as exhibited in Church history towards " unauthorized " prophets, constantly recalls the Pharisees. The attitude of politicians and men of business and governing classes towards moral principles constantly recalls the Sadducees and Pilate. The attitude of popular movements constantly recalls " the common people " of Jerusalem and Galilee. It is *the* tragedy of human life from the point of view of the believer in God. God comes unto His own and His own receive Him not.

And if the most tragic feature in the whole situation is the failure of the Twelve—if we can hardly bear to read the story of Peter's denial—yet we must not be scornful. The doctrine which they were required to embrace was a very new one—contrary always to flesh and blood, but to none so contrary as to the Jews. It is not easy to realize the depth of the requirement which our Lord made upon His disciples' hearts and minds when He bade them not only contemplate His own seeming failure and death, but also anticipate the doom which He so solemnly pronounced upon their nation and city and temple, and be prepared to witness its accomplishment even with joy, as the necessary prelude of the kingdom of God.[1]   No one, Jew or Gentile, can know his own mind or the mind of men and women in general without recognizing that the real strain on faith is the spectacle of the present seeming weakness of God and of good, which no prospect of future reversal seems able to counterbalance. Truly God " delivers His strength into captivity and His glory into the enemies' hands." [2]

[1] Luke xxi 28–31.
[2] Ps. lxxviii 61 (Bible version). The reference is to the capture of the Ark of God. Our Prayer Book version, " *their* power . . . and *their* beauty," is a mistake.

I

But a few weeks after the crucifixion and en-
tombment of Jesus, the company of " the brethren,"
numbering one hundred and twenty persons, and
centering upon the Twelve, are presented to us in the
beginning of the Acts in a wholly different frame of
mind.   They are now radiant and confident, and are
prepared to face an even world-wide mission, apparently of a most desperate kind, and to challenge the
world, with a clear understanding at least of the
ground of their mission.   I have contended in the
volume which preceded this,[1] that nothing can satis-
factorily account for their sudden, complete and
corporate change of mind, except a certain series of
facts, some of which are recorded in detail by the
Evangelists, and which are summarized at an earlier
date by St. Paul [2]—that is the finding of the tomb
of Jesus empty on the third day, and His repeated
appearances afterwards, with a humanity strangely
changed in physical condition, but still the same—
which had assured them, beyond possibility of mistake, of His actual resurrection from the dead.   On
the fortieth day after the Resurrection St. Luke
records that these appearances came to an end with
the Ascension,[3] which after another ten days was
followed by the promised effusion of the Holy Spirit.
I do not propose to go again over the ground of the

[1] *Belief in God*, pp. 262 ff.
[2] Edward Meyer, *Ursprung*, pp. 11–12, writes: "The bodily
resurrection of Jesus and His numerous appearances before the
disciples belong to the oldest traditions and those that were earliest
fixed in a definite formula.   Paul received this formula after his
conversion in his period of instruction (Lehrzeit), and reproduced
it in 1 Cor. xv. . . . That Paul says 'Kephas' not 'Peter'
is a proof that the formula . . . was originally composed in
Aramaic."
[3] There seems to me to be no adequate ground for the assumption
of Meyer (*op. cit.*, vol. i. pp. 40 ff.) that the narrative of the Ascension
is an interpolation.

" evidences " of these events having actually occurred. Without in any way blinding ourselves to difficulties or discrepancies of detail between our authorities— such as occur in all original testimonies by ordinary people, unless they have been artificially rectified—I do not think that it is possible either to reject them or to call them doubtful. It seems to me psychologically certain that such a rapid, simultaneous conversion of such unimaginative men as we know the Twelve to have been from the state of mind as described in the Gospels, both before and after the crucifixion of Jesus Christ, to the state of mind described in the beginning of the Acts, could not have occurred except by the impact of indisputable facts of experience, such as those to which they attributed their newly-won convictions.

Nor do I propose to recur to the question of the Lucan authorship and trustworthiness of the Acts of the Apostles. Some critics hold that in the earlier chapters (i–xii) St. Luke is dependent upon Aramaic documents. Dr. Burkitt has recently suggested that St. Mark's narrative may originally have extended over the period covered by them.[1] We can leave these questions aside as doubtful. What we are not justified in doubting is that, in his intercourse with Philip the Evangelist and Mnason, the " original " disciple, and some of the women of the apostolic company, and no doubt others at Caesarea and at Jerusalem, and with John Mark in Rome during St. Paul's imprisonment there—John Mark who had probably lived through

[1] *Earliest Sources for the Life of Jesus* (Constable, 1922), p. 79. " It may be well to remind ourselves that we do not know how far the narrative (of Mark) extended over the ground covered by St. Luke's *Acts of the Apostles*. The first half of the work ends with the name of ' John who was surnamed Mark,' and it is plausible to suppose it may have been in the work of Mark that the third Evangelist came across the life-like episode of Rhoda." Certainly, however, Papias' description of Mark's record does not suggest this larger scope.

all those early days in his mother's house at Jerusalem where the apostolic company assembled—Luke had excellent opportunities for knowing the facts with sufficient accuracy to enable him to write trustworthy history. In Rackham's *Acts* we have a very careful and thoughtful study of these early chapters. To my mind, one of the most convincing assurances of their trustworthiness lies in the exact account given of the nature of the early belief in Jesus. St. Luke published his record at least not earlier than St. Paul's release from his first captivity. He had been St. Paul's trusted companion all through the period when he was writing his epistles. He must have been quite familiar with St. Paul's full doctrine of Christ, and of justification and salvation in the Church which is His Body. I do not indeed see any signs that St. Luke assimilated St. Paul's theology very deeply—he was a historian with a vivid perception of the beauties of moral character, rather than a theologian, we should suppose; but he gives us touches of Paul's theology in the speeches in the latter part of the Acts. As we shall see, it is St. Paul who first in the record of the Acts calls Jesus the Son of God [1]; it is St. Paul who talks about justification by faith, as distinguished from works of the law [2]; it is St. Paul who talks about "the Church of God which he purchased with his own blood." [3] The circumstances of these speeches, as the Acts records them, do not give much opportunity for the characteristic Pauline theology. They consist of St. Paul's first approaches to Jewish and Gentile hearers, and of his *apologia pro vita sua* to the Jews and to the Church. But some of his characteristic phrases are there. Whereas

---

[1] Acts ix 20, cf. xiii 32. It is singular that in the Acts as a whole there is actually no mention of God as Father except in Acts i 4, 7 (the words of the risen Jesus) and Acts ii 33, where Peter refers to this promise.

[2] xiii 39.

[3] xx 28.

in the earlier part of the Acts they are quite absent.
This is very noticeable. It indicates that St. Luke
had good authorities for the early speeches he
records and did not write at random; thus we can
approach the first part of the Acts with reasonable
confidence to see how it represents the primitive
belief.

The disciples, as represented especially by their
leader St. Peter, are set before us as simply filled
with the thoughts forced upon them by the
Resurrection and later by the effusion of the Holy
Spirit. The central thought is that of the Lordship
of Jesus the Christ. Though God certified His
mission "by mighty works and wonders and signs
which God did by him in the midst of Israel," yet
Israel had crucified and slain Him by the hands of
the Romans. But now God had vindicated Him
by the Resurrection and exalted Him by His right
hand and to His right hand; and it was He who
had poured forth the promised gift of the Holy
Spirit, which He received from the Father. "Therefore let all the house of Israel know assuredly, that
God made him both Lord and Christ,[1] this Jesus
whom ye crucified."

So far as appears in the Acts, Peter raised no question concerning the divine Sonship or pre-existence of
Jesus.[2] He is content throughout, as in his discourse
in the house of Cornelius, to speak of Him as the
man "Jesus of Nazareth, anointed with the Holy
Ghost and with power, who went about doing good,
and healing all that were oppressed with the devil;
for God was with him." But now, risen and exalted

---

[1] Acts ii 22–36. This must not be taken to imply that he was
not the Christ when on earth. It was as the Christ that He suffered,
iv 10.

[2] We should notice that the glorified Christ is the man Jesus of
Nazareth who had lived and died on earth. There are no signs at
all of the pre-existent heavenly man-like being of the Similitudes of
Enoch.

to heaven, He is "Lord of all" and "ordained of
God to be the judge of quick and dead." It is in
His name, and through belief in Him, that men
must receive remission of sins and the gift of the
Holy Ghost.[1] It is in His name that miracles of
power are done.[2] There is indeed salvation in none
other : for neither is there any other name under
heaven that is given among men, wherein we must
be saved.[3] He is "the Prince" or "the Prince
of life," and the "Saviour." His is "the Name." [4]
This is their summary creed—Jesus is the Christ—
Jesus is Lord. The one name of salvation is the
name of Jesus. Beholding Him in the moment of
martyrdom, standing as Son of Man on the right
hand of God, Stephen addresses to Him the prayer—
" Lord Jesus, receive my spirit," and probably the
words following, " Lord, lay not this sin to their
charge," just as Jesus on the cross had addressed
the Father, "Father, into thy hands I commend
my spirit," " Father, forgive them." Before Pentecost, when the disciple who was to fill up the place
of Judas had to be chosen, they had prayed and said
" Thou, Lord, which knowest the hearts of all men,
show of these two the one whom thou hast chosen,
to take the place in this ministry and apostleship," and
it is probable[5] that the Lord Jesus just mentioned
is in that place also being appealed to, to make a
fresh choice in order to fill the vacancy in the number
of the twelve whom He had chosen when on earth.
It should be noted that " to call on the name of
Jesus," that is to invoke Him in prayer, is spoken
of (cap. ix 14, 21) as the characteristic habit of the
disciples.

Further it was " in the name of the Lord Jesus "

[1] Acts x 36–43.   [2] Acts iii 16.
[3] Acts iv 12.   [4] Acts iii 15, v 31, 41, ix 14–16.
[5] Acts i 21–4. The consideration to the contrary is that the
single Greek word for ' that knoweth the hearts ' ($\kappa\alpha\rho\delta\iota\alpha\gamma\nu\hat{\omega}\sigma\tau\alpha$) is
used of God, i.e. the Father, in xv 8.

that men were baptized [1]; and, if we accept the account of what occurred at the Last Supper as St. Paul declares himself to have " received " it and as the Synoptists relate it, we must believe that when the disciples met for " the breaking of the bread " [2] they celebrated, according to their Lord's institution, the sacrament of His body and blood, and in that solemn rite acknowledged that He who had given His body and blood in sacrifice for them upon the Cross, and who was now alive at the right hand of God, was also amongst them on earth, where they were gathered together in His name, to be their spiritual food, and to bind them together in one. Such a rite and such an accompanying belief seem to imply a conception of Christ's person beyond what, to judge from the record of Acts, they were at present explicitly entertaining or proclaiming.[3]

What then was " the faith in Jesus " or " in His Name " of the first Christian community, intellectually considered ? It was not, we should judge, an explicit faith in His deity, but faith in Him as Lord.[4] " Jesus is Christ and Lord " and " He has sent down upon us His Holy Spirit " was their summary creed. But to believe in the universal Lordship of Jesus, and His enthronement at God's right hand—to believe that He is to judge the quick and dead—that

---

[1] Acts viii 16. I have not cited the text (Matt. xxviii 19), " baptizing them in the name of the Father and of the Son and of the Holy Ghost," because, on purely critical principles, it is difficult to be sure of its being really a word of Christ on earth ; nor do I discuss the question of baptism only in the name of Jesus. The whole body of sacramental questions, with the question of the Church and its authority, is deferred to the next volume.

[2] Acts ii 42.

[3] On the doubts constantly being raised whether Jesus really in fact instituted any sacrament of His body and blood for future observance by His Church, see appended note A, p. 99.

I must not, of course, pass over the position of the critics who constantly inform us that it is in St. Paul that we first find the affirmation that Jesus is Lord. See appended note B, p. 102.

from Him the Spirit of God is received and in His
name sins are forgiven in baptism and wonders
done—that His name is the one name of salvation
given to all men under heaven—that He is to be
called upon in prayer—that He is present in " the
breaking of the bread " to be the spiritual food of
His disciples—all this taken together means certainly
that He had for them " the values of God." Not
indeed all the " values " of God, for they would not yet
have thought of Him, as far as we can see, as the
Creator or sustainer of the world. But with regard
to all that concerned their spiritual relations to God,
Jesus held towards them such a position as a mere
man, however highly endowed, could not have held.
How was this to be accounted for ? It was an
ambiguous moment. One can imagine an intelligent
Greek, who knew the severity of the Jewish monotheism, and was accustomed to constrast it with the
lax ascription of deity to eminent things or persons
in the Hellenic or Roman world, watching the Christians in Jerusalem with interest, and taking note
that these Jews were apparently abandoning what
he had always regarded as their chief religious
stronghold—their stubborn belief in one only God
and their stubborn refusal to worship any other
being. What was to be the end of it ?

II

It was not to end in any weakening of Monotheism. Among the fiercest of their Jewish enemies
was one who, converted to faith in Jesus, was to show
them how to conciliate their old faith in the One
God with their newly born faith in the Lordship of
Jesus.

I do not think it is an accident that St. Paul is
said by St. Luke, at the first moment after his

conversion to have proclaimed " Jesus that he is the Son of God." [1] Nor is it without serious meaning that St. Paul describes his own conversion as the revelation within him of Jesus as " God's son "— " to reveal his Son in me that I might preach him among the Gentiles." [2] That was the term, so solemnly used by Jesus of Himself, in which St. Paul saw the secret of His person. No doubt from the date of his conversion his soul went out in passionate faith toward Jesus as the glorified Christ and as the Lord. But he was, what no one of the earlier apostles had been, a man who had received the highest training of the Jewish schools " at the feet of " the renowned Rabbi Gamaliel, and we should judge from his Epistles that he was not only a Jewish theologian but also had imbibed at his native city of Tarsus something of the philosophical spirit for which it was famous. He could not be content to worship Jesus as Lord without understanding why such worship could be given Him, and how it was to be reconciled with the strict faith in one only God, one only object of worship, which retained his whole-hearted loyalty to the end.

He had the opportunity after his conversion of thinking out his position. After his first " act of reparation " at Damascus when, with all possible courage and at the greatest risk, he proclaimed his new faith " that Jesus is the Son of God " and " confounded the Jews that dwell at Damascus, proving that this is the Christ," he was hurried secretly out of the city and passed probably some years in Arabia. Then, three years after his conversion, he paid a brief visit to Jerusalem, where again " he preached boldly in the name of the Lord," but again was in risk of

[1] It must be remembered that Acts viii 37 (the only previous mention of " the Son of God " in our old version of Acts) is probably not part of the true text.

[2] Gal. i 16 ; cf. ii 20.

his life from the hostility of the Jews, and was sent
off to his old home, Tarsus, out of harm's way, and
must have been there perhaps some seven years.
But we hear little or nothing of any evangelistic
work there.[1] It is probable that his sojourn both in
Arabia and in Tarsus was on the whole a time of
retirement and thought. From the time when
Barnabas fetched him to Antioch, his life must have
been one of ceaseless strain. But before that he had
had time to think out the meaning of his new faith,
of which he had already, at Damascus and especially
at Jerusalem, received " the tradition,"[2] and he had
found in the doctrine of the divine sonship the way
of reconciliation between his old Monotheism and
his new belief in the Lordship of Jesus.[3]

But before we enquire into the sources of St.
Paul's doctrine of Christ's person, we must have it
clearly before our mind, and we should take notice
that the way in which it is referred to in his epistles
seems to show conclusively that, in its main lines,
it must have formed part of his first preaching

[1] He speaks (Gal. i 21) of going " into the region of Syria and
Cilicia," and of the Christians in Judaea hearing " that he that
once persecuted them now preached the faith of which he once
made havoc." We hear of " brethren in Syria and Cilicia," and
at the beginning of the second missionary journey " he went through
Syria and Cilicia confirming the churches " (Acts xv 23, 41).
But if these churches were of his foundation we should have been
likely to hear something of them. And we hear nothing.

[2] He tells us himself that he received the tradition concerning
the Resurrection (1 Cor. xv 1–3) and concerning the institution
of the Eucharist (probably there was more that he does not
mention). Galatians i 17, ii 6 must be read in the light of these
disclosures.

[3] I am glad to see that Eduard Meyer, *Ursprung*, vol. ii, p. 348,
recognizes the importance, not only of " the tradition " which
St. Paul received in Damascus and Jerusalem, but also of the
long period of subsequent reflection before he began his mission
work : " In der langen Zeit, die er nach seiner Bekehrung in
Damascus und Tarsus zubrachte, muss er über die neue Erkenntnis
gegrübelt haben, die ihm aufgegangen war, bis er mit seiner
Anschauungen in reinen war und sie sich in seiner Weise logisch
zurecht gelegt hatte, so dass er alsdann die Missionstätigkeit
beginnen konnte."

when founding his churches, for it is not introduced anywhere in his writings as if it were a new thing.

He is full of the familiar thought of the Lordship of Christ, and indeed occasionally the Lord (Jehovah) and the Lord (Christ) are unmistakably identified— that is, Old Testament language about the former is applied to the latter.[1] But St. Paul has—what the Church before him apparently had not—an explanation. Christ can be thus treated as divine Lord, or identified with Jehovah, because before He was sent into the world He was with the Father as His Son—" his own son " (Rom. viii 3), " the son of his love " (Col. i 13). The glorified Christ can be the very "image of God"[2] because, at the beginning of things, as Son of the Father, He had been God's " image"—the expression of the invisible God.[3] Through Him, the Son, has God done whatever in the process of creation He has done. He is " the heir of all creation "—" through him are all things "—" in him were all things created, in the heavens and upon the earth, things visible and things invisible, whether thrones or dominions or principalities or powers ; all things have been created through him, and unto him (he is their end) ; and he is (or ' he exists ') before all things, and in him all things have their coherence." He is not only the creator of all that is, but also the continuous, immanent principle of order in the universe.[4] It is He who was supplying the need of the Israelites in the wilderness as " the rock that followed

[1] See Romans x 9–15 (Joel ii 32) ; 2 Thess. i 9 (Is. ii 10, 19, 21) ; 1 Cor. ii 16 (Is. xl 13, lxx) ; 1 Cor. x 21 (Mal. i 7, 12). This identification has been described as "not proven" in any case in the N.T. But it seems to me beyond dispute. See Sanday and Headlam on Rom. x.

[2] 2 Cor. iv 4.   [3] Col. i 15.

[4] See 1 Cor. viii 6 ; Col. i 15–17. Nothing can better Lightfoot's notes on this passage.

them."[1] He it was who "when the fulness of the
time was come" was sent forth "born of a woman,
born under the law," "in the likeness of the flesh
of sin," but "knowing no sin,"[2] as man to redeem
mankind, whether Jews or Gentiles, who will believe
on Him. He was, as man on earth, their example,
and their propitiation before God, and now He is
continuously from heaven the source of their new
life by His spirit. For that divine Sonship which
was veiled during His mortal life and in His death,
was declared again unmistakably in His resurrection[3] ; and thereupon, being exalted to the heavenly
places, He communicates His own Spirit, which is
the Spirit of God, to the Church, which is His body,
and to all its members, so that " in Him " they may
live as sons in His sonship, and by Him be renewed
into His image, and remaining in Him,[4] whether
they live or die, may be prepared to meet Him when
He comes in glory, being already associated with
Him in the life of God.

This is St. Paul's doctrine of Christ in summary.
I think Dr. Allan Menzies (commenting on 2 Cor. iv
4) is right in saying "It was difficult for them
(Jews) to take in how one who had been a man on
the earth could be [a] God, and if this was not
accepted, all the other Pauline doctrines remained
incredible, a tangle of paradoxes and indiscretions.
The verse shows very clearly how the whole of Paul's
thought hinged on his doctrine of Christ's divinity."

St. Paul is not a scientific writer who exhibits
his thought accurately and consecutively stated.
If he had been this, he would have saved the

---

[1] 1 Cor. x 4. In this connection I am inclined to believe that
the A.V. of verse 9 gives the right reading : " Neither let us tempt
Christ, as some of them also tempted."

[2] See Rom. viii 3, Gal. iv 4, 2 Cor. v 21.

[3] Rom. i 3–4.

[4] " In the Lord," or " in Christ," or " in Christ Jesus," or " in
the Lord Jesus."

controversial and critical world a great deal of
trouble, but he would not have been St. Paul. He
does, however, incidentally give us what it is
hardly an exaggeration to call a careful theory of
the meaning of the Incarnation in the Epistle to
the Philippians, though the theory as given is only
incidental to an ethical exhortation. His theme
is humility, and his example of humility is Christ,
not only within the compass of His human life but
before that—in the act of taking humanity. For
" pre-existing in the characteristics [or nature]
of God, he set no store on equality with God, but
emptied himself, taking the characteristics [or
nature] of a servant, and being made in the likeness
of men ; and being found in fashion as a man, he
humbled himself, becoming obedient even unto
death, yea, the death of the cross. Wherefore also
God highly exalted him, and bestowed upon him
the name which is above every name ; that at
the name of Jesus every knee should bow, of things
in heaven and things on earth and things under the
earth, and that every tongue should confess that
Jesus Christ is Lord, to the glory of God the Father." [1]

[1] Phil. ii 5–11. This is one of the passages in the N.T. which
have been obscured by excessively minute scrutiny. I do not
think anything can better Lightfoot's commentary. Some people
are disposed to dispute that " emptied himself " or " annulled himself " is meant as a description of the act of the Incarnation at
all. They would apparently translate " he emptied himself,
having taken," i.e. He first took human nature and then humbled
Himself. But " emptied himself " here is surely parallel to
" beggared himself " or " made himself poor " in 2 Cor. viii 9.
Both phrases describe an act of abandonment by our Lord of the
state belonging to His divine nature which was involved in becoming
man. " Emptied himself " is therefore to be distinguished from
the " humbled himself " which follows in Phil. ii 7, and which
describes His conduct after He became man. See Menzies on
2 Cor. viii 9. " With the phrase ' chose poverty ' [or ' made himself
poor '] we may compare ' he emptied himself ' (Phil. ii), which
refers not to the act of Jesus as a man, but to the great act of
humiliation He performed when He gave up His existence in the
form of God, and took on Himself the form of a servant."
The word translated " characteristics " (or " nature," which I

This being St. Paul's doctrine of a real incarnation of the Son of God, who pre-existed in the essential characteristics or nature of God, we ask whether St. Paul believes Him to have been, and calls Him without qualification, God. What everywhere confronts us in St. Paul's letters is that he attributes to Him—always in definite subordination to God, the Father [1]—all the characteristic functions of God; the creation of all things in the universe and the maintenance of creation, as we have seen; the providence which directs the accidents of life; the "grace" that redeems men and holds them "in Christ" or "in the Lord" as the sphere in which they live; the final judgment which is unerringly to assess each human life; the crowning of the redeemed with glory and the consummation of the whole creation.[2] In the whole range of divine activities there appears to be no district in which

think is a better word) is literally "form"; but the English word is misleading. The original word describes the "permanent characteristics" or "kind" or "manner of being" of anything. See Lightfoot *in loc.* and Trench, *Synonyms*, pp. 247 ff. So the "form of the servant" describes the permanent characteristics or "nature" of manhood—with probable reference to the "servant of Jehovah" in Second Isaiah. The words "likeness" and "fashion" which follow affirm that the Son of God not only took the real nature but also the outward appearance and condition of manhood. The Son not only became really man, but ordinary man, like other men to look at, and like other men in all the changing conditions of life.

[1] Alike in (a) His cosmic activities, and (b) in His redemptive activities the Son is subordinate to the Father; see for (a) 1 Cor. viii 6, Col. i 15, and for (b) Gal. iv 4, Col. i 19, 1 Cor. xi 3. It is not necessary to multiply quotations. And the essential subordination of the Son to the Father, as recipient to source, has always been the Catholic doctrine. See Westcott on John xiv 28. In 1 Cor. xv 28 St. Paul speaks of the ultimate order, when the work of the mediatorial Kingdom of Christ is fully accomplished, and all resistance and rebellion is over for ever, and in that ultimate order the Son is subordinate to the Father.

[2] It is not necessary to multiply quotations, but see Col. i 14–18, 1 Thess. iii 11, 2 Cor. xiii 14, and Gal. i 3, 2 Cor. v 17, 2 Cor. v 10, Rom. vi 23, 2 Thess. ii 14, Phil. iii 21, ii 10, Eph. i 10.

7

God, that is the Father, is not associated with His Son, nor is it in St. Paul's mind apparently conceivable that the honour paid to the Son, the Lord Jesus, throughout the whole created universe, should be any derogation from or should be distinguishable from the honour paid to the Father, or that there should be anything given to the Father in the way of homage by His creatures which is withheld from the Son. On the whole the instinct of monotheism (and no doubt the pressing necessity to maintain the language of monotheism in churches of Gentile origin) leads St. Paul generally to speak of the Father alone as God and of the Son as Lord: " For us there is one God, the Father, of whom are all things, and we unto him ; and one Lord, Jesus Christ, through whom are all things, and we through him " (1 Cor. viii 6) ; but so completely is the Son represented as sharing in the divine life and activity that it is, I think, wilful to question the ascription to the Christ, who was born of Jewish stock " as concerning the flesh," of the words—which seem so plainly to suggest the antithesis of the glory of Christ to His humiliation—" who is over all, God blessed for ever " [1] or to question the phrase in St. Paul's speech at Miletus to the Ephesian elders, " the Church of God which he purchased with his own blood," or " the blood which is his own." [2] We should conclude, then, that as St. Paul constantly associates the Lord (Jesus) in all the strictly divine activity and glory, so occasionally he calls Him God.

We know that St. Paul would have attributed

---

[1] Rom. ix 5. See Sanday and Headlam *in loc.*

[2] Acts xx 28. In this phrase I think with Rackham God means the Father, but the blood of Christ is called " his own." In Titus ii 13, however, I think Parry, following Hort, is probably right in treating the words " Jesus Christ " as in apposition to " the glory of our great God and Saviour." Christ, that is, is " the glory of God " (see below, pp. 128 ff).

his doctrine of Christ to direct divine inspiration.[1] Just as our Lord would have St. Peter assured that his confession of His Messiahship was due to nothing lower than divine revelation, so would St. Paul have felt and claimed for his fuller conviction about Christ's person. But in neither case can divine revelation be taken to exclude human and external influences. Whence, then, we ask, did St. Paul derive, not his conviction, but the materials through which this conviction expressed itself?

It has been commonly suggested by those who are absorbed in the new study of " apocalyptic " that St. Paul's idea of the pre-existent Christ is derived from the Similitudes of the Book of Enoch or from similar sources which have perished. But this suggestion ought to be abandoned. The figure in the Similitudes is that of a quasi-angelic being in human form, who is being preserved in the secret treasury of God to be manifested only at the end of the world to carry out the Divine judgment and to usher in the world to come. If in the original document he is called " the son of man " (which I hold to be very doubtful), yet in no real sense has he ever been man, nor ever will be—that is, not in the sense of sharing the nature or experience, physical and spiritual, of the sons of men. It is a fundamentally " docetic " figure—that of these Similitudes—neither in any real sense divine nor in any real sense human. St. Paul shows, I think, not the slightest trace of such a presentation. He never speaks of the "Son of Man"; and the pre-existent " Son of God " of St. Paul is divine, subsisting in the " form " of God, and not yet in any sense human ; but at a definite moment in time, by a definite human birth of a woman, He became man. It was not that He appeared merely in human guise, but that He really became man, in the solidity of human flesh and reality of human character,

[1] Gal. i 12, 15, 16.

and as man lived, and was crucified and died, and was buried, and rose again and was glorified, and is " to come." [1] Nor is there any reason to think that St. Paul was influenced by Philo's hazy conception of the ideal man who exists among the ideas of the eternal world,[2] nor by any ancient myth of an eternal man. There is no trace in St. Paul of any " eternal man " at all. The only phrase pleaded on behalf of such a suggestion is the phrase " the second man is from heaven." In its context, I think, this phrase can only describe the coming of Christ in glory, not His first appearance on earth.[3] The Apostle is answering the question " with what manner of body do they [the dead] come," that is, at the resurrection day. And he answers that they will come in a spiritual body, like to Christ who has now become " life-giving spirit," and will come as the " second man from heaven." St. Paul was, in fact, not enunciating any old theory which he might be supposed to have learned as a Pharisee, but something which the resurrection of Christ (and his vision of the risen Christ) had taught him for the first time.[4]

To recur, then, to the question whence St. Paul derived the material for this conception of Christ : I think the answer must be in the first place that

[1] See for St. Paul's doctrine Phil. ii 6–10, Gal. iv 4. This verse in Galatians with Rom. i 3 implies the reality of His human flesh ; when St. Paul talks of His character as obedient, meek and gentle, he implies His full spiritual humanity. As He had the " form " of God, so He took the " form," that is, the real nature, of man. St. Paul was not confronted with any docetism. But there is no reason to think he would have made any terms with it. Christ in glory is still human and His " body of glory " is the pattern of the body of glory which we are all destined to enjoy, Phil. iii 21. On 2 Cor. v 16, " Christ after the flesh," see appended Note C, p. 105.

[2] See Lebreton, *Origines*, p. 216.

[3] 1 Cor. xv 47. See Robertson and Plummer, *in loc.* (*Internat. Crit. Comm.*). Also Dalman, *op. cit.*, pp. 251 f.

[4] On what has just been said, I must refer back for confirmation to the Note on pp. 30 ff.

he was much better acquainted than some people appear to suppose with the words of Christ. We must recognize, as has been already argued, that St. Paul, after his conversion, received " a tradition " which in certain respects was already formulated. I think this tradition probably included a record of the sayings of Christ. But whether this be so or no, we are bound to acknowledge that St. Paul had in his mind, if not in his hand, some record of the words of Christ, and assumes that the converts knew it also—for four times he refers to a particular " word of the Lord " as of final and decisive authority.[1] I think also St. Paul's ethical teaching shows unmistakable and close familiarity with Christ's teaching. His estimate of the law of love, and his description of love, and of " the fruits of the spirit," and his appeal to " the meekness and gentleness of Christ," and to His example of humility, will, if we meditate on them, convince us of this.[2] In the same way I think the remarkable phrase which occurs five times in St. Paul's epistles, " The Father of our Lord Jesus Christ," [3] and which is used side by side with phrases such as " our Father " or " the Father," means that St. Paul knew how it had been our Lord's habit to speak to His disciples—never of " our Father," [4] but of " your Father," and " my Father." " The Father of our Lord Jesus Christ " then, as St. Paul uses it, means Him whom Jesus Christ used constantly to speak of as " my Father." And if he knew how Jesus spoke of God as His Father, he must have known that He spoke of Himself as the Son. Thus I have grown to feel convinced

---

[1] 1 Cor. vii 10, ix 14, 1 Thess. iv 15, Acts xx 35. In the last two cases the " words of the Lord " have not been otherwise preserved. In the first two they have. See also 1 Tim. vi 3.

[2] So Dr. Rashdall, *The Idea of Atonement*, pp. 106 ff.

[3] Rom. xv 6, 2 Cor. i 3, xi 31, Eph. i 3, Col. i 3.

[4] " Our Father " (in the Lord's Prayer) is only put into the lips of the disciples.

that St. Paul must have had in his mind, and very possibly in written form before his eyes, such words as " I thank thee, O Father, Lord of heaven and earth, that thou didst hide these things from the wise and understanding, and didst reveal them unto babes ; yea, Father, for so it was well pleasing in thy sight.[1] All things have been delivered unto me of my Father : and no one knoweth the Son, save the Father : neither doth any know the Father save the Son, and he to whomsoever the Son willeth to reveal him," and " Of that day and that hour knoweth no one, not even the angels of heaven, neither the Son," and again the parable of the Husbandmen, suggesting so sharp a distinction between the servants of God (the prophets) and the only Son. Though, as I have said, the note of the divine sonship of Christ was absent apparently from the first Apostolic preaching, it is very difficult to doubt that there was thought and talk about such memorable sayings as these in their bearing on the mystery of Christ's person. And St. Paul was more quick than others to catch their full meaning.

Moreover it is plain that St. Paul's doctrine of the pre-existence of the Son, before the world was, and His co-operation with the Father in all His works, and His incarnation in the fulness of time, did not in any way shock or surprise the Church. There were, we know, aspects and elements in St. Paul's teaching which excited alarm and caused dissension. This is much more evident in St. Paul's own Epistles than in the Acts. But there is no such note of emphasis on his teaching about the person of Christ as to suggest that it was surprising by its novelty or calculated to raise antagonism. It is taken for granted as an accepted truth. And this could not have been the case if the idea of Jesus

[1] I suspect that 1 Cor. i 18 ff. is reminiscent of the context of these words : "I thank thee, Father," etc.

as Son of God, in a unique and pre-eminent sense, had not been in the tradition of the first Jerusalem Church, though for the time it appears to have been almost ignored, while attention was wholly concentrated upon His Messiahship and Lordship. Those who believe, as I do, that the author of the Fourth Gospel gives us real memorials of Jesus, and is no other than John the son of Zebedee, will remember that he was at Jerusalem at least during the earlier stages of St. Paul's career as an Apostle, and that St. Paul had converse with him as one of the "pillars." It is universally assumed that St. Paul influenced the author of the Johannine writings. I cannot help thinking it is possible that St. John may have communicated something to St. Paul.

I should not, of course, wish to lay any stress on this possibility. But I do wish to lay stress on the fact that St. Paul's doctrine of the Son of God seems to have caused no surprise or opposition; and this could hardly have been the case unless it had been already present in germ in the tradition of the Church, though it was not apparently much in evidence, while the whole attention of the Church was preoccupied with something else.

There is nothing in the Synoptists which very directly suggests the association of the Son in the activities of creation or of nature, though there is one saying in the Fourth Gospel which probably does suggest it [1]: "My Father worketh hitherto and I work." But as soon as ever the idea of the Son, as associated with the Father in His eternal life, had presented itself to St. Paul's mind, it would probably have clothed itself in the associations of the Wisdom of God as that is presented in *the Book of Proverbs* and especially in *the Wisdom of Solomon*, with which St. Paul in the Romans shows himself well acquainted.[2]

[1] John v 17-20.   [2] See Sanday and Headlam, p. 51.

he divine " Wisdom " in these books is not
conceived of as really a person, but it is strikingly
personified. It is represented as if it had separate
existence as God's effulgence or self-expression, before
ever the world was; and (perhaps in Proverbs,
certainly in the Book of Wisdom) as His agent in
creation and in His self-revelation to men. Much
of the language that St. Paul uses about the activity
of the Son in the creation and sustentation of the
world is paralleled in this literature. " The Lord
possessed me (or ' formed me ') as the beginning of
his way, before his works of old. I was set up from
everlasting, from the beginning, or ever the earth
was. . . . Then I was by him as a master work-
man (?); and I was daily his delight, rejoicing
always before him; rejoicing in his habitable earth;
and my delight was with the sons of men." [1] And
in the Book of Wisdom, Wisdom is called " the
artificer of all things . . . Yea she pervadeth and
penetrateth all things. . . . She is an effulgence
from everlasting light; and an unspotted mirror of
the working of God, and an image of his goodness.
And she, being one, hath power to do all things;
and remaining in herself, reneweth all things : and
from generation to generation passing into holy
souls, she maketh men friends of God and prophets."
" She reacheth from one end of the world to the other
with full strength, and ordereth all things graciously."
And Solomon prays, " Give me wisdom, her that
sitteth by thee on thy throne; . . . send her forth
from thy holy heaven, and from the throne of thy
glory bid her come." [2]

There can be no doubt that at least the Book of
Wisdom exhibits the influence of Greek philosophy.
The intellectual world, under the influence of
Platonists and Stoics, was full of the conception of
a divine Reason, immanent in the universe as its

[1] Prov. viii 22–30. [2] Wisd. vii 22 to ix 18.

order and law, and the source of the reason of man. St. Paul's own city Tarsus, where he was brought up, and to which he returned for a good many years after his conversion, was pre-eminently a philosophic city.[1] I do not suppose that St. Paul was a member of any of the philosophic schools. But I think it is impossible he can have been ignorant of the philosophical ideas which constituted the common intellectual atmosphere of educated men in his own city. And when we read such phrases as " in him (the Son) all things consist " or " in him we live and move and have our being," we cannot dissociate such an idea of an immanent God from the influences of current philosophy, or doubt that in St. Paul's mind this current conception of a pervading reason helped him to frame his conception of the activities of the Son of God in nature.

Nevertheless the influence of philosophy, or even of the Book of Wisdom, on St. Paul must not be exaggerated. St. Paul's attitude towards philosophy is not sympathetic or at all trustful. He delivers his solemn affirmations about Christ wholly as a revelation of God. As I have said, I believe him to have found in Christ's own words the source of his doctrine of His divine sonship, He *may* have found there also a foundation for his doctrine of the co-operation of the Son with the Father in the creation and main-tenance of nature. But as regards both doctrines, or, to speak more properly, both parts of the same doctrine, we shall note that the authors of the Epistle to the Hebrews and the Fourth Gospel are entirely at one with St. Paul. They all use the same language

[1] See Strabo, xiv 5, 13 : " The zeal of its inhabitants for philo-sophy and general culture is such that they have surpassed even Athens and Alexandria and all other cities where schools of philosophy can be mentioned. And its pre-eminence in this respect is so great, because there the students are all townspeople and foreign students do not readily settle there." Strabo was an older contemporary of St. Paul.

about the functions of the Son in nature. They reflect, no doubt, the language of the later Jewish theology about the Wisdom or Word of God. But the principle of such language is a fundamental principle of Old Testament religion. It is the refusal to separate the spiritual from the material, or God's work in men's souls from His work in nature. It would have seemed self-evident to a Jew that if the Son is the organ of God's revelation and communication of Himself to men's souls, He must also and equally be the organ of His work in creating and ordering nature. And in this principle we must surely see a real inspiration of the Spirit of truth.

III

Next, the Epistle to the Hebrews must claim our attention. Nothing can bring more clearly before our minds the *novelty* of literary criticism considered as a science than the fact that for so many centuries this Epistle should have been held to be by St. Paul. For though the ultimate theology is closely similar to St. Paul's, the tone of thought, as well as the phraseology[1] and style, is characteristically different. Who wrote this Epistle we do not know, but we are, I think, safe in saying that it was written for Jews and before, but not much before, the destruction of Jerusalem, and that it was written by one whose thought suggests Alexandria as his spiritual home.

[1] Thus God is scarcely called the "Father"; the idea of our being "in Christ Jesus" or "in the Lord" is absent; the doctrine of the Spirit is very slightly touched. There is (strangely) no assertion of the universalism of the Gospel. The antitheses "law" and "grace," "faith" and "works," "flesh" and "spirit" are not to be found. It is not certain that the author was acquainted with Philo's writings, but he certainly breathed in their atmosphere. For instance, for him heaven is the world of spiritual and intellectual realities and earth the world of shadows and images. People who say that for the early Christians heaven was definitely a place above our heads seem to forget the Epistle to the Hebrews.

It has one dominant purpose, that is to present to thoughtful Jewish converts, who were in danger of relapsing, the essential superiority of Christianity to the religion of the Old Testament and its finality, on the ground of its providing for men, through Christ, perfect and unhindered approach to God. That is to say, in other words, that its subject is the high-priesthood of Christ. But though this special doctrine of the Epistle is a fascinating subject, we are not at present directly concerned with it. What we are concerned with is simply the author's doctrine of the person of Christ, and this we shall find is almost identical with St. Paul's.

"Jesus," then, (for the writer most often used this purely human name,) had not the beginning of His personal existence when He took flesh. Before all creation He was the effulgence of God's glory and the very image of His substance.[1] These phrases suggest coeternity with God, but not directly personality. But they are coupled with the personal words "the son," and the "heir of all things"; and (as with St. Paul) it is the Son through whom God made the worlds, and it is He who bears along or upholds all things by the utterance of His power. As Son of the Father He builds the house of which Moses is the servant.[2] Again, as with St. Paul, all His activity in redemption is seen upon the background of His functions in the whole of nature. He is "God's Son, whom he appointed heir of all things, through whom also he made the worlds; who, being the effulgence of his glory, and the very image of his substance, and upholding all things by the word of his power, when he had made purification of sins, sat down on the right hand of the majesty on high."[3] But though there is thus unmistakable continuity of personal being and action between these different "moments" of the Son's life, yet

[1] i 2–4.　　　　[2] iii 1–6.　　　　[3] i 2–4.

there is no idea of any eternal *manhood*. He became man at a particular date. Thus He who had been so much above the angels was "made a little lower than the angels." [1] "He partook of flesh and blood." [2] "He taketh hold of the seed of Abraham." [3] "He sprang out of Judah." [4] And great emphasis is laid on the reality of His manhood in spirit as well as flesh. "He was in all points tempted like as we are, yet without sin." [5] "In that he himself hath suffered being tempted, he is able to succour them that are tempted." [6] "Who in the days of his flesh, having offered up prayers and supplications with strong crying and tears unto him that was able to save him from death, and having been heard for his godly fear, though he was a Son, yet learned obedience by the things that he suffered ; and having been made perfect, he became unto all them that obey him the author of eternal salvation." [7] His priesthood for men depends upon the reality of His manhood and human development : and it is in the perfection of His manhood that "he sat down on the right hand of God." [8]

Thus as He is properly divine, so He is properly human : but His personality is divine throughout —He is the eternal Son. That in which He offers Himself is "eternal spirit." [9] Whether, in the quotation from Ps. xlv,[10] He is called "God" is not certain ; but the words of Ps. cii, which describe the activity of the Lord (Jehovah) and His unchangeableness and eternity, are certainly ascribed to Jesus,[11] and apparently to Him is ascribed "the glory for ever and ever." [12] Certainly in this Epistle there is the full doctrine of the Incarnation, quite explicit.

---

[1] ii 9. [2] ii 14. [3] ii 16. [4] vii 14.
[5] iv 15. [6] ii 18. [7] v 7–9. [8] x 12.
[9] ix 14. [10] i 8. Westcott translates "God is thy throne."
[11] i 10. [12] xiii 21.

But before leaving this Epistle I should wish to emphasize its relative independence not only side by side with St. Paul's Epistles, but also side by side with Philo.

No doubt the author's intellectual equipment and outlook are those of Alexandrian Judaism, but the special value of his testimony to the doctrine of the Incarnation lies in this—that whereas the ideology of Philo and of other like Jewish thinkers would have come naturally to him, as a matter of fact his Christianity—his faith in Jesus—had given to all the current of ideas represented by Philo a wholly changed basis and tendency. He believed in the man Jesus : he clung with intense conviction and appreciation to His human sufferings of body and mind. The object on which his mind rested was, not an idea, but a person of flesh and blood, who has lived and struggled and suffered among the ordinary children of men. It is this strongly held historical basis of his faith which so deeply differentiates it from the ideology of Philo. It is not that he has transmuted the faith of the first disciples into something different by the use of Alexandrian ideas. It is that the first faith in Jesus, the actual historical person, accepted as what He declared Himself to be, the Son of God, has found in the Alexandrian tradition of Judaism ideas and terms in which it can express itself. This is to say that, by the side of St. Paul, the writer to the Hebrews stands with a very substantial originality, and with a very independent grasp upon the facts concerning Jesus; but, by the side of Philo, he stands on a different basis, and is travelling by a different road to a different goal.

I will leave to another chapter the rest of the New Testament books. But I feel that we have already traversed together—I and my readers— the most important and the most difficult part of our road. The task on which we set out was to

follow along the process by which the faith in Jesus
of the first disciples developed into a clear belief
in His person.

We watched how, unconsciously, the overmaster-
ing sense of authority resident and active in Him
brought them into an attitude towards Him which
cannot be otherwise described than that He came to
have for them " the values of God." We saw too
that Jesus Himself seems to have deliberately minis-
tered to this result. Then we watched their failure of
faith over the scandal of the cross and their recovery
in the light of the Resurrection. Again we saw how
their crucified Master, now raised to be the Lord of
all at God's right hand, comes to have, in even fuller
sense than before, the values of God for them. We
cannot doubt that there must have been deep questioning in their souls and probably in their conver-
sation as to the secret of His person and how the Man
could be thus exalted to the place of God. But we
catch no word about the divine Sonship in their public
preaching. It is St. Paul who, as far as our records
go, first appears to have brought the idea of the Sonship, grounded so securely in Christ's own language,
to explain the divine exaltation of the Man and to
give the Church the formula for its creed ; but we
have seen that the Church and its teachers, as
far as St. Paul's Epistles and other documents of
the New Testament[1] enable us to judge, appear to
have accepted this doctrine about eternal Sonship
and incarnation without controversy or demurrer.
We have seen the same doctrine a few years after
St. Paul's death unhesitatingly affirmed in the
Epistle of a man equal to St. Paul in intellectual
equipment, though independent of him in training
and in the character of his mind. What we have
still to ask ourselves is whether this process in the
disciples' minds, so far as we have followed it, is

[1] See below on the Epistles of Peter, James and Jude, pp. 127 ff.

for us really imaginable unless we suppose that the leading under which they were moving forward was the leading of God, and the conviction about Jesus to which they were led was the truth. But to that question we shall return, when we have considered the other documents of the New Testament.

NOTE A

On the doubts raised whether Jesus in fact instituted the Sacrament of His Body and Blood for the observance of His Church.

Bousset and the critics of his school maintain that the sacramental ideas and rites of St. Paul—in particular those connected with the Eucharist—were not derived from Jesus or from the early Jerusalem church, but had their origin in the Hellenistic churches of Syria, where sacramentalism was developed among the Christians under the influence of the Pagan mystery religions with which they had been familiar before their conversion. What St. Paul did was, with the help of a vision, recorded in 1 Cor. xi 23 ff., to formulate and give consistency to the sacramental principle on the basis of the Jew's belief in God and the newly-won belief in Jesus as " the Lord " and as " the Spirit." This theory must wait for fuller consideration till the next volume. But before Bousset wrote, and more widely than his influence has spread, it has been the custom (see Inge's *Outspoken Essays* (1919), pp. 227 f. and 249) among many critics to maintain that Jesus instituted no sacraments as He founded no church. Doubtless He celebrated a fraternal meal with His disciples before His Passion, which had a spiritual significance, as He was probably accustomed to do. But He instituted no rite for any future church, such as is implied in the words " Do this in remembrance of me " (1 Cor. xi 24, 25). The suggestion of these critics is that when St. Paul speaks of himself as having " received from the Lord " and " delivered to you " (1 Cor. xi 23) the account of the institution of such a rite at the Last Supper, with the solemn injunction

"Do this in remembrance of me," he means that he had received it *in a vision from Jesus*. This vision did not correspond at all closely to the historical reality, but its teaching and the practice based upon it spread rapidly through the churches. So that when the Synoptic Gospels were written it had become the accepted institution in all the churches and was related in the Gospels as history.

This theory seems to me to be in manifold ways arbitrary and improbable. For (1) St. Paul speaks also of having "received" and "delivered" the record of the Resurrection in 1 Cor. xv 2–4, and no one can reasonably doubt that he is there referring to the tradition of the Church (see verse 11). It is obvious, therefore, to interpret his words about the "tradition" of the Eucharist in the same sense (see Dr. Anderson Scott in *Cambridge Biblical Essays*, p. 337). It was "from the Lord" as its source, though through the Church, that St. Paul received it.

(2) If he had received it in a vision surely its form would have been different. It would hardly have come as an historical record. See Stanton, *The Gospels as Historical Documents*, vol. iii. pp. 273 ff.: "A passage earlier in the Epistle, where the apostle is interpreting [the sacrament] will suggest that Jesus [in the vision of Paul] might have said 'The bread which ye break is a communion in my body—the cup which ye partake is a communion in my blood.'" Nothing can read less like a vision than St. Paul's actual narrative.[1] Or if such a vision had been seen or imagined by St. Paul, which did not correspond to the facts as they had been hitherto received or to the practice of the churches already

[1] Eduard Meyer, *Ursprung*, vol. i. p. 175, is very emphatic that the account of the Last Supper, as St. Paul gives it, "belonged to the oldest element of the tradition, as Paul had received it in Damascus." It was as "a sharply formulated tradition" (fest formulierte Tradition) that he produced it. "He received the tradition of the institution of the Last Supper in the same sense 'from the Lord' as he received the Gospel as a whole. . . . In fact his information came naturally from the three years of his period of instruction in Damascus, which was completed through his intercourse with Peter and James in Jerusalem. Therefore it cannot be plausibly suggested that he here (i.e. in 1 Cor. xi) offers a special tradition about the Lord's Supper differing from the general tradition."

established, is it likely that such a vision would have altered the practice of all the churches, including the Jewish churches, for whom the first Gospel was written ? This seems very improbable.

(3) Curiously enough the critics are driven to seek the account of the original institution which has been least deeply affected by St. Paul's vision in the Gospel of his companion St. Luke, according to the shorter reading of his Gospel, found in some Western authorities, which leaves out all the words after " this is my body " —down to " poured out for you." I cannot but agree with Dr. Salmon that the words should not be omitted (see Dr. Salmon's *The Human Element in the Gospels* [Murray], pp. 492 f.). I think we can only suppose that their omission, like the omission of verse 17 in other authorities, is due to a desire not to duplicate the giving of a cup. It is utterly improbable that St. Luke meant to reject both St. Mark's account and St. Paul's belief and practice, with which he must have been well acquainted.

(4) Dr. Rashdall's pages on the Last Supper (*The Idea of Atonement*, pp. 37 ff.) are written to dispose of the idea that " a certain expiatory value was attached by our Lord Himself to His approaching death " in the phrases " This is my body [which is given for you]," " This is my blood of the covenant which is shed for many [for the remission of sins]." With the subject of the atonement we shall have to deal later on. But as far as the accounts of the Eucharist are concerned Dr. Rashdall's pages seem to me to represent that type of " criticism " which is least worthy of the name— the type of criticism which is resolved at all costs to eliminate what it does not want to accept. It is quite certain that the words in St. Mark, St. Matthew, St. Paul, and St. Luke (longer text) all alike postulate a Christ who believed Himself to be inaugurating a new covenant, according to the prophecies that so it should be ; and to be inaugurating it by sacrifice—by His blood —as the first covenant at Sinai had been inaugurated. And as it had been declared that the servant of Jehovah would, by " pouring out his soul unto death " as a guilt offering, redeem " many," so St. Mark and St. Matthew,

8

by the use of the words "for many," convey to us the thought that Jesus knew He was so doing.

(5) Some critics—influenced by Schweitzer—suppose the words of St. Matthew, "I will not drink henceforth of the fruit of the vine, until that day when I drink it new *with you* in my Father's kingdom," intimate that our Lord expected the immediate coming of the End and His union with His disciples at the heavenly feast of the Kingdom. In part they make this the ground for disbelieving that Jesus instituted any sacrament for constant observance in His Church. He had no thought for an intermediate period. But St. Mark, on whom St. Matthew is based, and St. Luke omit the words " with you." Without these words the saying has no suggestion of any immediate renewal of fellowship with His disciples. They only intimate that this is His last meal on earth, and that the new wine of the Kingdom lies immediately before Himself. And where the emphasis has to be laid on the particular words, we must prefer St. Mark and St. Luke in agreement to St. Matthew's version. But of the eschatology of our Lord we treat later in this volume.

NOTE B

*On the question whether the First Church in
Jerusalem called Jesus Lord*

We must not, of course, ignore the position taken by critics of the school of Bousset, and others, that the term " the Lord " (κύριος) for Jesus was due to the Hellenistic Christian churches at Antioch, Damascus, Tarsus, and the like, who passed through a rapid assimilation to the Pagan mystery religions, even before St. Paul began his public ministry. These Pagan adherents of mystery religions addressed their patron gods or goddesses as Lord or Lady—Lord Hermes, Lord Serapis, Lady Cybele, etc. Thus Bousset holds that the title (or its equivalent in Aramaic) was not used in the early Jerusalem community, but was first used in these Hellenistic churches.[1]

[1] Bousset, *Kyrios Christos*, pp. 77 ff.; cf. Glover, *Conflict of Religions*, p. 356.

On the other hand, let us hear Dalman[1]: "At first the title, used in speaking to or of Jesus, was no more than the respectful designation of the Teacher on the part of His disciples. As soon as Jesus had entered into His state of kingly majesty, it became among His followers an acknowledgment of sovereignty ; and when they addressed Him as the Son of God [which apparently was not commonly done in the days before St. Paul], then ' our Lord,' as applied to Jesus, was not widely separated from the same designation for God. But it must be remembered that the Aramaic-speaking Jews did not, save exceptionally, designate God as ' Lord,' so that in the Hebraist section of the Jewish Christians the expression ' Our Lord ' was used in reference to Jesus only, and would be quite free from ambiguity."

The question is this, then—Was the title Maran or Lord used of Jesus by the early Jerusalem community in a sense betokening sovereignty (" Lord of all ")—in a sense which, among Greek Christians of a few years later, easily merged into the sense of the same word as applied to God (Jehovah), but which at present would not have been precisely so used in Jerusalem ?

St. Luke plainly implies that it was, with the title " Christ," used by them as their special term for the exalted Jesus.[2] See Acts i 21, (?) 24, ii 36, (iv 33, v 14), vii 59, (?) 60, viii 16, ix (1), 10, 13, 15, 17, (29), (42), x 36, xi 8, 17, 20, (21), 23, (24).

There seems to me no kind of reason to doubt this, especially as St. Luke appears to be careful to avoid the title Son of God, till he comes to St. Paul. He seems to imply that the one title was, and the other was not, in use.

There are two other indications looking in the same direction.

(1) First, that even in the thoroughly Greek church of Corinth St. Paul assumes familiarity with the invocation " Maranatha," " Come, O our Lord ! " in Aramaic, which means clearly that it had an Aramaic

---

[1] See Dalman's *Words of Jesus,* p. 327.

[2] I have put in brackets ( ) the occasions where the word is used by St. Luke in his own person and not ascribed specially to some speaker other than himself.

origin. (The same Aramaic phrase occurs in the
Didachè, which is a document (I think) quite independent of St. Paul.) Bousset admits the force of this
as an argument that the title " Lord " goes back to the
original Aramaic-speaking church at Jerusalem, but
pleads that it is not *impossible* " that the Maranatha
formula had its origin, not on the ground of the original
Palestinian church, but in the bilingual region of the
Hellenistic communities of Antioch, Damascus, and
Tarsus itself." [1] No doubt it is possible : for we know
little or nothing of these communities and their manner
of speech. But the probability surely is that the
Hellenistic Christian communities there talked Greek.
Even in Jerusalem the names of the men chosen to
minister to the Hellenists are all Greek names. And
Bousset is surely mistaken in saying that St. Paul's
" tradition " goes back to these Syrian communities
only, and not to Jerusalem. Where St. Paul talks about
the tradition concerning the Resurrection (1 Cor. xv 3),
there he certainly means the tradition which he had
received from the earlier apostles—*i.e.* at Jerusalem—
for he ranks himself with them as " the last " and
irregular apostle, and adds, " Therefore, whether it were
I or they, so we preach." The tradition which he
received was therefore theirs before he came on the
scene. It came from Jerusalem. Again, in Rom. xv 19
St. Paul speaks of *Jerusalem* as his starting point.

(2) St. Paul was of course conscious that there were
" Gods many and Lords many," but certainly nothing
in his use of " Lord " as a title for Jesus Christ suggests
affinities with the heathen. It was, according to
St. Luke, used with special reference to the dignity of
the ascended Christ and His future coming. The phrase
" Maranatha," " Come, O our Lord," also suggests that.
St. Paul in his (probably earliest) Epistle to the Thessalonians constantly uses it with this suggestion : the
day of the Lord, the coming of the Lord, etc., see
1 Thess. ii 19, iii 13, iv 15, 16, 17, v 2; 2 Thess. i 7,
ii 1, 8, 14. But this is a distinctively Jewish idea. And

---

[1] P. 84. It is noteworthy that Bousset confesses " Schwieriger
ist es eine Alterbestimmung für das Vorkommen des griechischen
Kyriostitels in Syrien und seiner Umgebung zu gewinnen."

his characteristic phrase ἐν Κυρίῳ suggests something quite alien to the heathen cults.

On the whole, Bousset's position is singularly ill founded.

NOTE C

On the phrase of St. Paul, "Christ after the flesh."

It is difficult to feel sure what exactly St. Paul means by the words of 2 Cor. v 16 : " Wherefore we henceforth know no man after the flesh: even though we have known Christ after the flesh, yet now we know him no more." He is speaking, in a measure, generally of the ambassadors for Christ, not only of himself. That is (in part) the force of the plural " we." He is describing how the appreciation of the love of Christ involves for them death to their selfish selves, and to all the narrowness of natural affections. " To know men after the flesh " is to appraise them according to the standards of class, or race, or disposition. To " know Christ after the flesh " would be to appreciate Him as a Jew would naturally appreciate Him, as the heaven-sent Messenger who is to exalt the Jewish race and minister to Jewish pride. St. Paul had felt this pride in Christ, but before he recognized Jesus as the Christ. What he seems to mean is that all such narrow and partial prejudices have been abolished by the expulsive power of a love which is spiritual and universal. It is difficult, I acknowledge, to feel quite certain of St. Paul's meaning. But certainly he does not mean by " knowing Christ after the flesh," knowing Him as having become really and fully human in body as well as soul. That he could never repudiate. See Dr. Menzies' commentary *in loc.*

CHAPTER IV

ST. JOHN AND THE REST OF THE NEW TESTAMENT

I

THE doctrine of the divine Sonship and incarnation of Jesus Christ is given quite unmistakably in St. Paul's Epistles and the Epistle to the Hebrews, but it is given incidentally and by implication. But in St. John's Gospel, read in the light of the prologue and the conclusion,[1] it is given explicitly and directly; and the main, though not the only, object of the writing of the Gospel appears to be to affirm the doctrine with all the authority which the personal testimony of the author can give it.

I call this Gospel St. John's, and on the whole I believe it to give us at first hand the mature testimony of the son of Zebedee. But the widespread denial or doubt of his being the author, or the direct author, of the Fourth Gospel, and the consequent uncertainty about the authority to be attached to it, have seemed to make it wiser to build the structure of our argument independently of it in the first instance. So we have built it especially upon St. Mark and St. Luke, and upon the Acts, and upon St. Paul, and the Epistle to the Hebrews. But having done this we can supplement our argument with an appeal to St. John.

[1] John i 1–18 and John xx 30. Chap. xxi is evidently an appendix, by the same author, I believe, as the rest of the book, with an addition (verses 24, 25) by his companions.

Dr. Stanton has recently, in a very careful study of the Fourth Gospel, given us a theory of what one may call "mediate Johannine authorship." The actual author was, he supposes, a younger man than the Apostle, who had gone to Asia perhaps earlier than he, but had there become intimately associated with him, and who also had independent memories of his own—" who could remember having sometimes himself seen or heard Jesus, and who felt himself possessed of a knowledge, which was at least almost immediate, of the divine revelation made in the Lord, by intimate association with His personal disciples very soon after His departure." [1] I cannot be satisfied with this theory. It seems to me impossible to harmonize with the impression made by the Fourth Gospel. I cannot doubt that it at least claims to be in its whole bulk—and the same applies to the First Epistle—a personal testimony,

[1] Stanton, *The Gospels as Historical Witnesses*, Part iii (Cambridge, 1920), p. 281.
Since this chapter was written, I have noted that Ed. Meyer, *Ursprung*, i p. 312, treats as ridiculous any doubts that the author of the Fourth Gospel intended to represent himself as " the disciple whom Jesus loved " and as John the son of Zebedee. " This was the mask he assumed." He cannot understand how modern critics can have brought themselves to doubt this. Also he is confident that the author's conception of the Logos is derived from Palestinian Jewish sources (the " Memra " doctrine), and not from Greek philosophy, or Philo, though he may have known of the current Greek philosophical term (p. 318). I have also read Dr. Burney's *Aramaic Origin of the Fourth Gospel* (Oxford, 1922), who is (of course) insistent on its Palestinian origin, pp. 37 ff. In his opinion the author must have been an eyewitness of the events he describes—really " the disciple whom Jesus loved ": but he identifies him as " John the presbyter " and not the apostle. He thinks that he must have been a Jew of Jerusalem, belonging to the priestly circle, and well trained in the Rabbinical schools, and that he wrote the Gospel in Aramaic, probably at Antioch soon after A.D. 75, before he took up his residence at Ephesus. I am not without hopes that the essentially Palestinian, and not Hellenistic, origin and character of the Gospel, and its high value as an historical witness both to the events of our Lord's life and to His teaching, may soon come to be regarded as an " assured result " of critical enquiry.

so personal that it must be first-hand, and I see
no sufficient reason to doubt that the claim is true.
But Dr. Stanton's study at least shows very cogent
reasons for believing that both the narrative of the
Fourth Gospel and the discourses rest upon a real
apostolic experience, and I hope that critical students
will heed his arguments.[1]

Thus he seems to me to show convincingly that
the prologue to the Gospel, though of course it
stands first, is not by any means the governing
factor in the whole book.[2]   On the contrary, in the
bulk of the book, after the prologue, there is no
allusion to the doctrine of the (personal) Word of
God which is the characteristic feature of the prologue,
and " the word of God " is given, as in the First
Epistle, only its normal meaning of the divine
message.[3]   Jesus there appears only under those
titles which He certainly used of Himself—the
Son of Man and the Son of God—or the title which
was certainly ascribed to Him with His express
sanction—the Christ.   The substance of the book,
which is of a narrative character, must, Dr. Stanton
argues, be taken to represent the real experience
(and the conviction based upon the experience)
of an apostle or apostolic group, which was shared
by or communicated to the mind of the author,
supposed to be a different person.   To put this
experience on record was his primary object.   Only
at the last moment, so to speak, before he wrote
his " gospel " did the current idea of the Logos
(the divine Word or Reason or Power always active

---

[1] *Op. cit.*, chap. vi, p. 209.

[2] Pp. 166 ff.   This argument is substantially also Harnack's,
see p. 167.   See also D. C. Somervill, *A Short History of our Religion* (G. Bell & Son), p. 111: "A kind of preface or prologue,
which may also be regarded as an epilogue or summing up of the
whole matter."

[3] See John v 38, x 35, xv 25, xvii 6, 14, 17.   This is also the
sense of " the word " in 1 John i 2.

in the universe) suggest itself to the author as a suitable term to express the nature and functions of the Son. So he formulates his dogmatic prologue with the help of the new term with which both his Jewish training and his Asiatic experience had made him familiar. Thus the idea of the prologue must be thought of as having presented itself to his mind only after the narrative and ideas of the body of the Gospel were already formed and fixed, and, Dr. Stanton would say, after the First Epistle had been written. Further, the bulk of the Gospel must represent matter which had already become familiar in the oral instruction given to the congregations of Asiatic Christians.[1]

Dr. Stanton also indicates with admirable precision how closely akin the idea of the divine sonship of Jesus, as presented in the Fourth Gospel, is to what is found already in the foundation documents of the Synoptic Gospels [2]—to the conception of divine sonship implied in the narrative of the Temptation and presented in great sayings of our Lord which have been already examined ; and how the ideas of St. John vi about Christ, as through His flesh and blood the spiritual food of the world, are really implied in the language which He is recorded to have used, in the Synoptic Gospels and by St. Paul, at the Last Supper. On such grounds Dr. Stanton argues that the idea of the divine sonship of Jesus presented in the body of the Gospel must be accepted

[1] See pp. 50, 282.
[2] Pp. 267 ff. Cp. Harnack, *The Sayings of Jesus*, p. 302 : "If the first evangelist himself wrote the passage [St. Matt. xi 25–7] as we read it, then even with the most cautious interpretation of the passage, his own Christology approached very nearly to that of the Johannine writings in one of the most important points." In view of the fact that the saying occurs in substantially identical form in St. Matthew and St. Luke, and must therefore have so occurred in Q, we should substitute for Harnack's opening words something of this kind—"If, as we cannot doubt, the first recorder of our Lord's words, whose written record lies behind all our present Gospels, wrote the passage as we read it," etc.

as resting on genuine utterances of Christ, and he shows the reasonableness of believing that, if such utterances were really made as the Synoptists record, they were more frequently and more emphatically made than there appears. "It is improbable that such sayings could have been spoken, and yet have stood alone in the intercourse of Jesus with His disciples. Even in order that they might be rendered intelligible, and be duly impressed upon their minds, they would need to be repeated." Dr. Stanton also argues afresh with great force how well the Synoptic narrative can be fitted into the framework of the story of the Fourth Gospel, and I should add how much on the whole it gains thereby in intelligibility.

I have written so much by way of preface because writers are apt to assume that, if they reject the direct authorship of St. John the son of Zebedee, they can dispose of the whole Gospel as a work of pious imagination. I do not agree that the direct authorship can be rejected. But what I think is a prejudice against the authorship of St. John is still a very strong prejudice, and it seems to me very important that the world which especially claims to be critical should remember that it has still to reckon with the Fourth Gospel, both as to its incidents and its teaching, as making an historical claim which cannot be ignored, and representing a tradition quite independent of St. Paul.

I always find myself impressed by the fact that this Gospel four times calls attention to occasions when the disciples failed to apprehend at the time the meaning of some word of Jesus, and only afterwards in retrospect perceived what it had really been,[1] and also calls attention to our Lord's having promised His disciples that the Holy Spirit, whom they were to receive after His departure, would so

[1] John ii 22, viii 27, x 6, xii 16.

act within their minds as not only to interpret what
they remembered of His words, but also to bring out
of their "subconscious selves" what had been
forgotten or ignored.[1] That such should have been
their experience seems to me to be thoroughly in
accordance with human nature.[2] Thus I am disposed
to believe that the record of our Lord's words contained in the common matter of St. Matthew and
St. Luke represents the first memory of what He had
said, more or less exactly as He said it, but the
Fourth Gospel gives us what had been a gradually
growing recollection in the mind of St. John and
probably of others, viz. that the sayings of our Lord
about His divine sonship had been more frequent
and more emphatic than the earliest record had
implied.

Here in the Fourth Gospel, then, St. John, presupposing the Synoptic record, supplements it with
incidents and discourses especially intended to bear
on the point of divine sonship.[3] Thus, apart from
the comments of the Evangelist, so far as they can
be kept distinct from the words of Christ, we have
a discourse of Christ (cap. v) in which He asserts

[1] xiv 26, cf. xiii 7.
[2] D. C. Somervill, *op. cit.*, p. 106, quotes from Mr. Bruce Glasier's
memoir of William Morris, written twenty-five years after his
death, the following : " I have found that my memory is, on many
occasions, subject to what seems to be a sort of 'illumination' or
'inspiration.' Thus when I have fixed my mind on one, say, of
the incidents recalled in these chapters, the scene has begun to
unfold itself, perhaps slowly at first, but afterwards rapidly and
clearly. Meditating upon it for a time, I have lifted my pen and
begun to write. Then to my surprise the conversations, long
buried or hidden somewhere in my memory, have come back to
me sometimes with the greatest fulness, word for word, as we say.
Nay, not only the words, but the tones, the pauses and the gestures
of the speaker." My own belief is that in the Fourth Gospel the
memory of incidents and things seen is precise and clear cut. But
the memory of words, though true in its ultimate substance, has
become in its form transmuted and sometimes enlarged by meditation. In almost all cases, however, clear-cut sayings of our Lord
which are original and verbally genuine can be discerned.
[3] See xx 31.

at once, as always, His subordination to the Father,
but also His constant association with Him in His
works, in such general sense as, perhaps, suggests
His co-operation with the Father even in the processes
of nature. "My Father worketh hitherto, and I
work" (v 17–18). The co-operation actually asserted
(verses 19–29) is something quite transcending the
human level, though He who so works is called
"Son of Man." That is to say, there is asserted
a divine sonship belonging to the Son of Man under
human conditions, which yet can only belong to the
man, because He had come into His manhood out
of a pre-existence in God.[1] This is affirmed again
and again in the next chapter (vi 38, 41, 62), as
also that He is to return, in His manhood, to the
heaven whence He came. Again in the discourse
of chapter viii this pre-existent sonship is affirmed
and identified with the eternal existence of God
(verse 58). Again the Son and the Father are
declared to be one thing (x 30) and, as has been
explained above,[2] I do not think the apparent
minimizing of this claim (verses 33–36), when the
Jews rightly understood it as a claim of Godhead,
can be taken at its face value. The almost startling
incompatibility of the minimizing explanation of

[1] There are two assertions by our Lord that "the Father" is
"greater" than He (x 29, xiv 28). It has been long a matter
of controversy in the Church (see Westcott's note) whether this
superior "greatness" of the Father to the Son refers to the Godhead of the Son or to His manhood. It seems to me that the words
—so far like the words of our Lord recorded in St. Mark and St.
Matthew, asserting the Son's ignorance of the day and hour of the
"end of the world"—are spoken by the Son in His manhood
and with direct reference to His present human state, but that
it is not an *adequate* explanation of them to say that they describe
Him as "inferior to the Father as touching His manhood." For
they refer not to His manhood merely (which, according to the
teaching of the Church, had no separate personal existence) but
to Himself. They seem to me to describe an inferiority which
the incarnation of the Son has (so to speak) intensified, but which
depends upon and postulates an eternal subordination.

[2] See pp. 28 f.

His divine sonship with the general argument of the Gospel does indeed give us a guarantee that the Evangelist would not have preserved the words unless he had felt sure that they were really spoken by our Lord; but I think they must be interpreted, not as minimizing His meaning, but as intended to force the Jews to consider that, according to their authoritative Scriptures, something much less than Godhead would justify a claim of divine sonship in some sense. They could not, therefore, dispose of His inconvenient claim upon them merely by repudiating its full implication. More than this kind of meaning cannot be attached to this strange and isolated passage consistently with the constant tenor of the Gospel as a whole.

In the last discourses immediately before His passion our Lord is constantly represented as one who was conscious of having in one sense come from God—but without thereby leaving God, for He was still abiding in the Father and the Father in Him, and to see Him is to see the Father—and as being immediately to return to God to resume an interrupted glory and to fulfil the purpose of His mission by the bestowal of the Spirit, whom the Father is to send in His name and at His hands.[1] We shall have to return upon these last discourses about the Holy Spirit. All that we need now to do is to assure ourselves that in them, as in the rest of the Gospel, what we are presented with, in our Lord's words, is an indisputable and constantly reiterated assertion on His part of divine sonship. This is primarily an assertion of what He was then and there in His manhood; but it is also frequently and plainly implied that He has been through the ages the Son with the Father, dependent upon Him for His very life, but also belonging essentially to the divine being; that He came into the world

[1] xiv 16, 26, xv 26, xvi 7.

voluntarily in fulfilment of a divine mission of redemption—to accept death at the hands of men for
their salvation—and that He was about to resume
an interrupted glory on His return to heaven as
Son of Man, carrying thither His manhood to become
through the Spirit, whom He is to send down from
the Father upon His chosen body, the fountain head
of a new life.

Now I do not say that the author of the Fourth
Gospel was unacquainted with St. Paul. That can
hardly have been the case. But I say that all this
body of teaching appears to have grown quite independently of St. Paul. It has its own independent
phraseology and characteristic ideas, notably the
dominant ideas of " light " and " life " and " truth,"
of the conflict of belief and unbelief, of judgment
perpetually being enacted, and of eternal life already
enjoyed. And it must be held to rest upon the
foundation of a real tradition of the words of Jesus
in the churches of Asia and in the school of St.
John ; for myself I go farther, and believe it records
both the real memory and the deep meditation of
St. John as given us by himself. And I do not
see any point at which the record of the Fourth
Gospel—apart from the prologue, which has still
to be considered—suggests the influence of the
current Logos-philosophy of the Hellenistic world.
There is really nothing needed to account for it
but the Old Testament and the actual life and
teaching of Christ.

The outcome of this experience upon the author
has been to generate an idea of Christ as to the nature
of which he leaves us in no doubt. He believed
that Christ, the Son of Man, was the eternal Son of
God, who is very God. He identifies Him with the
Jehovah of the Old Testament, for he speaks of
Isaiah as having seen His (Christ's) " glory " when,
in his vision in the temple, he saw the form of Jehovah

sitting upon His throne[1]; and he represents the penitent Thomas as calling the risen Jesus "my Lord and my God." Also he plainly believes the eternal Son of God to have come or been sent by God into the world as man—the Son of Man. But there does not seem to me to be any trace of a belief in a pre-existent man or Son of Man. It was the pre-existent Son of God who was sent into the world (iii 16-18) as Son of Man, and who after His death and resurrection carried that manhood into heaven[2] in pursuance of a divine purpose of redemption. This alone gives a fair interpretation of the language of the Gospel as a whole. The author's mind is preoccupied with making it evident that Jesus was really the Son of God. But he leaves us in no doubt as to the reality of His manhood, both bodily and spiritual.[3]

All this belief of "St. John" concerning Jesus grew, I believe with Dr. Stanton, on the ground of a real historical tradition or (I should say) of a real memory, and in substance antedates the prologue. It is with this belief already in his mind that, when he came to give his Gospel written form, he found in the

---

[1] See Burney, *op. cit.*, p. 37.

[2] In vi 62 our Lord is represented as anticipating His ascension : "What and if ye see the Son of man ascending up where he was before." In iii 13 I think we must suppose that we have a reflection of the Evangelist and not a word of Christ. The ascension has plainly already occurred. The sense in which "the Son of man came down from heaven" is defined by the verses which follow. It is in the sense that "God sent his Son" (verses 16 and 17) and His "only begotten Son" (verse 18) into the world to save the world and that He came to save the world as man, the Son of Man.

[3] No doubt the reality of our Lord's manhood physically is what he sees represented symbolically in the blood from His pierced side, xix 34-5, see my *Exposition of St. John's Epistles, in loc.* ; see John iv 6 and xix 28 for His being tired and thirsty. Dr. Burkitt (*The Gospel History and its Transmission,* p. 233) has the courage to say that " In no early Christian document is the real humanity of Jesus so emphasized as in the Fourth Gospel." The reality of His human spirit and human sympathy appears in xi 33-8 xii 27, xiii 1, etc.

current idea of *the Logos* (the word or reason of God)
the best vehicle for expressing his doctrine in a concise
and dogmatic shape, such as would arrest the imagination and conciliate the sympathies of the world for
which he was writing. For his world was plainly
one deeply liable at the moment to be diverted by
the rising tide of " Gnostic " speculation from the
belief in the Incarnation, or (what is the same thing)
the belief that Jesus is the Son of God. It appears
indeed very vividly in St. John's Epistles that his
world was a troubled world—a world full of movements calculated to mislead and destroy this fundamental faith.[1] And all these movements would
recognize in the term " the Logos " one of their
keywords or favourite thoughts.

For the Hellenistic world was possessed with the
idea of a Law or Force or Mind moulding and governing the universe. This was the God immanent in
the world, "in whom we live and move and have
our being," of which the mind or spirit in each man
was a minute portion. This current belief was of
Stoic origin. Obviously, like the modern more or
less pantheistic utterances of Shelley and Goethe and
Wordsworth (in his earlier phase), this philosophy
responds to a widespread demand of the human spirit
that it shall be able to see God in all things and
to feel its own kinship with the divine. Before St.
John's days it had taken many different forms and
moved in many different directions. Thus a Jew of
Alexandria before our Lord's time, in the Book of

---

[1] The signs of trouble are apparent in 1 John i 18–26, iv 1–6,
v 6–10 ; 2 John 7–11. The precise nature of this hostile movement I have sought to describe in *Epistles of St. John*, pp. 109 ff.,
165 ff., 170 f., 191 ff. It denied St. John's central faith, viz. that
in the man Jesus the highest and lowest had become one—that
the man Jesus was really and personally the Son of God come in
the flesh, and it denied this by separating the man Jesus from the
divine Christ, who was represented only as coming down upon the
man at His baptism out of the heavenly regions and leaving Him
before His passion.

Wisdom, had assimilated this Hellenistic belief in a divine energy and law and spirit, immanent in the world, and had identified it with the Wisdom of God. As we have already seen,[1] in this beautiful little book Wisdom appears as something more than a mere personification of a divine quality. It is a living being, as well as a pervasive force throughout the whole universe. It is a spirit expressive of the inner being of God, and it is the revealer of God in nature and to man through His saints and prophets. Here we have an intermediate being presented to us—intermediate between the supreme and inaccessible God and the material world. And it is a very active power, which later on in the book, under the name of the Word of God, is described as leaping down from the divine throne to work His miracles of judgment upon Egypt, " a stern warrior into the midst of the doomed land." [2]

Later Philo, the Jew of Alexandria, elaborated this conception of an intermediate being, whether we are to call it person or no, who as the divine *Logos* is not only the immanent reason and law of the world, but also the active instrument of God and the revealer of His mysterious being. This idea of an intermediate being between the high and inaccessible God and the material world became exceedingly popular in all sorts of forms. But outside the influence of the Jewish religion it is almost always associated with the notion of matter as essentially evil, so that the supreme God could not be conceived of as either responsible for creating it, or enduring to come in immediate contact with it. Nor was the human imagination generally content with one divine or semi-divine intermediate being. The world teemed with beliefs in mysterious " powers " or " Gods," who in various ways represented a divine activity for man's enlightenment and salvation. These powers

[1] Above, p. 92.   [2] Wisd. xviii 15.

were identified with the Gods of old popular beliefs —for example with the old nature spirits who died in the decay of autumn and lived again in the rebirth of spring. These now reappear as Saviour Gods, who will redeem men from the endless flux and misery of material life and bring them by a new birth, symbolically represented, into the security of the heavenly life beyond death. All these kinds of beliefs—whether in the *Logos* as immanent mind or spirit of the universe, or in the *Logos* as an intermediate being between the supreme God and the material world, or in divine persons, vaguely conceived, through whom, by mysteries of initiation and sacramental participation, men can be saved from the miseries and fluctuations of material life and brought into the upper world of light and eternity —were already at work in the Hellenistic world, that is the world of mixed Oriental and Greek culture, when Christianity came into it. Obviously, this class of beliefs provided a condition in the souls of men, or a spiritual atmosphere, favourable to the spread of any religion of redemption or salvation, like the Christian religion. Obviously also, with its innumerable intermediate beings, or its one *Logos* neither really God nor really man, and with its almost universal belief in matter as so evil a thing that the high God could not directly touch it or be responsible for it, this whole class of beliefs was calculated, in its many movements, to pervert fundamentally the Christian tradition.

This St. John sees very vividly. Thus in the Prologue to his Gospel he accepts the term *Logos*, which has both its Hellenistic meanings such as we have been describing, and also its properly Jewish meaning, which we are very familiar with in the Old Testament—" the word of God " by which He created the world and proceeds forth to govern His people through His prophets, and to chastise the rebellious with His judgments. He seems to say to the Jewish world—" All that you have believed about God as proceeding forth by His word to create and govern nature, and to reveal Himself to man by His prophets, belongs to Jesus, and in Him is consummated." And to the Hellenistic world—" All that you have imagined of a divine activity in the world and a divine spirit, all that you have dreamed of a divine mediator or mediators between the highest and the lowest, and of mysteries of salvation, here have their justification and fulfilment, and also their correction."

Now I will attempt to paraphrase the prologue so as to bring out its general meaning,[1] referring from time to time to sayings in the Gospel which illustrate it.

At the beginning, before the world was, you must think of God as having already with Him His *Word*, the expression of Himself, God with God ; and the whole world of created things without exception was brought into being through this Word. Nor must you think of the Word as a mere quality of God, but as a person with God, in whom is life in its fulness. [As the Father hath life in Himself, so hath He given to the Son to have life in Himself.] Thus as all the life in creation is from Him, so specially is the life of men. To them as rational beings life is given in their reason and conscience as light— that is as illumination and guidance, as a " way " to be chosen and followed. So the light is given to all men. But men have loved darkness rather than light. They have followed their own desires and fancies instead of the divine leading. That is what we see in the world at large. The light is shining in the darkness and the darkness has not admitted it.[2] So it was when John the Baptist came, who was

---

[1] Where the reading is disputed, or the punctuation, I simply take what seems to me the better reading or stopping.
[2] Or " nevertheless the darkness has never overwhelmed the light."

not indeed the Light, but was a witness to the Light, calling men to faith in Another. And all the time that Other, the Word who is the True Light, lightening every man who comes into the world, was coming, and at last He came. The world to which He came was His own, as He was the creator of it, but it would not recognize Him. He came thither as to His own possession, but men—His own—refused to receive Him. That is, most men refused, but there were some who welcomed Him, and they received from Him the title to sonship of God, as all men receive it who believe on Him as He has disclosed Himself. This sonship is given by a new birth, not by the methods of natural birth. It proceeds not from mixture of human seeds, nor from carnal desire, nor from the will of a man, but purely from the will of God.[1] And all this coming of God into the world to enlighten and to regenerate those who would receive Him reached its fulfilment thus—the Word became flesh. Our creator and illuminator took our nature and tabernacled among us, as the glory of God tabernacled among the people of Israel[2]; and we His

[1] As will be seen, the phrases used, "not from bloods (i.e. the mingling of human seeds) nor carnal desire, nor the will of a man (a husband)," describe exactly the negative conditions of the human birth of Jesus of a virgin mother. Many of the early Fathers in fact had the singular, not the plural, in their text of St. John. They read it "who *was* born." Some modern scholars, including Dr. Inge and Dr. Burney, accept this as the original reading. I do not think this is probable. But I think it is certain (with Dr. Chase, Zahn and others) that the passage describes our new birth to divine sonship after the pattern picture of His birth who alone is in the fullest sense Son of God: so that the reader is reminded of a begetting and birth which took place without carnal impulse or the act of any man.

[2] In this phrase—"the *Word* was made flesh and *tabernacled* among us, and we beheld His *glory*"—St. John has brought together three characteristic Jewish ideas, which the Aramaic Targums lead us to believe were already in current use: *Memra* (the Word of God, constantly used to express God in action), *Shekinta* or (Hebrew) *Shekinah* (the tabernacle or abiding-place of God among His people, as above the cherubim in the Holy of Holies, and on special occasions besides), and *Yekara* (the glory which

witnesses who speak to you beheld His glory, beholding God in Him, as men see a father in his only son, full of the divine favour and truth. Here was one greater than John the Baptist and prior to him, as he himself bore witness : here was one who could do and give what Moses could not do or give. For the vision of God has been always unattainable to men : but here God only-begotten, the Son, whose place is in the bosom of the Father, hath interpreted Him [as He said, "He that hath seen me hath seen the Father"].

It is after this preface in which "the writer plainly announces the full and ultimate conclusion of beliefs to which he has come," [1] that he begins his story.

There is one point on which I ought to make my meaning clear before leaving St. John.

It has been for long a matter of ceaseless discussion whether St. John's term *the Logos* is derived from the Hebrew and Palestinian tradition or from the Hellenistic world of thought. I cannot but believe that in St. John's own mind its origin and meaning are fundamentally Palestinian and Jewish. I do not deny that he chooses the term as one familiar to the Hellenists. That I have already said. I do not suppose he had ever read Philo or any Stoic philosopher. But the idea and the word "Logos" were in the atmosphere of the Asiatic churches and St. John—with great discernment as it appeared— sees in it the best word to interpret to his generation the idea of the Son of God and His relation to the world both before and in the Incarnation. Nevertheless his own mind accepts and uses the term rather

under the cloudy veil shows itself in flashes). See below, p. 128, and cf. Burney, pp. 35 ff.

[1] See Dr. H. S. Holland, *The Philosophy of Faith and the Fourth Gospel*, p. 262. I was delighted to read in Dr. Armitage Robinson's recent lecture on the Fourth Gospel, given in Manchester Cathedral, an enthusiastic appreciation of the value of Dr. Holland's interpretation of the Fourth Gospel.

in the Hebrew than in the Greek sense. Not exclusively, but on the whole and first of all, the term in Greek meant *Reason* : while in the Old Testament the Word of God meant not reason at all, but the *utterance* of the will of God, or the *expression* of His mind. So as applied by St. John to the Son it means at bottom much what St. Paul meant by calling Him God's " image," and the author of the Epistle to the Hebrews by calling Him " the expression of his substance."

In the Targums, or Aramaic interpretations of the Hebrew Scriptures, " the Word (Memra) of God " is constantly used where the Hebrew speaks simply of God.[1] The " Word of God " is almost " God in action." In this sense, as has been already mentioned, " the Word of God " occurs in the Book of Wisdom,[2] and in a closely allied sense " the Wisdom of God." Dr. Rendel Harris[3] has shown how closely the phrases of St. John's prologue are modelled upon the description of the activity of the divine Wisdom in the Book of Proverbs and, still more, in the Book of Wisdom. St. John was probably acquainted with the Targums, which were already assuming fixed form, and with Proverbs and Wisdom. So it was from Jewish sources that he derived the term which he chose to express the scope and meaning of the Incarnation. But we cannot doubt that its familiar use in the Hellenic world, of which he cannot have been ignorant, partly determined his choice. In the generation after St. John it was chiefly in its Hellenic sense that the phrase came to be understood. But it was not so in St. John's mind, nor did his Gospel grow on any Hellenic soil.[4]

[1] See the passages quoted by Burney, *op. cit.* p. 38.
[2] Wisd. xviii 15, see above, p. 117.
[3] See his *Prologue to St. John's Gospel*, Camb., 1917.
[4] For the argument of Reitzenstein, who would trace the whole intellectual and mystical substance of the Fourth Gospel to a Hellenistic (Graeco-Egyptian) source, see appended note at the end of the chapter, p. 133.

II

We have passed in review the Synoptic Gospels, the Acts, the Epistles of St. Paul and that to the Hebrews, and the Gospel of St. John. In these Epistles and in the Fourth Gospel we have found a clearly expressed doctrine of Jesus Christ as an eternal and divine person, the Son of God, the divine agent in the creation and maintenance of all that exists, who at the last was incarnate for man's redemption in Jesus Christ. We have found the grounds of this doctrine in the Synoptic Gospels. Nothing else can explain the impression made by Jesus upon the disciples and His own language about His divine sonship. In the first part of the Acts, however, before the appearance of St. Paul upon the scene, we seem to find a situation in which Jesus, as the exalted and glorified Christ, is indeed treated as divine and worshipped as divine, but in which no question of pre-existence or divine sonship seems to be entertained. This situation is often represented as if the first disciples regarded Christ as strictly only a human person who, as Christ, had been exalted to divine honours on the throne of God, or deified. This is what is called the "adoptionist" theory of Christ's divinity. It played its part as a heresy among Jewish Christians in the second century under the name of Ebionism, and it was the clearly defined doctrine of Paul of Samosata in the third. But it is quite misleading so to describe the state of mind of the first Christians in Jerusalem. Ebionism, or Paul of Samosata's doctrine, was a clearly held theory. On the other hand, the Jerusalem church appears to have existed for some years without any theory, simply because their minds were absorbed in the sense of the glorified Christ, the Lord of all, at the right hand of God, and of the Spirit whom He had given them. Their creed was, "Jesus is Christ and Lord. He has given us the Spirit." But when, after a few years, the converted Saul felt at once the pressing need of a theory of Christ's person, and found this need satisfied in Christ's own language about His sonship to God, and so proclaimed the doctrine of the Incarnation, his words excited no dismay or dispute. Universally, as far as we know, the churches accepted his position. This means that, though hitherto they had not felt the pressure of the need for an explanation of their worship of the glorified Christ, yet, when once it was felt, they found it not in adoptionism but in the theory of the Incarnation ; and they found the warrant of this doctrine in Christ's own language. I cannot help thinking that in the memory and mind of some at least of the apostolic company this explanation must have been fermenting under the surface of their public witness before St. Paul appeared ; otherwise his teaching would have excited more comment. The celebration of the sacrament of Christ's body and blood, as well as the memory of some of His words, must, one would think, inevitably have led to such thoughts. What remains for us to do is to examine the rest of the documents of the New Testament, those especially which appear to be most independent of St. Paul, to see whether " adoptionism " is to be found in them, and first of all the most non-Pauline of all the books, the greatest expression of the spirit of Jewish apocalypse, the " Revelation of John the Divine."

(a) The Revelation.

There is no more thrilling book in the literature of the world than the Apocalypse of John. It is this quite independently of the question who John the Seer is, whether the " Son of Thunder," the apostle, or the supposed " Presbyter John," or whether the visions belong to an earlier or later date in the first century—problems which we need not discuss.[1] And it is also the most Judaic book in the New Testament, beyond all question. The God who there confronts us in all His majesty and all His tremendous activity of judgment, is the God of the Old Testament in His most fearful aspects. There are touches of tenderness, but they are rare. If this book is really written by the author of the Fourth Gospel and the First Epistle of John, then we must suppose that the acute crisis of persecution forced the Apostle to concentrate his mind for the time on that part of the truth about God which the Son of Thunder had never forgotten, but which had been pressed into the background by the fresher revelation of divine, self-sacrificing love. Now the tremendous God of Justice—God the almighty and God the avenger—occupies the whole stage. But with one startling difference. The One God of this uncompromising Jewish monotheism has a partner on His throne. It is now " the throne of God and of the Lamb," and the adoration of the whole world is directed towards His partner as to Him. There can be no question that Jesus, " the Lamb as it had been slain," is on the throne of God and treated as God. And there can be no doubt that this exaltation of the Lamb to divine functions and honours is explained on the principle of merit. It is the reward of His supreme self-sacrifice.[2] All this suggests the " Adoptionist " Christology sometimes ascribed to the Apocalypse. But we are pulled up short at the idea of such an ascription. Is it conceivable that in a book so intensely Jewish another should be equalled to God ? Has God, the God of Israel, forgotten His ancient " jealousy " ?

[1] Of course Burney's theory of the Aramaic original of the Gospel enables him easily to assign Gospel and Apocalypse to the same person—the presbyter John—for the Greek of the Gospel is not his Greek, but a translation.

[2] See Rev. v.

There is, we notice, twice in the book, when John would " worship " an angelic messenger, a stern repudiation on his part of the homage which only God must receive.[1] Well then, we are bound to be, as I say, pulled up short at the proposed intrusion into the heart of Judaism of an idea so alien to it. We look again at the language of the Apocalypse. Certainly there is no theory of Christ's person there. But there are two points which are enlightening.

(1) That the great phrase (in part taken from Isaiah), which is here heard from the lips of God to signify His activity from the beginning of time to the end of it—" the Alpha and the Omega, the first and the last "—is also heard from the lips of Christ.[2] This means unmistakably that the association of Christ in the activity of God had no beginning in time. No doubt it was only *in time* that He was glorified as God in His manhood. But what rendered that possible was His co-existence and co-ordination with God from the beginning.

(2) Such also is the lesson of the figure whose name is called the Word of God.[3] This surely is an intensely Jewish phrase. " The Word " here is not, I think, used as in the prologue to the Gospel. But it indicates something intensely active and energetic. It reminds us of the startling simile in the Book of Wisdom, already referred to more than once, where the Word of God is figured as a warrior leaping off His divine throne to rush in a moment to execute divine justice. It is the activity of God personified, as He has shown Himself in the government of the world. But we cannot question that the figure on the horse in the Apocalypse is Christ,[4] and this also means that the seer of the Apocalypse identified Jesus the Christ with the

---

[1] xix 10, xxii 9, and contrast i 17.
[2] See i 8, xxi 6, on the lips of God ; cf. Is. xli 4, xliii 10, xliv 6. On the lips of Christ, i 17, ii 8, xxii 13.
[3] xix 11–16.   [4] See Swete's and Charles' notes on the passage.

divine warrior of the Old Testament, that is with God the world ruler. Decisively then, we must say that the theology of the Apocalypse is not adoptionist. The person who is Jesus existed from the beginning with God and in God.

(b) *The Epistle of James*

When we pass to the Epistle of James we pass to another deeply Judaic document. And it is, as concerns both its origin and its date, a rather mysterious document, though, on the whole, I think we may still assign it to " the Lord's brother," and date it accordingly before he was executed (as Josephus tells us) in Jerusalem, under Annas the Younger, the Jewish High Priest, in A.D. 62. As to its spiritual and moral value, it speaks for itself as plainly as any document of the New Testament. It is full of the spirit of the Sermon on the Mount, and no less clearly of the spirit of the ancient prophets and the Wisdom literature. Theologically there is very little in it that is specifically Christian as distinct from what is Jewish. It is severely monotheist.[1] There is also plainly no trace of St. Paul's influence, and the writer appears to combat, not St. Paul's doctrine of justification, as written in his Epistles, but some perverted version of it.[2] His main interest is, I think, rightly interpreted by Hort. It is in the ideal for man disclosed by the word of God at his creation, to which his conscience bears witness, and which it is God's present purpose that he should recover. " Grace," St. James would say, " is not contrary to nature, but the restoration of nature."

As to the person of Christ, with which alone we are here concerned, there are three indications of St. James's mind. (1) In his initial greeting to his

[1] ii 19, iv 12.
[2] Fundamentally St. James' doctrine of justification is easily harmonized with St. Paul's.

Jewish readers he couples the Lord Jesus Christ
with God as He whose servant or slave he is; and the
more we think of this familiar phrase the more fully
it seems to involve the deity of Jesus, when it is
used by a faithful Jew; for it means that he can
surrender himself as wholly to Jesus as to God, and
that, in fact, the one surrender involves the other.
(2) At the end of the Epistle he speaks in one group
of connected sentences of the " coming (*parousia*) of
the Lord " (twice), of "the name of the Lord " in
which the prophets spoke; and of " the end of the
Lord," that is, His final dealings with Job.[1] Now
the first phrase must refer to the Lord Jesus [2] and
the second and third to the Lord Jehovah. But
no one could use the same name thrice in such intimate connection without practical identification of
the Lordship referred to in each case. (3) There is
a very interesting phrase which may be paraphrased
thus [3] : "My brethren, can you, while you keep
showing respect of persons, really hold the faith of
(or ' in ') our Lord Jesus Christ, the Glory ? " Let
us examine the phrase.

The Jews spoke much of the glory of Jehovah.
And in the latter days of Israel's religion, when the
dread prevailed of speaking of Jehovah at all, or of
connecting Him closely with earthly things, they
often—in the Aramaic, which had taken the place of
the old Hebrew—spoke of His *Word* [Memra], or
His *Glory* [Yekara], or His *abiding* [Shekintah or
Shekinah], for reverence sake, instead of speaking
of Himself. So we find it in the Aramaic interpretations of the Hebrew Scripture, which are called
Targums, and which were no doubt, if still unwritten,
yet in familiar use in our Lord's day. " The term
[Shekinah]," says Dr. Box,[4] " together with ' the

---

[1] v 7–11.   [2] So directly after (v 14) must "the name of the Lord."
[3] ii 1, following Hort.
    Hastings' *Dict. of Christ and the Gospels, s.v.* Shekinah.

Glory ' and ' the Word,' is used in the Targums as
an indirect expression in place of God. It denotes
God's visible presence and glorious manifestation,
which dwells among men, the localized presence of
the Deity. . . . The visible Shekinah, though distinct
from the glory, is associated in the closest way with
it. It was conceived of as the centre or source
from which the glory radiated." We understand the
idea, if we think of the words " the glory of the Lord
appeared in the cloud " or—the constantly repeated
phrase—" the Lord of Hosts which dwelleth between
(or ' sitteth upon ') the cherubim," or " the glory
of the Lord filled the house " (Solomon's temple), or
the phrase of the son of Sirach concerning Ezekiel's
vision : " the vision of glory, which God showed
him upon the chariot of the cherubim." [1] This
thought often explains uses of " glory " in the New
Testament, as when " the glory " is reckoned by
St. Paul among the privileges of Israel,[2] or Stephen
speaks of " the God of the glory," [3] or the Epistle
to the Hebrews of " the cherubim of glory." It
refers to the manifested or localized presence of God.
Thus either " the Shekinah " or " the Glory " would
be for a Christian Jew a natural expression for our
Lord, conceived of as the visible manifestation of
God among men. Thus when St. John says " The
Word was made flesh and *tabernacled* among us,
and we beheld his *glory*," he seems, as has already
been suggested, to be using all three current Jewish
expressions (Memra, Shekinah, Yekara) for the
Incarnate. And when St. Peter speaks of " the
spirit of the Glory and the spirit of God," he seems to
be using " the Glory " as a name of Christ.[4] And

---

[1] Exod. xvi 10, xxv 22, Numb. vii 89, 1 Sam. iv 4, 2 Sam. vi 2,
1 Kings viii 11, Ecclus. xlix 8.
[2] Rom. ix 4.   [3] Acts vii 2.
[4] 1 Pet. iv 14 ; cf. 1 Cor. ii 8.   Hort and Parry are possibly
right in rendering Tit. ii 13 " The manifestation of the Glory of
our great God and Saviour, that is Jesus Christ."

I think Dr. Hort must be right in so interpreting it here in St. James. He calls the Lord Jesus Christ the Glory, *i.e.* the visible manifestation of God among men ; and he would shame those whom he is addressing out of showing undue respect for wealthy persons by reminding them that " the Glory " dwelt among men in the guise of a poor man. On the whole, then, though James is almost wholly ethical in his interests and not theological, I think he indicates that, had he been bound to express himself, it would have been in the phraseology of St. Paul or St. John. The presence of his Epistle in the New Testament may be said to justify a Christianity that is almost purely ethical in its interests, but not an adoptionist Christology.

The Epistle of Jude, " the brother of James," is again deeply Jewish, though the Judaism is of a more apocalyptic type, and it is also predominantly ethical. " The faith once for all delivered to the saints " for which he pleaded must have been a faith which laid its stress on morals. But he seems to show much more affinity than James with St. Paul's language. " But ye beloved, building up yourselves in your most holy faith, praying in the Holy Spirit, keep yourselves in the love of God, looking for the mercy of our Lord Jesus Christ unto eternal life " is very Pauline phraseology. And " our only Master and Lord, Jesus Christ," is hardly compatible with any lower Christology than his.

(c) *The First Epistle of Peter*

This Epistle must be taken on strong external evidence as authentic, and on the internal evidence as written by Peter from Rome, which he calls Babylon, no doubt very shortly before his martyrdom. It is a beautiful and gracious document, a real treasure-house of ethical and spiritual teaching, very strongly reminiscent of the Gospels and very closely akin to St. Paul's ethical teaching. In fact the Epistle bears such unmistakable suggestions of the influence of the Epistles to the Romans and the Ephesians, that we do not expect to find in it any different theology. St. Peter is plainly at one with St. Paul.

The Epistle is written to men and women— obviously Gentiles in the main—who have been redeemed by God's infinite mercy out of a corrupt world and a most evil tradition into " the brotherhood "—the elect body, the only true Israel, royal and sacerdotal. This brotherhood is now exposed to obloquy and persecution and is to expect the hand of judgment more and more severely ; but it is to bear it joyfully and charitably, looking forward to the radiant glory in store for them, when the risen and ascended Lord Jesus Christ is revealed. He is now at the right hand of God, above all angels and spiritual powers, unseen but the object of their exultant faith. But He is to come. He is at hand to accomplish the judgment of God and the glory of His people. Thus the main stress, as in St. Peter's preaching in the Acts, is on the Lordship of Jesus at the right hand of God and on His coming.

This passionate faith in Him and expectation of His coming is the basis of an intensely other-worldly outlook, but it is the basis none the less of a conception of a social life to be lived in this world which is to compel the attention of those who are without the elect body. Besides the emphasis laid on the Coming in Glory there is strong emphasis on the present redemption from the evil world and atonement with God which has been wrought by Christ through His vicarious sacrifice and blood-shedding.[1] We notice the phrase " through Christ," which implies His mediatorship,[2] and the phrase "in Christ," [3]

---

[1] i 18–21, ii 21 ff., iii 16. [2] ii 5, iv 11. [3] iii 16, v 10, 14.

which here, as in St. Paul, implies His universal
spiritual presence. Again the Lordship of Jesus has
phrases applied to it from the Old Testament (" The
Lord is gracious," " sanctify Christ as Lord in your
hearts ") which were written of Jehovah, the Lord
of hosts.[1] Once more it is probable that in the
phrase " the spirit of the glory and the spirit of
God " (iv 14) Christ is described as " the Glory,"
that is the manifested presence of God—the phrase
which we have just considered in connection with
St. James.

When the question is asked whether Peter indicates
the pre-existence of Christ, I think the answer is
that he seems to *indicate* it, when he calls the spirit
in the old prophets " the Spirit of Christ," and also
when he is talking about the death of Christ and
the condition and activity of His disembodied spirit.
St. Peter speaks very clearly of the (human) spirit
of Jesus as separated from the body in death, and
of its activity in the unseen world ; and he seems to
speak of Christ—the person—as something distinct
from the human spirit in which He was acting.
He went among the dead, without His human body,
in respect of which He was dead, but in His human
spirit, which was quickened to a new life.[2]

On the whole I think this Epistle indicates a
mind predominantly ethical and practical and not
theological. But also a mind which was at one with
the theology of St. Paul in its main lines.

. . . . . .

The conclusion which we are bound to reach is
that in St. Paul's Epistles and in the Epistle to the
Hebrews and in St. John we get a definite and ex-

---

[1] iii 15 (see Is. viii 12–13) and ii 3 (see Ps. xxxiv 8).
[2] iii 18–19. This is a point made by Dr. Chase (see Hastings'
Dict. of the Bible, iii 793). But I cannot agree with him that i 11
does not seem to imply a pre-existent Christ.

plicit theology of the Person of Christ as the divine
Son incarnate. The different writers have each
of them his own point of view, but on the whole
their theology is identical. There are other documents of the New Testament which, taken by themselves, give us no clear theology of Christ's person,
but there is nothing in the New Testament which
indicates a rival theology to St. Paul's, or what was
later called an adoptionist Christology. Such a
Christology did appear in the second century in
the Jewish Ebionites and later in Paul of Samosata.
But it must be held to represent a falling away from
the standpoint which is either energetically maintained or implied in all the documents of the New
Testament. We cannot read the Epistle to the
Hebrews—which represents to us among a group
of Jewish Christians a "longing, lingering look
behind," and a movement back to the old Judaism
—without feeling that a half-instructed Jewish
Christianity must have existed fairly commonly,
and most probably would have existed in Palestine,
which would be very liable to relapse. Accordingly,
it is no surprise to find that a generation later than
the New Testament times such a relapse has occurred,
and that, outside the main streams of Christian life,
there are Christians who hold Christ for a mere man,
assumed by God. But we do not find that position
in the New Testament.

NOTE TO P. 122

Our studious friends, whose intellectual home is with
the German critics, have lately been murmuring in our
ears the name of the Strassburg scholar and philologist,
Richard Reitzenstein, as of one whose theories supply
a new and powerful explanation of the real origin of
Christian ideas and especially of "Johannine" ideas.
Reitzenstein[1] does in effect suggest that the source of the

[1] Richard Reitzenstein's *Poimandres* (Leipzig, 1904).

characteristic Johannine ideas and of much else in the
New Testament is to be found in the earliest documents
of the Hermetic literature, which he dates from the
first century of our era. The Hermetic literature he
regards as representing a religious community which
had its source in the identification of Hermes with the
Logos as the revealer of divine wisdom, and with the
Egyptian god Thot, venerated as the founder of Egyptian
wisdom. Hitherto the Hermetic books—the revelations
of Hermes Trismegistus—have been regarded as an example of Graeco-Egyptian syncretism, with Jewish and
Christian elements at work in it, belonging to the third
century, and presupposing the influence of Neo-Platonism;
and Reitzenstein appears to have failed in his attempt to
show cause to date any part of the literature in the first
century. His grounds for assigning it this earlier date
have been subjected by the Roman Catholic scholar,
E. Krebs (*Der Logos als Heiland*, Freiburg im Breisgau,
1910) to a very searching and careful examination, and
he has shown them to be highly precarious and improbable (*op. cit.*, pp. 133 ff.; cf. Ed. Meyer, *Ursprung*, ii pp.
56–7). This is the opinion of most of the scholars who
have examined the matter. And the whole conception of
a wide-spreading Hermetic sect or community appears
to be groundless. On the other hand Krebs has again
excellently laid bare the purely Jewish roots of the
ideas of the Fourth Gospel. As I have already said, in
examining the attempt to find a Hellenistic origin for
the faith in Jesus as Lord, and for the institution of
the sacrament of the Lord's Body and Blood,[1] I do not
think anything really lies at the *root* of the doctrine of
the New Testament except the tradition of the Old
Testament and the new experience which came to the
disciples of Jesus in His teaching and person, His life
and death and resurrection, and the mission of the Spirit.
All the New Testament grew from the Jewish root and
this experience of Jesus, including the Gospel of Paul
and the Gospel of John.

But when you come to the second stage, to the spread
of the Catholic Church, I think the new criticism which
calls our attention to Hellenistic syncretism, and sets the

[1] See appended notes to cap. iii.

Gnostic movement on its wider background, has much to teach us. With Christian *origins* Hellenism has very little to do. But the atmosphere of the mystery religions and of Hellenistic theosophy, with its yearning for divine fellowship and spiritual light and knowledge and salvation and a new birth, and its love of sacramental symbolism and fellowship, has a good deal to do with the *diffusion* of the Christian Church. It both provided its opportunity and constituted in part its peril; and we shall have to return upon the modern theory of the influence of the Hellenistic theosophy and the mystery religions, when we are dealing with the theory of the Church and the sacraments in the next volume.

CHAPTER V

THE APOCALYPTIC TEACHING OF JESUS

It is undeniable that the apocalyptic expectation formed a large element in the faith of the first Church, and that it was, on the lowest estimate, a considerable feature in the teaching of Jesus. By the apocalyptic expectation we mean the expectation that Jesus, the Christ, who had been crucified and now was risen and exalted to heaven, was " to come in glory " to " restore all things " and " to judge the quick and the dead." [1] The Church has long been accustomed to call this " the second coming " : and it is so referred to once or twice in the New Testament.[2] But almost always it is called simply " the coming " or " the presence " of Christ.[3] This is the word common to St. Matthew, St. James, St. Paul, and St. John. The birth, the ministry, the passion, the resurrection, the effusion of the Spirit—all these are indeed represented as moments or stages in His coming. But all these are viewed as incomplete. Then and then only will He in an adequate sense have come, when He comes into His own, or God comes into His own in Him, in fully manifested glory, so that " every eye shall see him," and every adverse power shall have been put under His feet. This is the old fundamental Jewish hope of the " day of the Lord." And this

---

[1] Acts iii 21, x 42, xvii 31. [2] Heb. ix 28 ; cf. i 6.
[3] παρουσία. See Matt. xxiv 3, 27, 37, 39, James v 7–8, 1 Thess. ii 19, iii 13, iv 15, etc., 1 John ii 28.

had, as we have seen, a very real and undeniable place in our Lord's own mind and teaching. No one therefore can think seriously about belief in Christ without fully facing this belief in the future coming of Christ in glory. But recently it has come to be widely and confidently stated and believed that Jesus Himself anticipated and proclaimed His *immediate* coming as the glorified Christ, within the lifetime of His own generation, and was in this (as in some other respects) deluded, or the victim of current ideas which were in fact illusions [1]; and there has been a great deal of discussion of the bearing of these delusions of the mind of Christ upon the theology of His person. But we had better, first of all, see whether there is sufficient reason to attribute delusions to Him; and we can only effectively do this if we have in view the Jewish expectation, Messianic and Apocalyptic, as it was before our Lord came, and take careful note of the way in which He both accepted it and also fundamentally altered its character. Then only can we estimate the justice with which delusion or mistake is attributed to Him as regards "the end" and the immediacy of the end.

The Jews, as we have already seen,[2] were conspicuous among the nations of the earth for their belief (i) in a divine purpose in the whole world, which was to be progressively realized and finally consummated, and (ii) in their own race as the divinely chosen instrument of this universal purpose, as it was said to Abraham, "In thy seed shall all the

---

[1] This however is of course not a merely recent difficulty for faith. I remember Professor Henry Sidgwick, shortly before his death in 1900, telling me that it had been a main reason with him for renouncing orthodoxy forty years before.

Other cases of presumed *error* in the mind and teaching of Jesus Christ—as regards the existence and activity of Satan and devils, and as regards the literary character of the Old Testament books—are dealt with below (pp. 189 ff.).

[2] See above, pp. 13 ff.

families of the earth be blessed." This is the root
of the Messianic hope as the prophets of Israel
announced it ; and it takes shape in the following
forms and features of the hope, which have been
already discussed and will here only be alluded to :

1. That the religion of Israel is finally to win
universal sovereignty and universal recognition.
"The mountain of the Lord's house shall be established in the top of the mountains and all nations
shall flow unto it. . . . Out of Zion shall go forth
the law and the word of the Lord from Jerusalem." [1]

2. That Israel is the elect vehicle of this true
religion, and that the anointed king of the family of
David, who is to bear the divine name, and to fulfil
the predestined glory of Israel, is to be the instrument
of this divine supremacy, this Kingdom of God.[2]

3. That this Kingdom to come is to be accompanied with, or be based upon, a new, more spiritual,
and everlasting covenant between God and His
restored people,[3] and the nations of the world reconciled to Israel.

4. That also it is to be accompanied with an
effusion of the Spirit of God, not only upon the
anointed king, but upon the whole people—upon
all flesh.[4]

5. That also it must involve a resurrection from
the dead of faithful Israelites who have died, that
they too may participate in the Kingdom ; and
this belief in the resurrection of faithful Israelites
becomes a belief in a resurrection generally of all,
good or evil alike, to glory or shame.[5]

6. This sovereignty of God requires for its establishment the infliction of the judgment of God upon

---

[1] See above, pp. 15 f.   [2] See above, pp. 16–17.
[3] See above, p. 18.
[4] Is. xi init. and Joel ii 28–9.   In Is. xlii and lxi the Spirit is
poured upon "The Servant," who begins by being the faithful
remnant of the people but seems to become an individual.
[5] Is. xxvi 4, Dan. xii 2.

every insolent and godless power in turn. The
prophets are full of "oracles of Jehovah" upon
Assyria, upon Egypt, upon Babylon, upon Edom,
upon Tyre, upon "the nations" generally. The
prophets announce like judgments upon apostate
and rebellious Israel and Judah; but on the whole
with a marked difference. The judgments upon
the nations are final and irreversible.[1] The judgment on Israel is, on the other hand, always figured
as a severe and just discipline, out of which at least
a faithful remnant is to emerge to fulfil the destiny
of the chosen people.

7. These particular judgments or dooms on particular nations are again and again thrown upon
the background of tremendous cosmic catastrophes.
Thus the doom on Babylon (Is. xiii 10–13) has this
background: "The stars of heaven and the con
stellations thereof shall not give their light; the
sun shall be darkened in his going forth, and the
moon shall not cause her light to shine. . . . I will
make the heavens to tremble and the earth shall be
shaken out of her place, in the wrath of the Lord
of hosts, and in the day of his fierce anger." Or
again the doom on Edom (Is. xxxiv 4–5) is thus
accompanied: "And all the host of heaven shall be
dissolved, and the heavens shall be rolled away as
a scroll: and all their host shall fade away, as the
leaf fadeth from off the vine, and as a fading leaf
from off the fig-tree. For my sword hath drunk
its fill in heaven: behold it shall come down upon
Edom . . . to judgment." I have chosen these
two quotations because our Lord so precisely repeats
the language of these two passages in His doom
upon Jerusalem.

What did Isaiah mean by such language? We
know that the Jewish seers and poets often represent nature as expressing sympathy, even violently,

[1] Except in Jeremiah; see above, p. 16 n. 3.

with the redemptive acts of God. "Why hop ye so, ye high hills?" "The hills melted like wax at the presence of the Lord." "The mountains and the hills shall break forth before you into singing, and all the trees of the field shall clap their hands." This is a kind of metaphor which we find in poets of many nations. It is akin to what Ruskin called the "pathetic fallacy." It is interesting to learn that mediaeval Jews in Spain commemorated thus the death of a certain Rabbi Isaac Alfasi, on May 12, 1103: "This day was a calamity: it was a day of misfortune and oppression, a day of darkness and gloom, a day of cloud and mist, a day when the heavens and their luminaries were obscured, when they were clothed with sackcloth. The stars put on mourning; the hills bowed; all Israel was terrified." And another epitaph on Rabbi Jona from the next century runs: "Son of Sion, before this stone weep for the sun buried beneath the dust of the earth; the firmament was clothed with darkness, the constellations were ashamed: the moon blushed; on the day when the glory and crown of the Law was buried." [1] Here we have, no doubt, nothing but conscious metaphor. All that is really meant is that two Rabbis died deeply regretted, and that nature must have sympathized with the sorrow of the Jews.

But though such expressions as Isaiah uses may be conscious metaphors, they are not mere metaphors. They mean at least that in the prophet's vision the physical world served the moral purpose of God, and might at any moment be expected to express it. And in the latter days of prophecy, when the triumph of Israel over the nations seemed more and more impossible by natural means, apocalyptic seers more and more clearly anticipate cosmic catastrophe

[1] See Lagrange, *Le Messianisme chez les Juifs* (Paris, 1909), pp. 49–50.

wrought by God in His omnipotence to end the
present world order, and usher in " a new heaven
and a new earth."

So we get the idea of an " end of the world "
followed by a " world to come," in the later literature.
But in all the books of the Old Testament, and indeed
in the New Testament, it appears to be always
in some sense this world which emerges, renovated
through cataclysm, as the sphere of the Kingdom
of God.[1] Only in some of the later uncanonical
Apocalypses, which seem in this respect to exhibit
influences from Persia, this world seems to be wholly
obliterated at the last day or wholly left behind,
and an altogether " other " world takes its place.
" The earth however purged and purified is no
fitting scene for an eternal kingdom. . . . God's
habitation and that of the blessed must be built
not of things earthly and corruptible, but of things
heavenly and incorruptible." [2] But enough has

---

[1] This will be obvious to anyone who will read Is. xxiv—seemingly
a late prophecy incorporated in Isaiah where, after " the earth is
utterly broken, the earth is clean dissolved," etc., it still appears
that Mount Zion and Jerusalem stand as the centre of the divine
kingdom.   So it is again in Joel ii after the cataclysm of verses
30, 31 (see verse 32 and iii 1 and 16–21).   So in Daniel vii 13
the sovereignty of the " one like unto a son of man who came
with the clouds of heaven " and was given universal dominion by
the " Ancient of Days "—which is interpreted immediately as the
rule of the saints of the Most High, that is of faithful Israel—
is still, like the previous sovereignties of the " great beasts," that
is the godless powers which it supplants, a sovereignty on this
earth (see verses 21–7).

And if the matter is frankly considered we must admit that the
expectation of the New Testament is still that of a return of Christ
to earth, a heavenly kingdom to come on earth—though it be a
new heaven and a new earth—a new Jerusalem which is to come
down from heaven as God's final dwelling-place among men (see,
e.g., Acts iii 20–21 ; 1 Thess. iv 16 ; Rom. viii 20–22).   In 2 Peter
iii the day of judgment by fire is conceived of on the analogy of
the earlier judgment by water : both judgments are represented
as destroying an old world and bringing a new one into existence—
which is still only the old one purged and renewed.   So also in the
Revelation.

[2] Charles, *Between the Old and New Testaments*, pp. 56–7.

been said about this already. Where this is so, the Messianic Kingdom, in the old Jewish sense, becomes very difficult to adjust to this " other world." It is either ignored altogether or becomes a rather meaningless temporary prelude to the Last Day.

The influence of these later Apocalypses has of recent years been much exaggerated. We have already had occasion to argue that all the literature of the New Testament tends to show that in our Lord's day the hope of the Messiah and His Kingdom was on the lines of the old prophetic hope of the King of David's line, who should restore the kingdom to Israel, whether this hope was more spiritually conceived, as it is represented in the opening chapters of St. Luke's Gospel, or was entertained on nationalist and militarist lines as by the mass of the people. When John the Baptist preached the Kingdom and the Christ as at hand, he sought to spiritualize the people's conception of what was coming, as being something so holy and awful as that only a new Israel, changed and purified in heart, could meet it; but this was only to renew the warnings of the old prophets. There is nothing in John the Baptist's teaching to suggest the later Apocalypses.[1]

What we have now to discover is the sense in which Christ both accepted and also transformed the old Messianic teaching.

To go back, then, to the headings under which we summarized the Jewish hope, and to deal very briefly with the earlier ones, (1) it must be granted that our Lord, while accepting the limitation of His own mission on earth to His own people, proclaimed a Gospel of the Kingdom which, having its roots in the Jewish religion (for " salvation is of the Jews "[2]), is now to become world-wide.

---

[1] Matt. iii 10–12 suggests no more than Mal. iii 2, 3, iv 1.
[2] John iv. 22. But the idea underlies all the Gospels.

The sayings " The gospel must first be preached unto all nations," " Wherever the gospel shall be preached throughout the whole world,"[1] the authenticity of which cannot reasonably be doubted, are enough to show this. And at the beginning of His mission, in the account of the Temptations, it is evident that the last temptation [2] would have no meaning except as addressed to one who in some sense was contemplating world-wide dominion.

(2) It does not seem to have been disputed that our Lord could rightly claim to be of the family of David, as being the reputed son of Joseph, and He certainly acknowledged Himself to be the Christ ; but it is plain that, in taking the title of " the Son of Man " and identifying it with the Suffering Servant of Jehovah, and criticizing for its inadequacy the current notion of the Christ as the son of David, He was turning His back in the most marked way on the Messianic hope, both as it was held in nationalist circles and as held among the Pharisees. He accepted, but He transformed in meaning, the Messiah's kingdom, so as to make it, in the most disconcerting sense, a kingdom not of this world.

(3) He solemnly, at the Last Supper at least, proclaimed the New Covenant as established in His blood.[3]

(4) As He declared Himself anointed and possessed by the Spirit,[4] so He led his disciples to expect His effusion upon them, at some definite moment after His departure, and the coming of the Spirit on the Day of Pentecost was at once identified as in some sense the coming of the Day of the Lord.[5]

---

[1] Mark xiii 10, xiv 9.   [2] Matt. iv 8.   [3] See above, p. 101.
[4] See Luke iv 1, 18, 21.   There is very little teaching about the Holy Spirit ascribed to our Lord in the Synoptists.   But St. Luke is explicit in xxiv 49 and Acts i 5, 8.   And it is, I think, impossible to doubt, in view of the belief of the first disciples, that teaching like that of John xiv to xvi must have been given by Him.
[5] Acts ii 17–18.

(5) Our Lord is represented in all the Gospels as constantly foretelling not His death only but also His resurrection : and the resurrection of the dead was, as we have seen, to be one of the signs that the Kingdom was come.[1]

Here then let us pause a moment. If it be agreed, as I think it should be, that our Lord, while He accepted the Messianic expectation, profoundly spiritualized it, declaring the " Kingdom of God " to be a kingdom of righteous men, such as must have its roots in the wills and hearts of men, and needs to be spiritually discerned, and is in actual process of establishment [2]; and if further He took three recognized notes of the Kingdom, the New Covenant of God with His people, and the Resurrection of the Dead, and the effusion of the Spirit, and led His disciples to expect the realization of these notes in the immediate future—that is in His own death and the immediately following events—if this be so, then there was certainly a sense in which He viewed the Kingdom as coming immediately. Thus when we find Him saying " Verily I say unto you, There be some here of them that stand by, which shall in no wise taste of death till they see the Kingdom of God come with power," [3] and again, before His Jewish judges, " Henceforth (not ' hereafter ' as in our old Bible, but ' henceforth ') ye shall see the

---

[1] St. Paul, in Rom. i 4, speaks of Christ's resurrection as " the resurrection of dead men "—i.e. it was the firstfruits and assurance of the general resurrection. There are several indications in the N.T. of this point of view.

[2] See Mark vii 15 ff., Luke xvii 20, 21, John iii 3.

[3] Mark ix 1, Luke ix 27, where the words "come with power " are omitted. In Matt. xvi 28 it stands " till they see the Son of Man coming in his kingdom." There was a tendency in St. Matthew to put all these prophecies in the form most suggestive of a visible coming of the glorified Christ. But where the reports differ in detail, one thing is quite certain—we cannot be sure of the *very words* of Christ on the particular occasion.

Son of man sitting on the right hand of power, and coming on the clouds of heaven "[1] (as in the vision of Daniel), we shall be disposed to find the fulfilment of these prophecies in the early chapters of the Acts. There we are given a picture of the little community of disciples absorbed in the sense of their Lord as already exalted by God's right hand and to God's right hand, and as acting upon them and through them with power from heaven, though there was a further coming to be expected. And so impressed were " the brethren " with the divine power working through the apostles that they regarded them, even in their own community, as a class apart. " Of the rest durst no man join himself to them : howbeit the (Jewish) people magnified them." [2] The disciples would have felt that they already saw the Twelve, according to Christ's promise, " sitting on thrones judging the twelve tribes of Israel." [3]

---

[1] Here Mark gives only " Ye shall see " (xiv 62). But both Matt. xxvi 64 and Luke xxii 69 give us the " henceforth " (ἀπ' ἄρτι or ἀπὸ τοῦ νῦν). In St. Luke the words are " From henceforth shall the Son of man be seated at the right hand of the power of God." But whatever the exact words, our Lord is recalling the vision in Daniel vii of one " like unto a Son of man coming with the clouds of heaven."

I do not think there is any need to suppose our Lord in these places to be citing the Book of Enoch. Daniel vii 13 satisfies all the requirements of the quotations. There is an excellent paper of the late Dr. Moorhouse, Bishop of Manchester, entitled *Did Our Lord Jesus Christ share the Popular Opinions of the Jews on Eschatology ?* (which he circulated but, as far as I know, did not publish), in which he answers his question in the negative, or in the sense that He " transmuted " the popular Apocalyptic. He says, and, I think, in the main, truly : " There is good reason to believe that our Lord invariably took his apocalyptic imagery, not from the later apocryphal writings, but from the books of the canonical prophecies." But I have argued above that our Lord's language assumes that the figure in Daniel had been already recognized as an individual person such as can be identified with the Messiah, and this identification probably came from Enoch.

[2] Acts v 12. See Rackham *in loc.*

[3] See Luke xxii 30.

Already the community of believers in Jesus as the Christ was the real Israel, and the Apostles were its princes, and Christ was not only reigning in glory in heaven but was so manifested on earth in judgments and wonderful works.

(6) But we have still to consider the two last headings (6 and 7) of the Messianic expectations, and first that of judgment on the hostile, godless powers. Our Lord, then, certainly, like the old prophets, pronounces a doom on a hostile power, but in this case the hostile power is the chosen people itself, who in their rejection of the Christ have shown themselves the enemies of God.

This is plainly the meaning of the parable of the vineyard [1] which appears in all three Synoptic Gospels. The sin of Israel has been consummated in the rejection of the Son of God, and God will come in judgment to destroy these unfaithful agents (I suppose the Jewish rulers in particular), and give His spiritual possession in charge to others—doubtless the " little flock " to whom Jesus said " It is your Father's good pleasure to give you the kingdom." [2] The same doom is recorded to have been pronounced with passionate anguish at the end of the woes upon the scribes and Pharisees in St. Matthew. " O Jerusalem, Jerusalem . . . Behold your house is left unto you desolate," [3] and, in St. Luke, with bitter tears when Jesus beheld the city and wept over it.[4] St. Paul, we notice, entertained no doubt that the doom on Jerusalem was irreversible—" wrath is come upon them to the uttermost." [5]

But, of course, the most detailed judgment on Jerusalem is in what is called our Lord's apocalyptic

---

[1] Mark xii 9.   [2] Luke xii 32.

[3] Matt. xxiii 37-8.   It is possible that verse 39 was pronounced before the entry into Jerusalem.

[4] Luke xix 41 ff.   [5] 1 Thess. ii 15-16.

discourse given in St. Mark xiii,[1] and the parallel
passage in the other Gospels. There we read how
our Lord had His attention called by one of His
disciples to the magnificence of the temple buildings,
and makes it the opportunity for denouncing upon
them speedy and complete ruin. Then when the
inner circle of disciples asks Him when this is to
happen and what sign is to presage the disaster,[2]
our Lord describes a time of spiritual confusion,
political unrest, and physical calamity, which is
to be expected before the judgment falls.[3] And
He warns the apostles that they are to find not
only the Jewish rulers but the world powers arrayed
against them in their task of preaching the Gospel
unto all the nations, and that they are to be objects
of universal hatred, and to be subjected to the
severest strain. Then, when they see an awful
profanation of the Holy Place occurring, such as
is obscurely described in the Book of Daniel, the
disciples who are in Judaea are to escape from the
doomed city at once, without a moment's delay,
and flee to the mountains. A scene of unparalleled
horror is to be expected from which they shall barely
escape, and the physical horrors shall be made more

[1] The critics have largely accepted the view that a considerable
part of the discourse (verses 7–8, 12, 14, 17–22, 24–7, 30) was
not pronounced by our Lord but was a "little apocalypse" due
to some prophet near the time of the destruction of Jerusalem—
about A.D. 66—and is the "oracle" which Eusebius (H.E. iii 5,
apparently on the authority of Hegesippus) declares to have warned
the Christians of Jerusalem to escape and remove to Pella, a city
of Peraea. I do not see sufficient reasons for adopting this view.
The "oracle" referred to by Eusebius may have been simply a
warning that *now* was the moment to act on the Lord's admonition
given to a few disciples privately nearly forty years before, and
carefully treasured in writing by the Jerusalem Church as its secret.
This would account for St. Mark here using a written document,
as he seems to do (see verse 14)

[2] In Matthew the question is made to concern *both* the destruction
and (as a separate event) the end of the world. St. Matthew tends
generally to heighten the apocalyptic colouring of our Lord's discourses. We cannot doubt that St. Mark rightly records their
question.　　　　　　　　　　　　　[3] Appended note, p. 160.

trying by the seductions of false Christs and false
prophets (verses 5–23). There are to follow " in
those days, after that tribulation," portents in the
heavens described in the words of Isaiah—darkened
sun and moon, falling stars, shaken heavens, and also
—what has no counterpart in Isaiah—the coming
of the Son of Man in power and glory, accompanied
with angels whom He will send to gather together
His scattered people from all quarters of the world
(verses 24–7). Then we are taken back to the time
of preparation, and the disciples are warned of the
certainty of the doom, and that this generation
shall see it accomplished (verses 30–31). Then, in
what appears to be sudden contrast, we hear of a
certain day and hour (" that day " and " that hour ")
which is veiled in complete uncertainty, of which
even the Son has no knowledge ; and the discourse
as it stands ends with a warning to them, couched
in a parable, that, though their Lord after
His departure should seem to delay His return,
they are always to watch, for it will be sudden,
when it comes, and they know not when to expect
it (32–7).

The main purpose of this discourse—apart from
its warnings of the spiritual trials which our Lord's
apostles are to expect—is to declare explicitly and
with imaginative [1] detail, such as we are familiar
with in the " judgments " of the old prophets, the
certain doom upon Jerusalem to be accomplished
before " this generation had passed away." This
was a definite prophecy, and it was fulfilled in A.D. 70,
amidst unimaginable horrors.

(7) But this doom upon Jerusalem is thrown, after
the manner of the ancient prophets, and in the

---

[1] The details appear to be details of the picture, as presented
to their imagination, rather than detailed prophecy of circumstances. Thus the Christians of Jerusalem did not "flee to the
mountains," but over the Jordan and just across it to Pella, opposite
southern Galilee.

words of Isaiah, upon a background of cosmic portents—darkened sun and moon, falling stars, shaken heavens, heralding the coming of the Son of Man as described in the vision of Daniel, but now as coming to earth to fulfil what had always been associated in prophecy with the Messianic kingdom—that is, the gathering of the true Israelites from all the quarters of the globe.[1] And there are other passages in which our Lord is recorded to have spoken of the coming of the Christ in glory to wind up the present world history in scathing judgment and abundant blessing, in phrases which are based upon Daniel's vision but assume that the figure of " one like to a son of man " has been already identified with the Christ,[2] and the final Day of Judgment a familiar prospect. The distinctive scenery of the day of judgment is more prominent in St. Matthew's accounts of our Lord's discourses than in those of the other Evangelists. But it is not, I think, possible to doubt that our Lord did not merely describe the destruction of Jerusalem in terms of celestial portents, after the manner of Isaiah, but did throw this judgment upon the background of the great and universal Day of Judgment with the glorified Christ for judge, thus adopting the latter apocalyptic imagery.

In what sense, we ask ? Well, it seems to me that any believer in the God of the prophets and of our Lord must believe with them in a Day of God, as bringing the present age, or human history, to its climax. God, for all His long tolerance of human wilfulness and arrogance, must one day come into His own in His whole creation, and everything must be seen in its true light as what it is

[1] Deut. xxx 3, Jer. xxiii 3, xxxii 37, Ezek. xxxiv 13, etc.
[2] Such passages are Matt. xiii 40–41, the conclusion of the parable of the Tares, Matt. xvi 27, Mark viii 38, Luke ix 26, Matt. xxv 31 ff., Luke xii 40 and 46, xix 15, John v 28. The first Church was plainly full of this expectation.

11

really worth. That is the "day of judgment" in its essence. And no believer in Christ can doubt that this final disclosure of things as they really are will be the manifested victory of Christ. His judgment on men and things will be shown to be the final judgment and the judgment of God. And this Day, like all the preparatory and partial "days of judgment," will speak the divine doom on all corrupt civilizations and godless and inhuman forms of power and institutions of cruelty and lust, and on all rebels against God and right, only now not partially and locally, but universally, in the whole created world. We cannot, it seems to me, hold any conception of progress which is consistent with the facts of experience, without recognizing that the divine purpose of progress works through cataclysms as well as gradually, and that the final coming of the Kingdom (if such an expectation is entertained) must involve a cataclysm also on the vastest scale. It seems to me quite certain that our Lord enforces this doctrine, and that He clothed this moral certainty in the tremendous imagery of the rending clouds, and the descending form, and the throne and the angels, and the judgment spoken on every soul. Certainly our Lord was ready enough to use imagery, and knew well enough how to distinguish symbolism from literal language. I cannot doubt that His picture of the Last Day is the clothing of an awful reality in symbolic forms. Only let us agree that our Lord, in this solemn imagery, did affirm that human history would reach its climax in what would be at once the coming of the Kingdom in full glory and the final Day of Judgment, and threw upon this background the immediate judgment on Jerusalem.

But now we come back to the question mentioned at starting this enquiry—did our Lord declare that the Last Day would follow immediately on the Fall of Jerusalem, and did He in this respect show Himself to be under the influence of a current apocalyptic expectation, and in fact mistaken ?

There was certainly, I think, mistake somewhere. St. Matthew with his " immediately " (xxiv 29) must be interpreted as meaning that the great day would follow the destruction of Jerusalem as a separate event without any considerable interval. And, in the sense intended, this certainly did not occur. But St. Mark's words are vaguer, "in those days, after that tribulation " (xiii 24), and St. Luke suggests an interval of indefinite length : " Jerusalem shall be trodden down of the Gentiles, until the times of the Gentiles be fulfilled " (xxi 24). Plainly we cannot rely upon having the precise words of Christ, and we seem to detect contrary tendencies in St. Matthew and St. Luke—in St. Matthew to accentuate everything apocalyptic in our Lord's words, and in St. Luke to minimize. If we are to form a sound judgment we must look at the general tenour of our Lord's teaching as a whole, and not lay stress upon single phrases in one Gospel.

I would say then that the extreme apocalyptic estimate of Christ formed (for example) by Schweitzer must certainly be rejected. He represents the Christ of current Judaism as simply the Heavenly Figure of Daniel and Enoch. He would have us believe that there was no question of our Lord while on earth being the Christ already. It was simply that He believed Himself, and was believed by others, to be destined to be the Christ from heaven. But that estimate alike of current Jewish belief and of the special belief concerning Jesus is, as has already been shown, quite contrary to the evidence. Holding this mistaken or very one-sided idea of the Messianic expectation, Schweitzer maintains that our Lord, when He first sent out the Twelve, expected to come as Christ in the clouds of heaven (without dying) before their brief mission was ended,[1] and that He had no idea of promoting any Kingdom of God in the world or establishing (what is the same thing) any new way or order of life among men. All His rapt attention was on the Last Day and the other world, as to come within the next few weeks. When He was disappointed about this, His disappointment, and the warning of the execution of John the Baptist, taught Him to think that He should offer Himself for death and that His sacrificial death would certainly move God to bring the kingdom from heaven at once.

All this picture of our Lord is surely violently one-sided and distorted. Our Lord assuredly proclaimed a kingdom of God, characterized by a new vision of God and a new conception of righteousness, which in one sense was already in being—a kingdom of God established in the hearts of men—already within men or among them.[2] Again, He certainly spoke of the growth of the kingdom under the figure of the growth of a plant and the diffusion of leaven; and again, as a mixed society on earth, which only

[1] This is founded on Matt. x 23 : "But when they persecute you in the city, flee unto the next : for verily I say unto you, Ye shall not have gone through the cities of Israel, till the Son of man be come." But the whole of this section in St. Matthew, verses 16–23, appears to be antedated. It belongs properly to the preparation by Christ of the apostles for their experiences after He was gone from them. (See Mark xiii 9–13, and Luke xxi 12–19.) The particular words quoted, which do not appear in St. Mark or St. Luke, probably in their original context meant "Never stay anywhere to press the Gospel on those who do not want it. There will always be unevangelized places to be given their chance before the Gospel is preached in the whole world and the end comes." I think we must conclude that St. Matthew, in adapting the words to a much earlier situation—a preliminary mission of the Twelve exclusively to Jews—has given them a misleading appearance. At any rate, whatever the words may be held to mean, it is an unreasonable thing to accentuate a solitary and unsupported saying so as to give to Jesus an appearance of being such a fanatic as is quite out of character with the general tone of His teaching.

[2] Luke xvii 20 ; cf. Matt. xi 12, xiii 44–6.

at the final day could be completely purified.[1] He
certainly prepared His " little flock " to become the
New Israel, and therefore (in some sense) the kingdom
of God on earth.[2] Again, He certainly spoke of a
preaching of the Gospel of the kingdom throughout
the whole world,[3] and He must have known, He who
was supremely sane, that this must be an affair of
a long time. Moreover, He speaks again and again
of the strain upon courage and faith involved in
waiting while God seems to do nothing—this under
the figure of the man of property who left the administration of his property to others and went
away " for a long time," and in other similar
parables [4] ; and He asked the startling question :
" When the Son of man cometh, shall he find the faith
on the earth ? " [5]—or will the strain have been too
much for it ?   It is plain that St. Luke is aware of a
tendency to misrepresent our Lord (as he thinks) as
having prophesied an *immediate* end, and desires to
correct it.[6]

Also we cannot ignore the teaching of the Fourth
Gospel. The final coming is there, and in the First
Epistle of St. John, still the object of expectation.[7]
But the writer also plainly thinks it his business to
remind the Church that the apocalyptic expectation was not the *whole* of our Lord's teaching, nor
(in his eyes) its most important element. Christ
also prepared for the establishment of His kingdom
here and now in the world, by the sending of His
Spirit, which was also His own return by the Spirit.

Thus, on the whole, we seem to me to have every

[1] Mark iv 30, Matt. xiii 33, 47–50, 52.
[2] That is to say, He refounded the Church. But this is reserved
for argument in the next volume.   [3] Mark xiii 10, xiv 9.
[4] Matt. xxv 19 ; cf. Luke xix 12, " into a far country."
[5] Luke xviii 8.
[6] Luke xix 12. " Because they supposed that the Kingdom of
God was immediately to appear."
[7] John v 28–9, vi 39, 40, 54 (" the last day "), xi 24, xii 48, xxi
22–3 ; 1 John ii 28, iii 2, 2 John 7.

reason to believe that our Lord's teaching about the coming of the kingdom was much more complex and many-sided than the apocalyptic school acknowledges. He accepted, but He transmuted, the apocalyptic hope. He prophesied an immediate coming by the Spirit. He prophesied a speedy coming in judgment on Jerusalem. He also threw this "doom" upon the background of a final coming or Day of Judgment. No doubt the first disciples expected this final day immediately, and the expectation has coloured the report of our Lord's words in St. Matthew and perhaps somewhat in St. Mark also. But it is in both these Gospels that we read the indisputably authentic words of Christ: "Of that day and that hour knoweth no one, not the angels which are in heaven, neither the Son, but the Father." This certainly means that our Lord had not—at least in His mortal state—a map of the future spread before Him. We should take these words in connection with those recorded of our Lord by St. Luke, before His ascension, in answer to a question of the disciples, which shows them still clinging to the old Jewish hope in its fallacious form: "Dost thou at this time restore the kingdom to Israel?"—"He said unto them, It is not for you to know times or seasons which the Father hath set within his own authority."[1] These last two sayings mean, I think, unmistakably that our Lord gave no teaching at all upon the time of the end. He left it wholly vague and indefinite.

Thus, we must, on reviewing the whole evidence, give a negative answer to the question whether our Lord was mistaken about the time of the end. I think we have seen cogent reasons for saying that our Lord refused to give any teaching on the subject, and declared it not to be within the scope of His knowledge, as He then was. There was mistake—

[1] Acts i 6, 7.

but it was on the part of the disciples, and not of our Lord ; and we have, I think, to admit that it has somewhat discoloured some expressions, especially in the first of the Synoptic Gospels, but not sufficiently to prevent our correcting the discolouring out of the total impression left us.

I think, also, that this answer to the question is the one suggested by the attitude of the disciples, especially St. Paul, in the matter. Plainly he at first shared the expectation of the end within his own lifetime,[1] and plainly also he grew out of it [2]— not out of the expectation, but out of its immediacy —simply by the growth of his experience and reflection, and without any shock. It would appear as if the expectation was to him *not* an "article of faith" and *not* something for which he had a word of Christ. Otherwise there would have been the sense of shock. And St. Paul's attitude is reflected in that of the whole Church. Jerusalem fell—by wholly natural means, but according to the prophecy of Jesus : yet "the end" did not come. Then we find the seer of the Apocalypse making another prophecy. The hostile power is now not the apostate Israel but the Roman Empire turned persecutor ; and the seer pronounces upon it the doom of God, and again throws that doom upon the background of the End. The Church, we gather, like St. Paul, had experienced no shock in seeing that the Day of God did not "immediately" follow, as they had expected, the doom on Jerusalem. They prepared to see another doom on another hostile power, persecuting Rome, and again to throw it upon the background of the final and universal judgment.

This represents the attitude which our Lord would have His disciples take. Because they believe in God, they must take it for granted that in no

[1] 1 Thess. iv 14, 1 Cor. xv 51.   [2] Phil. i 23, 2 Tim. iv 6.

department can evil be finally victorious. The end is certain and is to be eagerly expected. God must come into His own. That is " the day of the Lord," or " day of judgment." In the world's history there are many days of judgment. Over long periods indeed God seems to do nothing and the world-power to have it all its own way. But there are also days when the world-power seems to be cracking and dissolving, and then it falls. God has bared His arm. Sooner or later the judgment of God falls " naturally " on every institution which ignores, persistently and defiantly, the law of righteousness. " Wheresoever the carcase is, there will the eagles be gathered together." Thus we have many " last days," [1] or " days of extremity," followed by " days of the Lord." But all these days of the Lord, of which the Bible record is full, are the prelude of something final and universal—*the* Day—after which God is to be all in all. Of the date of this we know, and are to know, nothing, and of its character and manner of coming we hear only in apocalyptic imagery and symbolism, as a reflection in a mirror, or in a riddle. Only we know it is certain to come, and as we belong already to the kingdom of God we most passionately and eagerly desire to see it fully consummated.

．　　．　　．　　．　　．　　．

It is from such a point of view as this that, though it is going somewhat out of our way, we can attempt a brief answer to the question which is continually being raised afresh, whether Christianity is a religion of this world or an other-worldly religion—whether Christians are to labour for the gradual upbuilding of the city of God on earth by the transformation both of individual characters and human institu-

---

[1] I think Westcott (on 1 John ii 18), and Hort (on 1 Peter i 5), and Parry (on 2 Tim. iii 1) are right in distinguishing "*the* last day" from "last days" and "a last hour." "There is clearly a distinction to be drawn, according as the article is used or not."

tions, or whether they are to look forward to the
destruction of this wicked world and all that belongs
to it, and the perfecting of man's hopes in a quite
different world called heaven ?

The problem is generally stated in somewhat misleading terms—as an alternative—but there can be
no question that for a very long period of time
popular religion has contented itself in the main
with the latter expectation : and that the apathy
of religious people in the face of social injustice
—all that has given point to the charge that
"religion has been the opium of the poor"—has
been due in great measure to the hold that this
idea has had on the religious imagination. But I
think that any frank consideration of the New
Testament will lead us to the conclusion that the
New Testament, as well as the Old, is on the other
side.[1] There the aim is that the kingdom of God
should come " on earth as it is in heaven." [2]   The
end is always pictured as the Return of Christ in
glory and triumph from heaven to earth with the
angels and saints—all the treasures of heaven to be
fused with a purged and renewed earth : it is the
redemption of " the whole creation " : it is the
New Jerusalem coming down from God out of heaven
to be God's dwelling-place upon the " new earth "
and under the " new heaven " : it is " the kingdom
of the world " made "the kingdom of the Lord and
of his Christ." We will not concern ourselves with

[1] See above, p. 141 n. 1, with references. I find in Hastings' *Dict.
of the Bible*, art. " Heaven " : " In the N.T. the heaven which is
to be our final home and the goal of our hope is a heaven that is
above this world and beyond time, not only superterrestrial, but
supramundane, the transcendent heaven which is brought to light
in the Gospel " (p. 323). This seems to me a quite remarkably
perverted statement.

[2] It would be an immense gain if Christians in general could be
brought to realize that in the Lord's Prayer the words "in earth as it
is in heaven " refer to all three previous clauses, and if the Lord's
Prayer were printed and recited so as to make this evident.

the question of the meaning to be attached to the
preliminary millennium of the Apocalypse. But there
can be no question, I think, that the ultimate kingdom is in the New Testament, on the whole, figured
not only as including this world, purged by scathing
judgment, but in some sense as centring upon it.
Let us allow as fully as possible that all the language
about the last things is highly figurative : nevertheless it is intended to impress and affect our
imagination, and it makes the greatest possible difference if our imagination becomes rightly coloured—
if what we come to anticipate with assurance is
not our being carried away to some other remote
world, but the victory of God in the creation and
world that we know.

And not only is this the truth about the end of
the world, but it is also true that the Church—
which is the old Israel renewed and refounded by
Christ—is, or is the representative of, the kingdom
of God on earth here and now, albeit not yet perfected,[1] the kingdom which is "righteousness, peace,
and joy in the Holy Spirit." So the ethics of the New
Testament are predominantly *social* ethics—the ethics
of brotherhood ; its discipline is primarily moral
discipline. The aim of the Church is to show here
and now the true human fellowship realized in Christ.
It is bound to make war, in the name of Christ, on
all injustice as much as on all impurity. It must
take all human life for its province. It must de-
velop its philosophy, its art, its principles of social
economy. It exists in the world, but not of the
world, and that means that it must vigorously and
combatively maintain the true principles of human
brotherhood and human life against " the lusts of the
flesh, and the lust of the eyes, and the pride of life "
—that is, against the social aims and practices of
the selfish, avaricious, and lustful world. This seems

---

[1] " Non adhuc regnat hoc regnum," St. Augustine says.

to me indisputable.   The only question which remains
to answer is whether the idea of a gradually and
progressively realized kingdom of God in this world
—a Church gradually appropriating the world, and
consequently a world progressing towards perfection
—is to oust the apocalyptic idea of a Christ manifested
in cataclysm and judgment at the end—whether the
two conceptions are mutually exclusive.   Many of
our Christian socialists appear to think so, and among
the radical reconstructors of the Gospel men as unlike
one another as Harnack and Schweitzer take it for
granted that the apocalyptic hope is gone beyond
recall and for good.

But I think we must not accept as mutually
exclusive alternatives the idea of a progressive
realization of the kingdom here and now and the
apocalyptic hope.   Both seem to me to find their
place in the teaching and mind of Christ ; and both
seem to me to be equally warranted by experience
and needed for the equipment of human souls all
down the generations.   We are to labour for the
establishment of the kingdom of God in the name of
Christ and in the power of His Spirit here and now.
But neither Christ nor experience warrants us in
believing that we are to see the extinction of the
power of evil within the present world order.   Progress, as we recognize to-day, is an exceedingly
fitful and chequered process.   There is no security
against the collapse of civilizations and Churches.
The powers of evil do not seem to be worn out or to
be weakened—only to take new shapes.   Now, as
of old, there appears to be the most fearful waste
of the best human efforts.   It seems to me that
Jesus Christ would prepare us for all this by the
apocalyptic, other-worldly hope.   He would have us
believe that no good effort for the cause of truth
and righteousness will ever really be lost.   Their
" works follow with " the suffering servants who

seem to die defeated, but "in the Lord." With them (or in them) the fruits of what they have thought and done and suffered are gathered into the treasury of God in the heavenly world unseen, and one day we shall see them with our eyes. We shall see the fruit of all true human effort integrated in the perfect fellowship, when Christ comes again—when the City of God descends. But we are not led to expect the City of God as the culmination of a gradually progressive movement to perfection. The present world order will always present the aspect of a more or less desperate struggle. It is on the other side of Armageddon that the City of God will appear. And that final battle will be won, as it seems, by the pure act of God, and the New Jerusalem will appear from heaven, so that we cannot imagine that we have fashioned it.

This is metaphorical teaching or symbolism, no doubt: but only in metaphor or symbol can we envisage the truth about the future. And the apocalyptic metaphors, which possess the hearts of men in days of seeming moral disaster, correspond, we may be persuaded, with spiritual realities.

NOTE TO P. 147.

An Illustration from Tacitus

It is instructive to read, in connection with Mark xiii 7–13, Tacitus' introduction to his *Histories*, in which he is to describe the events of A.D. 68–70, and amongst them the Jewish War and the capture of Jerusalem, from the point of view of the Roman Empire: "The story I now commence is rich in vicissitudes, grim with warfare, torn by civil strife, a tale of horror even during times of peace. It tells of four emperors slain by the sword, three several civil wars, an even larger number of foreign wars, and some that were both at once. . . . Now, too, Italy was smitten with new disasters, or disasters which it had not witnessed for a long period of years.

Towns along the rich coast of Campania were submerged or buried. The city was devastated by fires, ancient temples were destroyed, and the Capitol itself was fired by Roman hands. Sacred rites were profaned, and there were adulteries in high places. The sea swarmed with exiles, and the cliffs were red with blood. Worse horrors reigned in the city. . . . Slaves were bribed against their masters, freedmen against their patrons, and if a man had no enemies he was ruined by his friends. . . ." Then, after describing some better features of the life of the time, he continues : " Besides these manifold disasters to mankind there were portents in the sky and on the earth, and the warnings of thunderbolts, a premonition of good and of evil, some doubtful, some obvious. Indeed, never has it been proved by such terrible disasters to Rome or such clear evidence that the Gods were concerned not with our safety but with vengeance on our sins."

CHAPTER VI

IS THE DOCTRINE OF THE INCARNATION TRUE ?

THUS far we have been pursuing a purely historical method. Thus, after duly taking into account the distinctively Jewish background of beliefs and expectations in which the faith in Jesus had its origin (cap. i), we occupied ourselves in tracing the growth of the idea of His person as it appears in the New Testament. We began from the first undefined belief of the Twelve, which the scandal of the Cross temporarily overthrew (cap. ii) but which revived under the experience of the Resurrection and the coming of the Spirit and took shape in the enthusiastic conviction of the original Church in Jerusalem that Jesus was truly the glorified Christ, the Lord of all, the object of worship, appointed to be the final judge of quick and dead.

This passionate faith, which might have seemed to be moving in the direction of the deification of the man Jesus, was interpreted to the Church itself by Saul of Tarsus—the scourge of the Church who was converted to become its glory—in the light of the title which in momentous utterances Jesus had used to describe Himself—the title of the Son of God. Not the deification of a man, but the Incarnation of the pre-existing Son, St. Paul declared to be the interpretation of His person. And though no teacher of the Church before St. Paul can be shown to have given it expression, yet it appears that the whole

162

apostolic group and all the young churches welcomed the interpretation as the truth, quite without controversy. They must have felt that St. Paul was only giving clear utterance to what the language of Jesus implied about Himself, and what alone could explain or justify the unreserved faith they reposed in Him. The same doctrine of Christ's person is expressed from a rather different point of view by the Alexandrian author of the Epistle to the Hebrews (cap. iii).

We saw that the Fourth Gospel gives this doctrine of incarnation its fullest and most deliberate expression, and makes the most decided claim to find in the language of Jesus Himself its indisputable justification ; and it was pointed out how strong the grounds are for believing that the Fourth Gospel presents us with a real historical tradition supplementary to the earlier Gospels. Finally we examined the language of the seer of the Apocalypse, and of James, and of Jude, and of Peter, and, though they do not plainly state any theory of Christ's person, we found it almost impossible to believe that they could have been satisfied with anything short of the Incarnation doctrine, in view of the indications of their faith which they give us.

There is, we saw, no rival adoptionist theory—no doctrine that is of a man adopted into the Godhead (apotheosis)—to be found in the New Testament, whether previously to St. Paul's activity or after his appearance on the scene. What had happened was that the years immediately succeeding the death and resurrection of Jesus saw the Church concentrated upon the worship of the glorified Christ and Lord, and treating Him as having "the values of God" for them, without apparently finding it necessary to form or proclaim any theory of His person. When St. Paul was given to the Church to do this service for them, they appear to have accepted his interpretation unanimously. It must have been already at work, we feel, under the surface in the apostolic company, though it does not find expression in the Acts. Later, in Jewish Ebionism and in Paul of Samosata's Adoptionism, we are given positive theories—rivals of the Incarnation doctrine—as that Jesus was an inspired man and no more, or a man assumed into the Godhead on account of his excellence—but these were certainly deteriorations from the level of the whole New Testament, even from the unformulated belief of the first Jerusalem Church. Indeed it is impossible to read the Epistle to the Hebrews without feeling that the writer's mind is full of the fear that any clinging to antiquated Jewish rites and ceremonies, on the part of those who have once confessed Jesus, will involve a lapse, not only morally but intellectually, from their first faith. And this is what actually occurred, if not to the group overseas to whom the Epistle to the Hebrews was apparently addressed, yet certainly in Palestine and nearer home (cap. iv).

After this we devoted special attention to the apocalyptic element in the New Testament—the expectation of the future coming of the Christ in glory—and endeavoured to see it in its relation to the whole Messianic idea; and we saw that there are no adequate grounds for the often repeated assertion that Jesus Himself entertained the delusion of the immediate coming of the end of the world (cap. v).

We shall have to pursue the course of the faith to its formulation in the creeds of the Church and the decisions of the Councils. But we had better pause here. The theologians of the later Church are unanimous in declaring that they were not originating anything, but defending and defining the faith of the New Testament—the faith of the apostles. This, no doubt, may be disputed and must be examined. But I think we shall find that they were justified in their contention in the sense that where we pass off the ground of the New Testament we leave behind us, already accomplished, the fundamentally creative work in Christian theology.

But, whether this be wholly true or no, there is at any rate enough truth in it to justify us in pausing at this point to ask whether the doctrine of the incarnation of the Son of God, as we find it in St. Paul and the Epistle to the Hebrews and St. John, is really the only legitimate way of thinking of and accounting for the historical person—Jesus of Nazareth.

I

At the beginning of our inquiry[1] I described certain rival interpretations of His person which at present are largely in occupation of the intellectual field, and which are associated especially with the names of Harnack, Schweitzer, and Bousset. It is common to the maintainers of all these rival interpretations that they approach the Gospels with what I think we must call a dogmatic prejudice. On general philosophical and historical grounds they peremptorily refuse to admit the credibility of miracles, so far as these go beyond healings of the sick effected by suggestion, and apparently quite as peremptorily they refuse to entertain, as even an hypothesis to be fairly considered, the traditional conception of Jesus as the incarnation of a divine person. At all costs the Christ of history must for them be found non-miraculous and (however much inspired by the Spirit of God) purely a human person.

I have laboured (in the volume preceding this) to convince my readers that these presuppositions are unwarranted—that we can approach the Gospels open-minded. I also insisted that any treatment of

[1] See above, pp. 35 ff.

the Gospels which refuses the strictly miraculous is forced to eliminate so much out of the foundation documents as to discredit them deeply as historical records. The narrative has to be rewritten from the point of view of each new critic, accentuating this and leaving out that, as his particular judgment dictates. The proof that this is so lies in the extraordinary differences between the various critical reconstructions of the historical Jesus, notably between the three to which I specially called attention. My answer, therefore, to those " critical " estimates I have attempted to give in this way—I have urged the high claim of our foundation Gospel documents and the Acts of the Apostles to take rank as credible history. I have begged my readers to approach the study of these documents with an open mind. Taking them, not as exempt from error, but as good history, and seeking to give an impartial attention to all the elements of the narrative, I have sought to trace the growth of the belief in Christ's person as it is represented in these narratives and as it reaches its coherent expression in the Epistles. The picture of the development of a belief which such impartial study discloses is to my mind very convincing. The facts as they are recorded account for the developing belief, and the belief interprets the facts. It alone can interpret the facts as a whole. In proof of this I must go back to Harnack and Schweitzer.

Harnack admirably describes the ethical teaching of Christ, but there are three elements in our fundamental records which he perforce refuses to admit as historical, not on critical but on *a priori* grounds : the claim of a divine Sonship which, as it stands (both in St. Mark and Q), Harnack admits to be superhuman ; the tremendous apocalyptic claim, which he minimizes towards vanishing-point ; and the miracles, especially the real Resurrection. That is to say that out of four elements in our foundation Gospels, which are all equally and obtrusively present, Harnack chooses one and fashions his picture out of it alone, with the result that the Jesus of history, as he represents Him, seems altogether inadequate to account for the results which have flowed forth from Him. Jesus, the ethical and spiritual prophet, was a fact of history, but it appears that there was much there besides.

I would advise anyone to read Harnack's account of the faith in Jesus of the apostolic band immediately after His death [1] and, without stopping to criticize it in detail, ask himself whether it does not require the actual fact of the Resurrection, and what followed, to account for it. The picture in the Gospels and Acts is lifelike and unmistakable. A hesitating, vacillating company who deserted their Master in the hour of His seeming failure and death are, after a brief interval, transformed into a radiant, confident band who can face the world with unflinching courage. The change is accounted for by certain facts—the fact of the Resurrection, made evident by the repeated appearances of the risen Lord, and His ascension to the right hand of God and His mission of the Spirit. Harnack himself dates St. Paul's conversion, herein differing from most authorities, as early as a year after our Lord's death. He does not question that the record which St. Paul gives us of His resurrection on the third day and His subsequent appearances [2] was what he received from " the primitive community." It was a record of a succession of solid and distinct events. But in Harnack's estimate these supposed events were the projection upon the outward world of their own vivid imagination. Their state of mind produced the supposed events, not real events their state of mind. They felt that Jesus had really, as He said,

[1] Lecture IX of *What is Christianity?*   [2] 1 Cor. xv.

died for them. They felt that He must have sur-
vived death, and that God must vindicate Him.
Their Messianic beliefs invested Him with supreme
Lordship. And all this, though in reality their faith
had failed them under the scandal of the Cross, and
God had not vindicated Jesus by any outward event,
and He did not come in glory as they expected.
Granted the primitive faith, solidly grounded on
the experiences recorded in the last chapters of the
Gospels and the opening chapters of the Acts, the
Church can start on its course, as we see it, in the
enthusiasm of conviction. But it was the facts
which created the conviction. And apart from the
impact of indisputable facts, the moral transformation
of the apostles and the triumphant certitude of the
Acts are quite unaccountable. Also, I cannot believe
that St. Paul's doctrine of the divine Son incarnate
would ever have received the unquestioned acceptance which the evidence shows it received, if it had
not been grounded beyond question on the Lord's
own witness to Himself.

It is almost comic to pass from Harnack to
Schweitzer, for what is all in all to the one is nothing
to the other. For Schweitzer Jesus is hardly an
ethical teacher at all. He is an apocalyptic seer
of what we cannot but call a fanatical type. He is
that and almost nothing else. He created a flaming
expectation in the first Jerusalem Church of His
speedy coming in the clouds of heaven. Again we
note, as with Harnack, that there is nothing admitted
to have occurred which accounts for the transformation of the character of the Twelve from
utter despondency to confident enthusiasm. But in
Harnack's account the first Christians have at least
a task before them. There is an ethical gospel—
a gospel of divine Fatherhood and human brotherhood—to be preached, and a life to be realized on
earth by the community of believers. Christianity

is "the Way." But according to Schweitzer they appear to have nothing to do—no divine legacy left them, except the expectation of the Christ coming in the clouds to judge the world, which was not realized. The Christ who has been so potent a factor in human history, who has given to men so new a sense of the worth, here and now, of human personality and human life, has, according to Schweitzer, hardly anything to do with Jesus as in fact He was. He again, like Harnack, only more one-sidedly, has fastened upon one element in the record—the apocalyptic—and has sought to fashion out of it the complete picture, again with the result that the supposed Jesus cannot supply any intelligible explanation of the Church which was called by His name.

In Bousset's and Kirsopp Lake's estimate of history there is even less in the historical Jesus than Harnack or Schweitzer finds there. There is even less any adequate historical cause of the great effect. On the showing of these very radical critics the Catholic Church owes comparatively little to Him except His prophetic teaching about God and the example of His noble life and self-sacrificing death.

Now, is it not the most effective argument against all these three schools of interpreters to show that there is a picture of Jesus of Nazareth, which is formed by taking our records seriously as historical documents, which takes in what each of these groups of interpreters wishes to emphasize, but by taking in also what they severally or all together repudiate (though without any critical ground for their repudiation) can combine all the elements in one strangely compelling and convincing whole, which moreover is obviously adequate—as no one of these partial or one-sided estimates of the "Jesus of History" is—to explain the effects which are summed up in the religion of the New Testament ?

II

Certainly it is easier to examine the views of the critics whom we have been considering than those of our English Modernists. The German and French scholars at any rate express their views as lucidly as possible, and show us quite clearly what they mean and whither they are moving. But the greater number of our English Modernists do not give us this intellectual satisfaction.

The Report of their Conference at Cambridge in the summer of 1921, on Christ and the Creeds,[1] seemed to me to be more markedly characterized by strong statements of what the speakers do not believe than by clear exposition of what they do. It was unfortunate also that the question, what is the best intellectual expression which we can find for the truth about Christ, was crossed and confused by a quite different issue—what is the intellectual obligation involved in the honest recitation of the Creeds. These two issues had better be kept quite distinct, and with the latter we are not concerned in this book. It was also apparent that the speakers at the conference were men holding very different views. Nevertheless the Report made certain things evident.

(1) The Modernist movement as a whole is not, as Dr. Sanday used to try to persuade us to believe, a movement which would be satisfied with eliminating from the Christian creed the affirmation of certain miracles, leaving the ideas about God and the Incarnation untouched. It is a movement which as a whole demands a trenchant rehandling of our doctrine of God and of the person of Christ. It is a clear gain to recognize this. The really root

[1] Report in *Modern Churchman*, Sept. 1921.

question is the question of what sort is the God in whom we believe.[1]

(2) Some of those who took part in the conference " differ " (as one of them says) " from the Chalce-donian Fathers by holding that the substances of deity and humanity are not two but one. Perfect humanity is deity under human conditions."[2] I have already sought to make it evident that such an idea as this was familiar enough in the Greek world, but is quite contrary to the fundamental Hebrew doctrine of God the Creator, always essentially and fundamentally distinct from all His creatures, which our Lord and His apostles take for granted.[3] That men are portions of God in respect of their reason or spirit—that God would not be complete without man—that a man by becoming good and realizing himself as a rational being would become God or a god—are familiar propositions in certain types of Hellenism and (except the last) in certain types of modern philosophy. But they are flatly contrary to the root conceptions on which our religion was based. The first matter (intellectually speaking) on which we have to make up our minds is whether the Hebrew conception of God, which is the foundation of the Christian religion, is valid—i.e. due to a real self-disclosure of God through the Hebrew prophets and Jesus Christ. We only lose time by trying to evade this question. In the volume which preceded this I have sought carefully to examine it, and to give the reasons which seem to me to justify the belief in a positive self-disclosure of God on which the Christian Gospel is based.

[1] This is admirably emphasized in an article by the Rev. Richard Hanson, " Anglicanism and Modern Problems," *Church Quarterly*, April 1922.

[2] *Report*, pp. 196–8. Again, p. 293. The idea thus expressed, " They treat God and man as two distinct, real existences (substances) each with its own special characteristics," is repudiated as unsatisfactory.

[3] See above, p. 5 ; and *Belief in God*, chaps. v and vi.

(3) Others in the Conference repudiated very emphatically the conception which we find so decidedly expressed in St. Paul and St. John of a divine person, pre-existing, who in the fulness of time became man for our salvation.[1] Language is used which suggests the ancient idea of Adoptionism —the idea of a perfectly good man and singularly inspired prophet raised to divine honours and identified with God. Now I associate myself wholly with a remark made by Dr. Kirsopp Lake[2]: "Adoptionism seems to me to have no part or lot in any intelligent modern theology, though it is unfortunately often promulgated, especially in pulpits which are regarded as liberal. We cannot believe that at any time a human being, in consequence of his virtue, became God, which he was not before, or that any human being will ever do so. No doctrine of Christology, and no doctrine of salvation, which is Adoptionist in essence, can ever come to terms with modern thought." I do not think there is any doubt that we have in our day to choose ulti-mately between the incarnation doctrine of St. Paul and St. John and the Creeds and, on the other hand, the conception of Christ as the best, or one of the best, and most inspired of men, who left to men the heritage of the grandest teaching about the fatherhood of God, and the possibilities of humanity, and the purest example of love and sacrifice, and who, after His death, was deified only in the imagination of His disciples. But I cannot square the record of Jesus, as it stands, with such incontestable evidence of reality, in the Gospels, or the record of the impression which He made on His disciples, with any merely humanitarian estimate of Him. The bedrock of the Catholic conviction about Jesus is in these earliest records. But on this

[1] *Report*, pp. 287, 288, 276 f.
[2] *Landmarks in Early Christianity*, pp. 131-2.

I have already said what seems to me the certain
truth[1]; and I can only ask my readers to concentrate
on this point all their powers of spiritual apprehension, with the sincere desire to reach a decision.
Before I take leave of them, I shall ask them to
estimate the importance for human life which is
involved in that decision.[2] But all that I ask for
now is a frank and conscientious exercise of the
responsibility of judgment on the facts of the case.
Dr. Bethune Baker at the Cambridge Conference
spoke of men being "hypnotized by orthodox presuppositions." I seem to see more intelligent people
to-day who are hypnotized by unorthodox presuppositions. However, there is no question at
present of orthodoxy or unorthodoxy. These words
imply an ecclesiastical authority, and no question
of ecclesiastical authority has been raised at all.
I have been trying to proceed simply as an individual
doing his best to form a true judgment in view of
all the facts. That seems to be for many minds
to-day the first necessity. And I ask for a like
frankness on the part of my readers.

III

But there is no doubt that the New Testament
doctrine of the person of Christ, while it has inspired
and still inspires the faith of millions, also rouses
a sense of antagonism in a great many minds—an
antagonism of a kind which is peculiar to our time.
They feel what can perhaps best be expressed by
saying that the doctrine in effect dehumanizes
Christ, even if in theory and formally it safeguards
His manhood. This Christ, they say, whom you
describe as sinless, and who certainly, if the pages

---

[1] See above, p. 46 ff.
[2] See below, pp. 314 ff.

of the Gospels can be taken to give an undistorted picture of Him, appears as never betraying any sense of error, moral weakness, or insufficiency—this Christ moreover whom you describe as personally the eternal Son of God manifested in human flesh, and at no moment therefore merely man—makes no appeal to us. His example is of no use to us. What we need for our help and encouragement is a man who is only a man and has no resources but such as are common to men, and no exemptions from human frailties. Only such a Christ could encourage us to believe that we can become as he was.

Words like these are often used with deep sincerity and real passion. When like words were used to Augustine many centuries ago, he pressed his Pelagian antagonist with the inquiry whether he meant that he wanted a Christ who starts precisely from the common human level of sinfulness; and whether, therefore, he would not, if he were logical, find the most encouraging Christ to be one who had to start with the most evilly disposed nature to tame, and the most unruly lusts and passions to subdue.[1] This is a very shrewd question which the objector would not have found it easy to answer. In fact, if it is merely a question of an encouraging example, the most valuable example for each of us would appear to be the person who starts most completely on his own level. But it is impossible to read the Gospels and not feel that Jesus Christ did not appeal to men primarily or chiefly as an example they

[1] Augustine, c. Julian. op. imperfect. iv. cc. 48-57. These are very interesting chapters. See c. 49: "Christus . . . sicut in virtute omnium hominum maximus, ita esse in carne libidinosissimus debuit"; and c. 52: "Sic es amator egregius castitatis ut tibi castior videatur qui concubitus illicitos cupit, sed ut non perpretret, suae cupiditati resistit." Again Christ, according to Julian, should be represented as saying, "Estote ergo casti, quia, ut vobis ad me imitandum obstacula excusationis auferrem, libininosior vobis nasci volui, et tamen maximam libidinem meam concessos fines nunquam transire permisi."

could follow. They felt Him to be in some formidable sense above them—teaching and working with a quite extraordinary authority—drawing them with a tremendous claim as from above—claiming, controlling, saving, judging. About this there can be no question, if the Gospels are in any sense historical. And it is no use fashioning a Christ of our own fancy.

We must not, of course, minimize the reality and value of His human example. Certainly, as St. Peter says, He left us an example that we should follow in His steps. This cannot be too strongly or constantly insisted upon, and we will come back to it. But first of all let us think out the meaning of this plea for an example on our own level. Let us realize the limitations of mere example. The mere example of one individual man upon his fellows tells most when men are living close together under similar conditions—as amongst the crew of a ship, or the soldiers of a regiment, or the boys of a school, or the members of a profession. Anything which suggests difference of conditions weakens the force of mere example and speedily annihilates it. The example of a respectable clergyman's temperance has no effect upon a man living in an uncomfortable cottage with no refuge but the public-house. Difference of race, again, or remoteness of time, almost at once destroys the force of example. An Englishman is not commonly much impressed by the hardness of ancient Spartans or the asceticism of Indian fakirs. Once again the strong sense of what we call genius in another, in proportion to the feeling of uniqueness which it arouses in us, destroys the appeal of his example. In all these ways, it must be acknowledged, the mere example of a Christ who lived nearly two thousand years ago in remote Syria, under conditions utterly unlike ours—one, moreover, who was on all showing a supreme moral genius—would have little effect on us to-day, and indeed would hardly have survived in the memory of men but as a remote legend.

In fact, if you look to the men of supreme moral and religious influence in our race, you find that this influence has depended upon their power of perpetuating themselves in some sort of institution or system of teaching and discipline. The Buddha perpetuated himself in " the way " which he taught —the way of escape into the ultimate Nirvana out of the endless and weary succession of existences ; and the success of his method for those who accept his premiss—that life is an evil to be escaped from— has been made evident down the generations in constant examples. What we have to take note of in the case of our Lord is the actual manner in which his example and teaching were in fact perpetuated, and we shall be astonished, and perhaps at first irritated, to find how in fact it was the belief in Him as a person essentially superhuman and divine which alone enabled His influence to become permanently powerful.

As a teacher, living as man among men, it appeared that neither His teaching nor His example was effective with His first disciples. He was altogether too high for them—too unworldly. They failed under the strain He laid upon them and deserted Him. What recovered them was their hardly won faith in His resurrection, which convinced them of His supernatural Sonship, and their consciousness of the divine Spirit—His Father's Spirit and His own—received as a distinctive gift at a memorable moment. Thereby they realized Christ as their living Lord who from heaven was inspiring, guiding, governing and enriching them with an inward life ; in virtue of which His outward example, their memory of which is recorded in the Gospels, became something quite different from the mere example of a departed hero. The example living in their memory was the pattern of humanity, or " the way," in accordance with which He was moulding them from heaven by His Spirit. It was only " in Christ " that they could follow Christ. But it was only because He was something more than man—something in respect of which they would have felt it madness to equal themselves with Him—that He could be living in them and they in Him—that He could thus have access to their inmost souls, and remake them, and " dwell in their hearts by faith."

And this has been true for all successive generations of Christians. The example of Christ has been of supreme importance. He called Himself the Son of Man, or the Man. That pattern of glorious man-hood—glorious in all its relations, Godward and man-ward, and not least in its matchless self-control—has appealed to men in each successive generation as presenting an ideal before which all cynicism is put to flight. Here is the man whose life is alto-gether worthy of fullest admiration. If He is the real man, there remains no manner of doubt in our hearts that the life of a man, even under extremest conditions of failure and suffering, is altogether worth living. But in its supreme perfection it would seem to us, as it seemed to the first disciples, an example of despair. It postulates for life forces and powers which we seem to lack. And, in fact, He appears in the Gospels as claiming a mastery over other men's lives which it is not for a mere man to claim. But He did not end by setting an example. He died, but He is still alive. That is the point of the Christian belief. It concerns " one Jesus who was dead, whom Paul," and all Christians since, have " affirmed to be alive." Yes, alive in the heavens— the same Son of God who came down from heaven to redeem our nature from within by Himself taking it, and exalting it into the glory of God ; and who thus alive in the heavens is alive in us also by His Spirit, moulding us inwardly into the pattern of the life He showed us outwardly in word and work. There is no possibility of question that this is the way in which Christ's example has in fact appealed to men in the succession of generations. They have studied " the life," " the way," in the pages of the Gospel, as described in His words and as lived in His conduct, and also as reflected in countless saints who were His true disciples ; and however low the level at which they may have started to become His disciples and to imitate Him, however degraded and polluted they have felt their manhood to be, they have not despaired because they believed in Him, not only as their pattern of manhood, but as their Redeemer, in whose name they were set free from all the guilt of the past and were granted that incomparable blessing, the forgiveness of their sins—that is, the opportunity constantly renewed of a fresh start free from all the guilt and burden of the past— and also that without which example and absolution would have been alike useless—the gift of the Spirit, the Spirit of His Father and His own Spirit, poured into them out of His heavenly manhood to purge them and strengthen them and renew them inwardly after the pattern which in His human life He had shown them outwardly. No one can doubt that that has been the way in which Christ has exerted His influence and made His example effective down the centuries like the example of no other man. This sort of influence has a sort of analogy in the influence of other men over their fellows. But in His case there has been an " influence " or " inflowing " of Him into all those who have accepted Him as their Master which has been quite distinctive. Of no mere man could it be said that he could thus gain effective entry into the very centre of the personalities of all other men, so as to renew them from the roots of their being by his spirit, and make them " in him " new men. That is a recreative act which, in the full sense in which it has been experienced from the first, can be assigned to none other than Him " in whom we live and move and are."

Unless I am very much mistaken, there is singularly prevalent to-day, especially in the English-speaking world, what is, I am persuaded, at the bottom an irrational pride—the sort of pride which is rooted in a wholly false view of human independence—which is only willing to accept a doctrine of incarnation if it be understood as the incarnation of God in humanity at large, of which the incarnation in Christ is only what I may call the foremost specimen. According to this presentation, I am to see in Christ what I have it in me to become. He demonstrates the power of the divine Spirit in humanity in a sense which, without Him, I should never perhaps have suspected, but which, once instructed by Him, I can realize in myself without needing from Him anything but the light of His example. He says to us, in effect, " You can all be Christs like me, if you will." But this is the most astonishingly unhistorical representation. I do not mean merely that the matter is not so represented in the New Testament, but that it has not so been realized in Christian experience.

However, the highest type of Christian experience may be found in the New Testament. And what we find there does, to a degree which startles us, negate the manner of thinking and speaking which I have just tried to describe.

In the New Testament there is scarcely a hint to be found of a universal gift of the Spirit of God to men because they are men.[1] There *is* suggested a

---

[1] James iv 5 is, of course, very difficult. If it means " He [God] jealously longs for the spirit which He [at our original creation, when He breathed into our nostrils the breath of life] caused to

universal presence to all men of the divine Light which is the Word of God,[1] but the Spirit, who makes the light effectual, is, as a matter of fact, represented as given only through the Risen Christ to those who believe in Him, and as a gift communicated at a definable moment.   Let us confine ourselves to the historical or literary facts for the present.   I am *not* saying that the New Testament excludes the idea that the Holy Spirit is in such sense "the giver of life," as that wherever life is, and especially wherever rational and moral life is, He Himself must be.   This is indeed suggested in the Old Testament. There God's spirit or breath is in all things and inspires the natural gifts of all men, as well as the special endowments of the prophets.   As the Book of Wisdom says, "the spirit of the Lord filleth the world."   And I think the orthodox Christian theology of the Holy Trinity makes such an assumption inevitable.   Thus we are *not* to agree with Origen, who would seemingly have actually *limited* the activity of the Holy spirit within the circle of "the saints," or the believing Church.   It is not for us so to limit God's activity.   The Spirit, like the wind which represents Him, "bloweth where it listeth." Nevertheless, from end to end of the New Testament the gift of the Spirit is only contemplated first as given to John the Baptist, the prophet who is to prepare for Christ,[2] then as especially the agent in the conception of Christ,[3] then as imparted to Christ for the fulfilment of His mission,[4] and, finally, as to be expected from Him and as actually poured out by Him upon those who believe in Him.   Thus in the Gospels men are expected to see in Christ the action of the Holy Spirit, and it is blasphemy against

dwell in us," as Dr. Hort interprets, then there is no reference here to anything but the spirit of man, which is distinct from the Spirit of God.

[1] John i 9.   [2] Luke i 15, also ii 25 ff. to Simeon.
[3] Luke i 35.   [4] Mark i 10.

the Spirit to attribute His works to the evil one. And the disciples are to expect the Spirit as a future endowment which they have not yet received. This, of course, is in a very marked way the teaching of the Fourth Gospel : "The Spirit was not yet (given), because Jesus was not yet glorified." [1] "My Father will give you another helper in my name," or "I will send him unto you." [2] But it is equally the teaching of St. Luke at the beginning of the Acts. There the disciples are anxiously to await a gift which they have not yet received, and the gift is represented as communicated in an objective form under memorable conditions on the day of Pentecost. Afterwards, also, the gift appears as given in an objective manner in baptism and the laying on of hands.[3] The disciples of John the Baptist at Ephesus need to be instructed about the gift of the Holy Ghost and to receive Him in due manner.[4]

Even the saintly Roman soldier Cornelius, with the pious group around him, though his prayers and alms have already gained him acceptance with God, and though God makes evident by a visible manifestation that He has given him His Spirit, must receive at least the outward form of baptism.[5] So important it is to make it evident that the New Israel only, the Church of Jesus Christ, is the home or sphere of the Spirit. I suppose that if you had asked a New Testament disciple what it is to be a Christian, he would have given one of two replies—either that a Christian is one who believes that Jesus is Lord or that he is one who has " received the Spirit " of God. St. Paul uses the phrase as equivalent to being a Christian. " Received ye the Spirit," he asks, " by the works of the law or by the hearing of faith ? " It is not possible to state too strongly

---

[1] John vii 39.   [2] John xiv 16, xv 26.
[3] Acts viii 17–18.   [4] xix 1–6.   [5] Acts x 24–47.

that the Spirit is, in the New Testament, regarded as possessing the Church, and as not to be expected or looked for except as received from Christ and within the membership of His society.

Let us then sum the matter up. Thank God the New Testament sets no limit to the activity of the divine Spirit. Nay, it may truly be said that it is blasphemy against the Spirit to deny His activity wherever we see active goodness among men. But it is true that the New Testament deliberately concentrates our attention upon the new gift of the Spirit as given in Christ and through Christ. It tells us that all that we see in the man Christ is to be made common to all men of good will—but it adds " in Christ " and " through Christ." It addresses mankind as needing to be redeemed, and the effective evidence of such redemption is found in the gift of the Spirit communicated to them as a newly-given gift from Christ. We are all to be anointed by the same Spirit which possessed Him—we are all (if you will) to be Christs—but it is not as individuals in our own right. That right we are left to suppose we have lost and can only recover in Christ.[1] It is idle to dispute that this is the message of the Bible. Thus there is truly to be an incarnation of God in humanity, but it is in the New Humanity, through Christ, by deliberate faith and conscious incorporation into His society. That is the message declared and covenanted and open. What lies in the secret counsels of God for humanity beyond the area of this message, or where the message has been misunderstood because misdelivered, is not part of the message, though it may be part of the hope of the human heart which has been taught in Christ that God is justice and love, and that there is no limit to His love.

[1] John i 12, " As many as received him, to them gave he the right to become children of God."

Then to wind all this up. I think no one who considers how the Catholic Church has blurred the full message of Christ's humanity and His human example—of which we shall have sad occasion to speak—can be anyway surprised if such unfaithfulness has led to violent reactions of feeling against the Church and the message of the Church. But after all, what we want to know is the truth about the Christian message: and also we make an eager appeal to the specifically Christian experience. Of the Christian message then as the New Testament expounds it and as Christian experience over the centuries has on the whole confirmed it, I say this without hesitation: that it does not proclaim a Christ whose human example would have sufficed for us: or a Christ who is only a specimen of the forces of manhood which we all already carry within ourselves. It proclaims Christ the Man indeed, but the man whom we need as our saviour as well as our example—whom we need to make us new men, through faith in Him and by the receiving of His Spirit, in such a way as is inconceivable unless He is all along something much more than man. So that the very features of the Person which seem to remove His example furthest from us appear at the last as the very conditions of its being brought close to us in permanently effective power.

IV

There is another kind of objection to the idea or doctrine of Christ as really the manifestation of God in manhood, on the ground of doubts about His moral perfection. I am sure, for instance, that there are a good many honest people who feel that our Lord's tremendous denunciations of the scribes and Pharisees [1] are indiscriminating and violent—that

[1] Matt. xxii, Mark xii 38–40, Luke xx 45–7.

they would indeed be in the spirit of the Old Testament, but that, if Christ really uttered them, they
were not worthy of Him.

Again, the " cursing of the barren fig-tree," taken
as it stands in Mark, is described as expressing a
spirit of sudden anger, unreasoning and revengeful ;
so that the critics, who are very skilful in getting
rid of what they do not like, very commonly seek to
exclude it as a historical incident from the narrative,
and represent it as a parable misunderstood. I do
not think they are successful. For it stands a very
vividly described incident in St. Mark's narrative,
with details which seem singularly precise and convincing.[1] It is true that St. Mark's explanatory
phrase, " for the time of figs was not yet," appears
to be misleading. What our Lord was apparently
expecting to feed upon was the green knops (the
" green figs " of Cant. ii 13) which appear on the
fig-tree before the leaves, and without which any
leafy fig-tree will, of course, be barren for the year.
These green knops are, we are informed, still
commonly eaten in Palestine. Not finding any,
our Lord discerned in the fig-tree the type of an
outward show of life (the leaves) which is in fact
unfruitful, and He pronounced a solemn doom on
this deceitful show. It seems to me a miracle of
judgment very penetrating in its significance. I do
not feel the least inclined either to doubt the fact
or to apologize for it.

As to the denunciations of the scribes and Pharisees,
they may perhaps have been directed, not against
all the scribes and Pharisees, but against a certain
class or section of them. But if the Gospels and
St. Paul represent the historical situation with any
fidelity, these rigid maintainers of Jewish orthodoxy
and tradition were as a class deeply corrupted by
formalism, self-righteousness, hypocrisy and self-

[1] Mark xi 12 ff., 20 ff.

seeking.[1] Our Lord does not appear anywhere to
have denounced the principle of ecclesiastical
authority or ceremonial observance—to this question
we will come back in the next volume—but, if we
consider what the characteristic vices of ecclesiastical
authority have been in many ages when the Church
was seemingly powerful, and the awful hindrance
to the spiritual influence of Christ's religion which
these characteristic vices of ecclesiastics have proved
themselves to be, we shall surely feel that the Master
of human life, who discerned so deeply its tendencies
and dangers, had good cause to utter even the
tremendous denunciations which are ascribed to
Him of pride and selfishness parading itself in the
guise of religion. Again I cannot apologize or
explain away. I know indeed that there is a spirit
in our age which would like to eliminate out of its
conception of God the whole element of fiery indig-
nation, whether against false religion or any other
kind of sin. " I believe," writes one of our
modernists, " that we shall come to see that it is
precisely those contemporary ideas of the wrath of
God and His ultimate avenging activity as destroying Judge, which are the unauthentic elements in
the teaching ascribed to Jesus." [2] Language like
this, I confess, makes me shiver. I feel sure in my
conscience that if God is really as the prophets
disclose Him, and sin is essentially what the Bible
represents it as being—and the deepest spiritual
experience of Christendom has given its assent to
the representation—the wrath of God against sin
and the awfulness of final judgment remain a quite
essential and permanent element of " the truth as
it is in Jesus." Thus I read our Lord's tremendous
" dooms " with awe and terror indeed, but not

[1] See Rom. ii 17–23, and, besides the passages in the note on
p. 183, Luke xvi 14.
[2] Dr. Emmet in the *Modern Churchman*, p. 221.

with any expectation that the enlightened conscience of men will ever have cause to wish them
away. Without them the picture of Jesus would
fail altogether to represent the whole truth about
God.

It is, of course, sometimes pleaded that we have
no right to claim for our Lord moral perfection in
the fullest sense—that in fact He disclaimed such
goodness when He said to the young man " Why
callest thou me good ? None is good save one,
even God." [1] But it is, I think, certainly a mistake
so to interpret His words. In the Gospels generally
our Lord seems to present Himself to His disciples
as an infallible guide and teacher and pattern.
There is not in all our Lord's words (other than the
words in question) the slightest sign of the consciousness of sin or of the fear of going wrong. Certainly
He cannot have disclaimed goodness, even in the
highest sense, with any kind of consistency. And
the saying in question admits of a very natural and
suggestive interpretation. This young man came in
a spirit that was both self-complacent and flattering. Doubtless he both wanted to make himself
agreeable and to receive commendation. It was a
cheap thing to say " Good Master," and our Lord
pulls him up. " Young man, think what goodness
means when you call me good." I do not think
our Lord either disclaims goodness, nor, on the other
hand, that He means, as some orthodox com-
mentators have suggested, that He is good because
He is God. I think He simply means that the
goodness the young man is in search of is to be
found in God only, and he is not to give flattering
titles to men.

There are at least three occasions where our
Lord appears in the Gospels as simply challenging

[1] St. Mark x 18 and Luke xviii 18.   St. Matthew seems to
tone the saying down (xix 17).

men to think before they speak—not to make glib
statements, or use convenient arguments which
intellectual or moral consistency ought to make
them shrink from. Thus He confronts the glib
and constant statement of the scribes, that the
Christ was to be the son of David [1] with the language
of the psalm, held to be David's, where he appears
to address the future Christ as Lord, and He asks
how David could call His future son his "Lord."
I do not think it is at all necessary to suppose that
Christ was here making any pronouncement on the
authorship of the psalm. He was simply pressing
the scribes with the duty of thinking before they
spoke—His meaning being that their account of
the Christ was inadequate in the light of their own
Scriptures. So in the same way we should interpret
the strange passage, referred to earlier, in St. John,[2]
where our Lord, so contrary to His general teaching in this Gospel—which is quite unmistakable—
appears to minimize the meaning of the title "Son
of God." He seems to have meant that, at least in
some sense, His opponents must recognize its legitimacy in the case of anyone who represents in any
way the authority of God. In all these cases
mistaken conclusions have been drawn from the
words of Jesus—as that He did not claim goodness,
or that He disowned sonship to David, or that He
meant little by calling Himself Son of God. These
conclusions are shown to be mistaken by the general
sense of His teaching. What He was doing in these
cases was to insist on men's thinking before they
spoke—thinking whether a convenient argument or
lightly uttered word was not really incompatible
with what intellectual consistency or moral seriousness would force them to acknowledge. And this
is surely a very important lesson.

But we return to our main thesis. It is indeed

[1] Mark xii 35.   [2] John x 36. See above, pp. 5-6.

the case that we could hardly believe the doctrine of the Incarnation, if we saw evidence of hasty passion and moral imperfection in Jesus, or if He appeared to have confessed to being deficient in goodness. But such evidences and confessions are not really to be found. The character of Jesus, as the Gospels describe Him, remains in the moral region supreme and perfect—so impressive, I think, in its majesty, that it hushes in our minds the first suggestions of criticism.

V

Finally we have the suggestion to consider, that Jesus showed Himself in certain respects unmistakably deluded—the victim of current errors. Without asking what kind of belief concerning Jesus would be compatible with the acceptance of such a suggestion, let us first of all consider carefully and frankly the facts of the case.

We are bound to recognize in Jesus a real limitation of knowledge. He Himself—in a saying which cannot be supposed to have been invented for Him, but which is assuredly authentic—declared Himself ignorant of the day and hour of the end of the world. He had no map of the future spread before His eyes. He, the Son of God—at least in His mortal life— was limited in knowledge and knew His limitation. Thus there is no sign whatever that He transcended the knowledge of natural things common to His Palestinian contemporaries. Also, there is no pretension of knowledge on any such subject. There is in His teaching none of the " science falsely socalled," which abounds in the contemporary apocalypses. He cannot be said to have given any teaching at all on any subject except on the great spiritual subjects. And on these He seems to speak with a sense of full authority amounting to infallibility.

I cannot resist that impression. "Verily, I say unto you." That is enough.[1]

But there are certain points on which our Lord is commonly supposed to have given positive teaching which was in fact erroneous.

1. He is supposed to have proclaimed His own immediate coming in glory and the end of " this world." I have dealt with this point at length.[2] The conclusion which the facts seem to me to warrant is that our Lord expressly disclaimed knowledge of the time and season of the end, and expressly warned His disciples against supposing that God intended such knowledge for them, though His disciples, or some of them, misunderstood Him. There is no real warrant for ascribing delusion to our Lord's mind on the subject. Under this head no more will be said here.

2. He is perceived to have shared the current belief in devils and diabolic possession ; and this, it is taken for granted, was no more than a superstition which we have outgrown.

Now I am not disposed to deny that in this matter also there may have been occasional misunderstandings on the part of His disciples. As I read the account of the healing of the Gadarene, or Gerasine, demoniac in St. Mark (Mark v 1–17), it suggests itself somewhat readily that the supposed permission given by Jesus for the entry of the " legion " of demons into the swine may have been a misinterpretation on the part of the disciples. And sometimes, when our Lord is speaking of evil spirits, He undoubtedly uses metaphorical language.[3] But I think it is quite certain that He did believe in evil and in good spirits, and in their activity among men ; and not only did He believe this, but

---

[1] On our Lord's use of " Amen," see Dalman, *Words of Jesus*, pp. 226 ff.

[2] Chap. V.   [3] *E.g.* Luke xi 24–7.

He made it a quite distinct element in His teaching.
He would have His disciples look out upon the world
as a scene in which the conflict of good and evil
is not merely carried on among men.   Behind the
activities of bad men He sees an awful invisible
agency organizing and maintaining a kingdom of
evil and enslaving the souls of men.   " An enemy
hath done this "—an evil will or army of wills, set
to thwart the good purpose of God.[1]   And in various
widespread kinds of disease He recognized evil
spirits as possessing men and women, and constantly
dealt with them accordingly.

But have we the right to class all this as delusions
which we have outgrown ?   Certainly, as to the
existence of spirits and their activity among men
there has been a very widespread assent given by
the conscience of men, and of men of the profoundest
spiritual insight.   The testimony of such a man
as Frederick Denison Maurice is very impressive.[2]
I do not think our knowledge authorizes any denial
of it.   It seems to me that not only the personal
experience of individual souls but the spectacle of
the organization and continuity of evil influences in
the world, suggests the truth of the explanation
which our Lord certainly adopted as His own.   And
as to the reality of diabolic possession, I have been
again and again deeply impressed by the testimony
of missionaries in non-Christian countries, that they
are not able to doubt it.   " It may or may not
exist in England," they say, " but it certainly
exists in India or China or Africa."

On the whole—in view of the deep mystery of
evil in the world—I fail to see what right men have
to treat the belief in evil spirits and their activity,

[1] See Mark iii 22–30 ; Luke xi 17–26 (the obvious metaphors
do not conceal the also obvious intention of teaching truth) ; Matt.
xiii 28 ; Luke x 18, xiii 16, xxii 31, etc.
[2] See my *St. John's Epistles*, pp. 145 ff.

or the belief in good spirits or angels, as error and delusion, or as childish fancy which the mature mind outgrows. But one point must be kept steadily in view. The whole world in our Lord's time, and Palestine not less than other districts, was weighed down by the terror of evil spirits, just as a great part of the world is to-day. Jesus no doubt affirmed that they really existed and were the cause of numberless moral and physical evils. But He would not suffer men to remain in dread of them. His whole teaching was of redemption. If men would trust God, they could be free—free from the fear of evil spirits and from the fear of death. And He was come to lead them to this liberty. As He is recorded to have said to the Seventy: " I beheld Satan fallen as lightning from heaven. Behold, I have given you authority to tread upon serpents and scorpions, and over all the power of the enemy : and nothing shall in any wise hurt you." [1] No doubt it was this sense of victory over the powers of evil among Christians which, as much as anything, promoted the spread of the Church. The characteristic of Christians should not be their belief in the activity of evil spirits, but their belief that they are impotent against the Redeemer of men.

3. There is lastly the assertion to be considered that our Lord gave positive teaching about the Old Testament which identifies Him with traditional ideas about that literature which modern critical science has shown to be untrue. I think this is an exaggeration. On the whole our Lord's teaching about the Old Testament is most remarkable for its profound spiritual truth. No doubt, as He spoke of the sun rising, so He spoke of the Books of the Law as by Moses and the Psalter as by David, and drew lessons from the narratives without any question being raised of their historical character.

[1] Luke x 18–19.

It would have been impossible to do otherwise, if He was freely to use human language intelligible to the people of Galilee or the Rabbis of Jerusalem. I should suppose that He did not know what the progress of critical science has made fairly evident to us, but I should suppose also that there was in His own consciousness a great distinction clearly present between what He did know—the spiritual content of His message—and all the popular assumptions of knowledge on matters which were not within His scope. On matters not within the scope of His mission, He appears as giving no positive teaching at all.

The only occasion on which it seems to me that it can be plausibly pleaded that He laid stress upon a question of authorship or literary character in books of the Bible was in His argument about Ps. cx. On that occasion the verbal difference between the narratives of the three Evangelists makes it evident that we cannot rely on having the precise words of Christ. On the other hand His purpose is quite plain. It is not, as some moderns would have us believe, to repudiate the Davidic descent of the Christ, but to make it plain that the Scribes, if they were true to their accepted principles, would not be able to speak as if the Christ was to be the Son of David and nothing more. They must recognize Him as David's Lord as well as David's Son. I think it is quite enough for the fair interpretation of the passage to represent our Lord as confronting the Scribes with the requirements of their own lore, without laying any stress on it Himself. I have already pointed out that this sort of *argumentum ad hominem* appears to have been characteristic of our Lord. I should like to repeat that I believe there must have been in His own consciousness a vast region of common assumptions which He was content to take for granted without confusing them with the things which He *knew*.[1]   Thus as concerns the argument about Ps. cx, I do not think we are compelled either to force men in the name of Jesus to accept a theory of authorship which seems to us very improbable, or to declare Christ mistaken. It belonged to a region of knowledge in which He knew that He had no commission, and in which knowledge beyond that of His contemporaries would, in fact, not have helped but hindered His mission.

As to the bearing of our Lord's limited human knowledge on the theory of the Incarnation, more will be said in the next chapter.   Here I want only to draw a distinction, which I think the facts warrant, between limitation of knowledge which must be acknowledged in Him and anything which can be called delusion or the teaching of error, of which I cannot see the traces.

I know there are many good men who would say that we can believe that our Lord was really the victim of certain current delusions and taught in accordance with these delusions, without affecting our faith in the reality of the Incarnation as St. Paul and St. John believed it.   Here I admit I stumble. But I need not pursue the question, because I dispute the premiss.   I see no positive delusion or error in the teaching of Jesus.   The truth of what He can fairly be said to have taught seems to me to stand secure, in spite of all the developments of science and changes of human circumstance.

I have been seeking in this chapter only to show what seems to me the essential weakness and one-sidedness of each of the various humanitarian estimates of Christ, and to obviate the objections which are made against the doctrine of His person as St. Paul and St. John present it to us.   There is

[1] On the limitations of our Lord's knowledge within the sphere of His mortal life as man, see below, pp. 225 ff.

always, however, something unsatisfactory about the result of saying no to a string of objections. Each answer may seem in turn fairly satisfactory, but there remains the sense that there is or may be " something in them." And, in fact, on a subject so great and mysterious as the person of Christ, it is absurd to suppose that everything will be clear. I have done my best with each of the objections in turn, and I am not without hope that the answer in each case will be felt to be stronger than the objection. But it is quite certain that it is not by any such negative process that any real conviction will be won. The real conviction must come from the study of the positive picture in the Gospels. It must be the gradually growing assurance that this picture is not one which can be due to human invention or imagination. It must overwhelm us with the sense of its truth, and with the sense that only the doctrine of the Incarnation can really interpret it or account for it. And toward this sort of conviction the removal of objections and the consideration of particular literary problems only make a very partial contribution. The conviction itself must be of the sort suggested by Jesus Himself when He said of Peter's first conviction of His Messiahship : " Flesh and blood hath not revealed it unto thee, but my Father which is in heaven," and of the sort which St. Paul meant when he said, " No man can say *Jesus is Lord* but in the Holy Spirit."

Certainly it is not the case that our deepest and most important convictions are those which involve least difficulty, or those against which fewest objections can be plausibly urged. Certainly also, as concerns the faith in Christ's person, the Evangelists do not, on the whole, give us the impression that they sought to remove difficulties for faith out of their records. On the whole they give us the impression

of candour and naïveté in a high degree. It is not
pleaded therefore that there are no difficulties about
the traditional faith in Christ. What is pleaded is
that, if all the facts are frankly faced, the only con
ception which adequately accounts for them is the
conception which the first Church was led to form—
the conception of the incarnation of the Son of God
—the doctrine of " the Word made flesh."

CHAPTER VII

THE DEFINITIONS OF THE COUNCILS CONCERNING
THE PERSON OF CHRIST

WE have been carefully reviewing the New Testament, and we have seen good reason for reaching the conclusion that only the conception of Jesus as the eternal Son of God incarnate is adequate to account for the facts of the case—that is especially the spiritual authority claimed and exercised by Him, which so plainly passes the limits of legitimate human influence, and His own occasional utterances about Himself; or, to view the matter from the side of the disciples, the awestruck devotion passing into worship which they experienced, and which they expressed after the Resurrection by calling their Master " the Lord " in a sense which certainly involves divine sovereignty. And we noted how carefully this conception of the Lord's person was expressed by St. Paul and St. John and in the Epistle to the Hebrews upon the background of, and consistently with, the traditional monotheism of the Jews, and how it was apparently accepted throughout the apostolic churches without controversy or demur—how it is implied in the New Testament writings where it is not explicit.

I

Merely considered as literary documents—the earliest which remain to us concerning the origin of Christianity—the books of the New Testament, or almost all of them, stand by themselves in importance. They alone represent the creative period of the Christian Church, in the sense that all the later literature represents an attitude of conscious dependence upon a message already delivered. Thus (1) we know practically nothing about our Lord except what we find in the New Testament. Among the few sayings ascribed to Him which are preserved outside the New Testament only one has any bearing upon the question of His person—that which occurs among His sayings in a papyrus discovered not long ago on the site of Oxyrhynchus in Egypt[1]: "Where one is alone, so am I with him. Raise the stone and there you will find me; cleave the wood and there am I too." This, if it were a genuine saying, would seem to ascribe to our Lord Himself a declaration of His universal presence in nature. But he would indeed be bold who would assert its genuineness. As Dr. Burkitt says, these brief sayings seem to represent an early Egyptian amalgamation of Hellenistic and Christian ideas. And the apocryphal "Gospels" which remain to us serve no purpose at all except to show how poor a thing the early Christian imagination proved to be when it sought to invent further accounts of our Lord's infancy or childhood, or of His appearances after His resurrection. Again (2) there is no other record of the first life of the Christian Church except St. Luke's in the Acts. (3) As to the Epistles, it would be impossible to make a brief statement about the signs of their early diffusion and influence which would be sufficiently accurate. Certainly some of St. Paul's most characteristic ideas as concerning justification by faith and the relation of Grace to Law did not deeply influence the early Church. Plainly they had not understood

[1] See Grenfell and Hunt, *Logia Iesou* (1897), p. 12.

him. But as far as the conception of Christ's person
is concerned, the doctrine of the incarnation of the
pre-existent divine Son in Jesus the Christ is the
accepted tradition behind the earliest sub-apostolic
writers—Clement, Barnabas, Ignatius, Hermas and
the Apologists.[1] It holds the field before the Christian
Church had any New Testament.

This is what the ordinary Christian has not grasped.
The earliest Christian Church had a collection of
Holy Scriptures ; but it was simply the Old Testament canon. It is marvellous with what unanimity
the Gentiles, who very soon swallowed up the Jewish
element in the Church, accepted the Jewish foundation and the Jewish Scriptures. It was long before
they collected their apostolic writings into a canon.
The history of this formation of a canon is obscure,
as very much is obscure in the earliest Christian
history. But by the middle of the second century
the four Gospels were practically canonized, and
doubtless from very early days the apostolic Epistles
were read in the churches to which they were addressed,
and began to pass from church to church. However, for the first hundred years of the Church's
existence it had no Bible—no standard of reference
—except the Old Testament and " the tradition "—
that is, the teaching first given in each local church
by its apostolic founder, fortified by the constant
intercourse between the different churches. We
have already seen that the writers of the Epistles
can take for granted a certain " tradition " as known
to those they wrote to ; and from what they take
for granted we can more or less gather the content
of the tradition in the different churches.[2]

So equipped, then, the young churches started on
their career in a world singularly well adapted to

[1] See appended note at the end of the chapter, p. 228, on Hermas,
the Didache, etc.
[2] See *Belief in God*, pp. 207 ff.

puzzle and bewilder them. For the Hellenistic world of the Roman Empire was in a state of intellectual ferment. It was not a day of great philosophers, but it was a day when intellectual interest was keen. Men were widely seeking some doctrine of the " whence " and the " whither "—some doctrine of how the world which seems so evil was made and is governed—and how the hapless soul of man is to escape from the changes and chances of this mortal life into some region of calm and security and immortality. And the cities were full of teachers and lecturers—who had each of them a " gnosis," a " knowledge " or theory of his own, which was either divulged to all who would come and listen, or reserved as a secret for the initiates into this or that " mystery-cult." Christianity spread rapidly because of its moral attractiveness, and especially probably because of its practical spirit of brotherhood. And there were multitudes of " gnostics " who were ready enough to adopt the Christian ideas and sacred names, and adjust them to their cosmic theories. So the Christian churches found themselves in a bewildering world of speculation and of fusion between different systems and traditions, and they were forced to clear up their ideas and to know their own mind. Moreover, though Christianity had qualities which made it popular, it had others which rendered it profoundly unpopular. It was suspected of being a secret society, disloyal to the Emperor and the Empire. It was thus always subject to persecution, because it was supposed to encourage the dangerous elements in society. And the darkest stories were told about its nocturnal gatherings and secret orgies. So, not only was it driven by its inner necessities to obtain a clear account of its own doctrine, it was also driven to explain itself to those outside, and to seek to remove the suspicions of the authorities. This is the origin of the " Apologies," and it is the apologists of the second century who made the first attempt to present, in terms acceptable and intelligible to the outside world, an explanation of Christianity as a doctrine and as a way of life.

Of these apologists let us take Justin Martyr as an example. He had found his way to Christianity through disappointment with the various philosophies. But he retained his philosopher's dress, and would still present the doctrine in which he had found satisfaction so as to be intelligible and acceptable in the world that he had left. He made great play with the *Logos*-doctrine, that is the doctrine of the divine reason and energy immanent in the universe, which, as we have seen, was the popular idea of the day, and one which Christianity could use in its own sense. But he is not by any means a sure-footed theologian, and he falls into modes of expression which he had much better not have used, and which the Church after him had to repudiate—as when he talked of the Word or Son of God as a " second God."[1] So it was with the pious but somewhat stupid prophet Hermas, of Rome. He too means well and gives fervent exhortations to his fellow Christians through the medium of his visions. But again he is not at all a clear thinker, and his phraseology is loose. But all the while the Christian churches in the different cities were closely knit together and intensely conscious of unity. Thus as we survey the early period we seem to see the Church as a whole standing before the world, with grand moral steadfastness and an intense sense of practical security in its tradition of religious belief and practice, but subjected to an intellectual cross-questioning of a very puzzling kind. Will you admit this ? Do you believe that ? Will you accept this suggestion ? Will you accommodate

[1] See below, p. 242.

yourself to that popular theory ? And the Church made many mistakes in its haste, and corrected them somewhat painfully at its leisure. Only gradually and hardly did it fashion its terminology, chiefly by the help of certain men who relatively deserve the title of great men : Irenaeus,[1] whose intellectual perceptions were very sure ; Tertullian, the African, who was much more brilliant and also much more rhetorical and one-sided ; and Origen of Alexandria, who, in spite of certain very precarious speculations and excursions into the unknowable, was the greatest of all.

Now it is obvious that this process cannot be described in detail in one chapter in a small volume. I propose to make only one or two general observations before we approach the age when the Church, in formal councils, gave certain dogmatic definitions of its doctrine of the person of Christ, to which we must pay more precise attention.

The chief intellectual difficulties of the Church were (1) with regard to the doctrine of the Trinity—that is especially the relation of the Son, conceived of as an eternal and divine person, to God the Father and to the Holy Spirit. It was in this region that it found the greatest difficulty in fixing its termin-

---

[1] See on Irenaeus *Belief in God*, p. 47. Dr. Rashdall has strangely accused him of what later was called Apollinarianism (see *Jesus Human and Divine*, p. 13). But Irenaeus gives us an account of our Lord's temptations, according to which the divine Word left the man or the manhood in Jesus to struggle and suffer unaided in those dark hours. ὥσπερ γὰρ ἦν ἄνθρωπος, ἵνα πειράσθη, οὕτως καὶ λόγος ἵνα δοξασθῇ· ἡσυχάζοντος μὲν τοῦ λόγου ἐν τῷ πειράζεσθαι, etc. (iii 19, 3). The phraseology may be easily criticized. But it certainly quite clearly means that Irenaeus thought of Christ as having a properly human mind and will in which to be tempted and struggle. Again, he says : " He struggled and overcame : He was man fighting for His fathers, and by His obedience paying the debt of their disobedience. . . ." And in order to fight the human fight fully " He passed through every age, from infancy to manhood, restoring to each communion with God " (iii 18, 6, 7). He was what He seemed—really man (ii 22). See my *Dissertations*, pp. 108 ff. I cannot think what caused Dr. Rashdall to make such a statement.

ology : (2) in maintaining its hold on the real humanity of Christ. The Hellenistic world was still possessed with the sense that the source of spiritual contamination for souls lay in the body and the material world, and that the redemption of the soul lay in its exemption from matter. And following on this conception of matter as evil was a horror of the idea of any real incarnation of God. The Church could not remain uninfluenced by this tendency. Thus we have a whole series of attempts— Docetism and all the varieties of Gnosticism—to explain away the reality of Christ's physical manhood ; and all such attempts appear to have met with a great deal of sympathy and success. Tertullian, looking back on the history of Gnosticism at the beginning of the third century, can speak of the dismal experience which the Church had passed through of seeing " one and another, the most faithful, the wisest, the most experienced in the Church, going over to the wrong side." [1]   Meanwhile there was comparatively little difficulty in maintaining the originally divine nature or deity of Christ. The popular instinct was all on this side.

The ablest opponent of this fundamental article of faith was a brilliant but morally disagreeable man—Paul, the bishop of Samosata, the favourite and courtier of Zenobia, the Queen of Palmyra. His doctrine is broadly the same as one we are made familiar with to-day—that the person Jesus did not exist till He was born of Mary ; that the divine Word or Wisdom (conceived of as a quality or aspect of God and not as a person) dwelt in him as it dwells in other men, but in a unique degree, so as gradually to deify him, till from having been a man he became God.   The support which Zenobia gave her favourite made it very difficult for the local episcopate to secure his deposition. But as

[1] de praescr. 3.

soon as Zenobia was defeated by the Emperor Aurelian his strength was gone. It would seem that he had no popular support in the Church, though he became indirectly the parent of an intellectual school of which Arianism was the fruit.

This very rough sketch must suffice to bring us to the period of the Councils. The reason why we must consider their dogmatic definitions is not because they represent the action of ecclesiastical authority, for with that at present we are not concerned, but because, viewed historically, the teaching about the person of Christ which we get in the New Testament, and which we find from the first as the tradition of the Church, seems here to reach its intellectual expression, or at least its technical formulation. That at least was the claim made for these formulas —that they represented no new doctrine and no addition to the doctrine of the Bible and the tradition of the Church, but were simply its expression in an articulate form with a view to defending it against the invasion of proposed interpretations of Christ which would have fundamentally destroyed the Church tradition in its real meaning. The question for us is whether this is really so, or whether, on the other hand, the definitions are encumbrances which the faith of the New Testament would have done better to dispense with, or which, even if they were once necessary, are now certainly to be regarded as antiquated expressions of the faith in terms of a philosophy which has been long outgrown, and for which we can surely find better substitutes in the language of modern thought, retaining the ancient formulas only as historical records. This is a very insistent question to-day; and though we are not yet in a position to pay regard to the question of ecclesiastical authority, we can discuss these formulas very profitably on their merits.

II

The first occasion for an ecclesiastical dogma was found in the heresy of Arius. He was a clever and influential parish priest of Alexandria who was one of the numerous pupils of a famous teacher, Lucian of Antioch, a martyr in the Diocletian persecution (about 311), and also the parent of an Antiochene school of teachers, some of whom it is fair to call rationalists. Arius' theory of the person of our Lord was a complex one,[1] but it is mainly with one startling feature in it that the Church concerned itself. He affirmed that Christ was indeed the incarnation of a pre-existent being, the Word or Son, who was "divine" in a popular sense and could be called God and worshipped, but who was not really of the nature of God the Creator. He was a creature who had a beginning from the divine will, and was the created medium through whom God made other creatures. Arius, like the rest of the Church, held fast to the old doctrine of God the Creator derived from the prophets of Israel. He was not a pantheist. He recognized that there can be no confusion between the Creator and the creature. Christ in His original nature must be either one or the other. He must come from one side or other of the line which separates the creative nature from the created. And he quite definitely put Christ on the side of the creatures. He was not of the nature of God, but He came into existence by His will. Thus to account for His exalted and quasi-divine character and position, he would have had the Church regard Him as something like a demigod or created God in His first being, and as a divinized hero in the human

---

[1] It is carefully described by Harnack, *Hist. of Dogma* (Eng. trans.), vol. iv, cap. i, and by Robertson in his admirable Introduction to the translation of Athanasius in *Nicene and Post Nicene Fathers* (Parkers, Oxford, 1892).

guise which he afterwards assumed. He seems to have been a thorough intellectualist in love with his own theory, and to have thrown himself zealously and successfully into the task of propagating it. Doubtless he saw in it a bridge by which the non-Christian intellectual world could be persuaded to accept Christ and worship Christ without abandoning its own familiar categories.

This is what the Church saw from another point of view—that Arianism was a bold attempt to assimilate within the Christian Church the pagan idea of a demigod. Arius' first opponent was his bishop, Alexander; and it was the commotion stirred by Alexander's resistance to Arius which alarmed the Emperor Constantine—persuaded that this was merely a question of words, and anxious above all things to promote the peace of the Church in which he had recently learned to see the hope of the empire. This led him to try the expedient of summoning a General Council, which should represent the bishops of all the Christian churches of the empire, to settle the matter. The Council met in 325 in Nicaea and condemned Arius almost unanimously, and, as an expedient to make the condemnation effective, modified an existing baptismal creed, especially by introducing into it the word *Homoousios*, " of one substance with the Father " ; which henceforth became the test word of orthodoxy, being selected, we observe, because of its *exclusive* power, because though Arians would accept a word which sounded very like it—*Homoiousios* (of like substance with the Father)—they simply could not say that Father and Son were of the *same* substance or reality.

This choice of a word—and that a word not found in Scripture—to exclude from the Christian Church a group of men believed to be in error, but in a highly metaphysical region, when the word which they were prepared to accept differed from the word selected only in a single letter, is a proceeding naturally repulsive to moderate men at all times, and especially to the modern Englishman. Nevertheless, we must confess that it was necessary. To tolerate the Arians was to tolerate both the pagan conception of a created God or demigod, and also the conception of a deified hero : that is to say, the Church, in tolerating them, would have turned its back on the foundation of its religion—its belief inherited from the prophets of Israel that there was only one God, and there could be none other than He, and that none but He might be adored as God. It is only to say the same thing in other words to say that, if the Christian Church had not been in fundamental error for nearly three hundred years in worshipping Jesus the Christ as its Lord and calling Him God, that must be because He came originally from the other side of that unfathomable gulf which divides the self-existent God the Creator from all His creatures, even the highest—because He belongs to the only eternal reality, the being of God. The long-persecuted Church was just being called to assume the rôle of the established religion of the empire. It was about to enter upon the tremendous charge of guiding the half-converted tribes who were beginning to pour over it and were destined so soon to overwhelm it. It is very easy to see that if it had consented, however reluctantly, to tolerate what Arianism asked it to tolerate, polytheism, both philosophical and popular, both civilized and barbarous, would have effected its lodgment securely within the Church. The Church did not, in fact, keep its doctrine wholly free from deleterious matter derived from paganism. Far from it. But if it had done what the Arians asked of it, its belief in one only God, one only object of worship, would have been submerged in the flood of pagan polytheism.

I will venture to quote once more the remarkable

acknowledgment on the part of Thomas Carlyle which Froude relates [1]: "He made one remark which is worth recording. In earlier years he had spoken contemptuously of the Athanasian controversy—of the Christian world torn in pieces over a diphthong; and he would ring the changes in broad Annandale on the *Homoousion* and the *Homoiousion*. He now told me that he perceived Christianity itself to have been at stake. If the Arians had won, it would have dwindled away to a legend."

The speedily won decision of the Council of Nicaea proved to be a surprise rather than a victory. Owing to a variety of political and other causes, for more than fifty years of bewildering controversy, the fate of its momentous decision hung in the balance. So far as the controversy was really theological at all, it was a struggle of religious faith holding on to a tradition and a revelation, against an ingenious intellectual theory, supported by a closely knit *coterie* of scholars of the school of Lucian, and aided by a mass of mere conservatism which was only reluctant to accept the new word *Homoousion*. Athanasius, who was the champion of orthodoxy from the time of the Council, when he was still a deacon, till the day of his death, makes the real nature of the struggle constantly evident. In his first writings, when he was a very young man, he had shown himself fascinated by the current philosophy of the *Logos*— the divinity immanent in the world—and had interpreted the Incarnation in the light of it.[2] But

---

[1] Carlyle's *Life in London*, ii 462. See also the similar judgment in Harnack, *Hist. of Dogma*, iv 43: "Had the Arian doctrine gained the victory, it would in all probability have completely ruined Christianity," etc.

[2] Dr. Rashdall, in *Jesus Human and Divine* (Melrose, 1922), p. 14, reproduces an earlier paper in which, with astonishing emphasis, he accused Athanasius (like Irenaeus, see above, p. 201) of being Apollinarian: "It cannot be too strongly asserted that Athanasius was an Apollinarian." In a note to the republished paper, in consequence of protests, he modifies his statement thus: "In his

through all the long years of conflict his philosophical interests are almost wholly swallowed up in his passionate but also deliberate and rational zeal for Christianity as a religion resting on a person who can be wholly believed in and worshipped as the Redeemer because He is really God as well as man [1] —a religion, moreover, which is essentially the same religion as had its beginnings in the Old Testament, the religion of the one God, who is not less truly one because He has come nearer to us in His incarnate Son, and we have recognized a distinction as of persons in the one divine being. Athanasius argues elaborately and persistently, but never as a philosopher contending for his theory, always as one put in charge of a revelation and a tradition, always with his eye fixed upon the strictly religious interests and loyalties. It is a great mistake to speak as if

earlier days." What should we think of an historian of to-day who should speak of Mr. Gladstone in retrospect as " a strenuous Tory," or of a distinguished bishop, still alive, as " a pugnacious High Churchman," and then explain that he was referring to his hot youth ? Dr. Rashdall then says that in the *Orations* there is " no trace of any distinct recognition of a human soul in Jesus," and that his later distinct repudiations of Apollinarianism were " formal " and " that it may be doubted how far this admission really affected his general way of thinking."

The truth behind all this is that the circumstances of current controversy and the tone of the Alexandrian atmosphere both alike tended towards a one-sided emphasis on the Godhead of Christ, as compared with the manhood. But Athanasius was on his guard. I have quoted in my *Dissertations*, pp. 122–6, many passages from the *Orations* dealing with our Lord's assertion that He *did not know* (Mark xiii 32) and similar texts. Athanasius' explanation of the texts may be regarded as more or as less satisfactory. But, at any rate, they make it quite evident that he recognized in our Lord's manhood, or " flesh," a human mind which must be in itself limited and susceptible of progress and liable to ignorance. This is plain through the whole course of his controversial life, as well as in his later utterances when Apollinarianism was specifically in question. No doubt Athanasius was always reluctant to give up old friends on account of their excesses, whether Apollinarius or Marcellus. But he was himself precisely *not* Apollinarian.

[1] Harnack and Robertson give us excellent accounts of Athanasius' doctrine, and Dr. Bright (*Church of the Fathers*) is ncomparable in his vivid estimate of Athanasius as a person.

the outlook of the Church in the matter was mainly philosophical. All that the Church did was to choose the best available term to express the truth that Christ was God, and that there could not be any being conceived of or worshipped as God except the one God without abandoning the foundation of the revelation on which the Church rested. Certainly Athanasius against Arius stands for permanent and practical religion against an intellectual theory which in fact turned out to be a very transitory phase of philosophy indeed.

III

But before the death of Athanasius the balance of interest had shifted from one aspect of the person of the Redeemer to the other—from His Godhead to His manhood. A hundred years earlier Origen had prefaced his most speculative book—on *The Principles of Things*—by pointing out that there was a Christian tradition which it was the first business of the Church to hand down, and that (among other necessary points) it proclaimed a Christ who was both eternally and permanently God and also, by His incarnation, really man. In the traditional religion of the mass of the Christian people it was in ancient days always rather the belief in His manhood that was in peril than that in His Godhead. But the Church's duty was always to be true to the double idea or double fact and, in spite of one-sided tendencies, it fulfilled this duty. This is illustrated by the history of the Councils. One of the most zealous of the Athanasians and one of the ablest, Apollinarius of Laodicea, in his zeal to maintain the moral perfection and immutability of Christ, embraced the notion that in Christ the divine reason and will took the place of the changeable human will and fallible human reason. So that the manhood of Christ which He took at the Incarnation was not a full and complete manhood, but a manifestation of the divine reason veiling itself and expressing itself in a human flesh and animal soul, or principle of life.[1] This idea, which ought indeed to startle anyone who has read the Gospels, including the account of the temptation and of the agony in Gethsemane, Apollinarius made more plausible apparently by the idea that in the divine Word lies the eternal archetype of all created things,[2] and in particular of human nature, which was made in the image of God—so that the eternal Word can even be spoken of as the archetypal or eternal man, and we may suppose that He was always destined to act as man in a human body. But there is a good deal of uncertainty about the date and the nature of this refinement.

It must be confessed that zeal for the full meaning of the manhood of Christ was not a very conspicuous characteristic of Greek theologians. Nevertheless, when thus challenged by Apollinarius the Church was true to itself. The Council of Constantinople—the history of which is very obscure in many respects—certainly followed the lead of an earlier Council at Alexandria and condemned the Apollinarians, but without any special definition. When the Council was later reckoned for ecumenical, this[3] was what it was chiefly credited with—that it had affirmed that the Church must proclaim a Christ who was not only truly God but also perfectly and completely man, with all the complement of properly human faculties, spiritual as well as physical. Once again

[1] He adopted the psychological theory which would describe man as made up of body, soul, and spirit.

[2] The Fathers mostly read John i 3, 4 as "Without him [the Word] was not anything made. That which hath been made was [eternally] life in him."

[3] As also that it gave completed expression to the doctrine of the Trinity by bringing the Holy Spirit as well as the Son under the term *Homoousios*.

the Church had behaved, not as a group of philosophers or psychologists seeking to frame a satisfying theory of Christ's person, but as the trustees
for a religion rooted in historical facts, bound to
the full reality of Christ the man.

To-day it is not necessary to argue the case against
Apollinarius. All our modern Lives of Christ, and
books about Christ, give the fullest interpretation
to His manhood and call attention to the overwhelming evidence which the Gospels give us of the
human spirit—reason and will and feeling—in Jesus.
Present-day enthusiasm is all for the full manhood.
The question with us is only whether this reality of
His manhood is consistent with personal Godhead.
In ancient days, however, Apollinarius and His
followers found much more popular sympathy than
those who were accused of denying the personal
Godhead of Christ.

IV

Then once more the balance shifts. There was a
school of theologians, already alluded to, who had
their centre at Antioch and did honour to Lucian
as their master, amongst whom the most famous
names were those of Diodore of Tarsus and Theodore
of Mopsuestia. They were scholars with whom
modern Englishmen would have natural sympathy.
Their zeal was for a critical and historical interpretation of the sacred books, and for the reality of
the manhood of Christ. In strenuous opposition
to the tendencies of Alexandria, and especially of
Apollinarius, they emphasized the freedom of Christ's
human will and the reality of His human growth
and human limitations in mind as well as body,
even to the point of postulating for Him, as it seemed,
an independent human personality, at any rate to
start with. The " connection " between the divine

Word or Son and the human person of Jesus, the adopted Son, was, in their estimation, so close as to involve actual identification of the man Jesus with the Son of God. But this was apparently a gradual process and was the reward of a continually fuller moral perfection. Fundamentally and originally the man Jesus was a separate person from the eternal Son.

One of the disciples of this school, Nestorius, a fiery and pugnacious character, became Bishop of Constantinople in A.D. 428. His "chaplain," Anastasius, took an early opportunity vehemently to repudiate the term *theotokos* which it was customary to apply to the Blessed Virgin Mary, signifying precisely that her infant Son was personally God. "Let no one," he cried, "call Mary Theotokos; for Mary was but a woman; and it is impossible that God should be born of a woman." Nestorius threw himself into the defence of the Antiochene doctrine in special antagonism to the influences from Alexandria, where the great Cyril was archbishop. In particular, he was said to have committed himself to the assertion that "the child of two or three months old I cannot call God." At once a tumult arose in the Church, and controversy was fierce. Few things in the history of the Church have probably harmed it more than the bitterness and uncharitableness of its controversialists. Nestorius was bitter. But what has mostly harmed the Church was the bitterness of its protagonist Cyril. And there is no question that the theology he poured forth was distinctly one-sided and ill calculated to satisfy the reasonable scruples of the Antiochenes. But with these matters we are not here concerned. Nor are we really concerned with the question whether, after all, Nestorius ultimately meant to deny what the Church was at pains to affirm. There is now ground for believing that, had he lived a few years longer, he might have been satisfied to accept the decision of the Council of Chalcedon in 451, in which he could have recognized the safeguarding of what he valued.[1]

But the obscurity of many of the details of the controversy, and the painfully uncharitable tone of it, which leaves a most disagreeable impression on our minds, cannot be allowed to obscure the real importance of the issue. The Creed of Nicaea affirmed that it was the eternal Son of God, Himself very God, who for us men and for our salvation had come down and taken flesh of Mary and been born and suffered for us. And long before Nicaea that was the passionate faith of the Church. It was really God, the eternal Son, who was born of Mary, and who lived and died under conditions of a real humanity. And this continuity of personality was the very thing which Nestorius seemed to deny. Thus once more a Council, reckoned as ecumenical, was held at Ephesus in 431, and Nestorius was violently condemned and the title *Theotokos*, as applied to the mother of Jesus—that is, strictly, "the bearer of God"—was made obligatory for acceptance by the officers and teachers of the Church. And I do not think it can be doubted that here again the Church, in refusing to admit that Jesus was a separate person from the Son of God, and affirming, on the contrary, that it was the same person—the Word or Son—who was eternally in the being of God and through whom all things were made, who was born as a baby of Mary and lived and died upon the Cross—in affirming this and denying its contrary the Church was certainly only reaffirming the doctrine of St. Paul and St. John and the Epistle to the Hebrews.

[1] On the subtle and difficult question what Diodore, Theodore, and Nestorius actually and precisely meant to affirm and deny, I would refer to the very just summary, as it seems to me, given by Dr. Kidd in his just published *History of the Church*, vol. iii, chaps. xi and xii.

The spiritual importance of the question at issue may be made more apparent by four considerations.

(1) The sum and substance of Christian redemption lies in the real union of Christians with Jesus, the man who lived and worked and suffered on earth and now reigns in heaven. And the point is that in being made one with Him—baptized into Him and receiving into ourselves His very life, His flesh and blood—we are really made one, not with any created or intermediate person, but with God Himself. And it is only because He is verily and personally God that His manhood can have imparted to it this capacity for universal participation and assimilation. St. Cyril is always recurring to this point.

(2) Christians from the beginning, and notably St. Paul, have insisted upon the pre-eminence and uniqueness of the self-sacrifice of Christ. Now, judged by an objective standard, the measure of Christ's self-sacrifice within the limits of His mortal life cannot be said to be greater, at any rate, than that of multitudes of martyrs. But it is not within these limits that the uniqueness of Christ's self-sacrifice is found. It lies in the region of His pre-existent life. It consists in this, that one who existed in the glory of God consented to abandon this to us inconceivable glory of life, in order to accept the conditions and limitations and sufferings of real manhood. This act of self-sacrifice is strictly unique, and it is so only because the person who sacrifices Himself is very God—not closely united to God but personally God. His acts are strictly God's acts and His love God's love.

(3) Herein lies also the clue to the *finality* of the Christ. Intellectually considered, nothing is more essential to a full faith in Christ than this recognition of His essential finality—to which we shall have to recur later on. This means that He is not only the

greatest prophet and the most conspicuous saint and the noblest leader of humanity who has ever lived; for if that were all, obviously we could " look for another " as great as He, possibly greater than He.   And if Jesus be, as at the last analysis Nestorianism always asserts, a human person, one among millions of human persons, whom the divine Word united to Himself and even (finally) absorbed into Himself, there is no reason in the nature of things why the process should not be repeated.   It is, in fact, only the highest example of what occurs in its measure in every good man.   There may be another Christ, even conceivably a higher and more enlightened one.   There is no real ground for asserting the finality of the Christ, unless He be personally God in manhood.   Then, and then only, must He be essentially and necessarily final.   For there can be no disclosure of God in manhood or of manhood in God even conceivable which should be completer or fuller (at least under the conditions of this world) than is given us in Him who is the Word made flesh.   Nor in the nature of things can there be another such.   There can be no other such person as the only-begotten Son of God.

(4) This, too, is important—the " Nestorian " conception is exceedingly difficult to grasp with precision.   It is deeply evasive intellectually considered, and appears to pass from one form to another. But the Creed of the Church is a creed for common men, and must be able to express itself, in those points for which it claims popular acceptance, in broad affirmations—broad as well as true.   The orthodox creed—that for us men and for our salvation very God, the Son of God, consented to come down from the bosom of the Father to become man and for us to die—has this broad intelligibility.

But freed from refinements and reduced to a like broad intelligibility, it is impossible to doubt that the teaching of Nestorius would have inevitably taken shape in the proclamation of Jesus as the deified man,[1] which from every point of view would have been a disaster.

V

Once more, and for the last time, the balance shifts. It is now an old Constantinopolitan monk called Eutyches, who affirmed that though Godhead and manhood were separate before the Incarnation, yet in Jesus the manhood was in some sense absorbed and swallowed up in the Godhead. There was a widespread tendency towards this sort of " monophysitism "—this doctrine of the absorption of the manhood in the Godhead—and the Eastern Church might easily have overbalanced on that side. But the West, in the person of the great Leo, Bishop of Rome, put its weight on the other side, and at Chalcedon, in 451, the last of the great definitions was made which affirmed that the manhood remained in Christ, not only complete, but permanently unconfused—that as Christ was consubstantial with God according to His Godhead, so He became and remained consubstantial with us according to His manhood. So the doctrine was fixed that in Christ incarnate there is one person and that divine, but two natures, divine and human, the one original and the other voluntarily assumed by incarnation but permanent and distinct. This —the Chalcedonian—may be considered in principle the final definition of the Church. If a century later the Church had occasion to affirm that in Christ was the reality of a human *will*, and the whole rational activity of manhood, that was only a reaffirmation—

---

[1] If Nestorianism among Syrians and Assyrians has not taken any such shape it is, I think, because their so-called Nestorianism is really not Nestorianism at all, but in part simply a difficulty of language and in part loyalty to a persecuted leader.

important enough in itself—of what was really secured in principle by the definitions which excluded Apollinarianism and Eutychianism.

VI

We need pursue the history of ecclesiastical dogma no further. In this volume we are in no way concerned with any question of the *authority* which these decrees have as dogmas of the Church. The whole idea of Church *authority* will be ignored till we reach the subject of the Church in the next volume. At present we are simply taking these decrees as important facts in the historical development of the doctrine of the person of Christ. And we cannot fail to be conscious that they have at different periods, and especially to-day, been the subject of widespread criticism in intellectual circles, often violently and contemptuously expressed, especially at their culminating point in the formula of Chalcedon which demands our acceptance of the conception of Christ as throughout, from eternity to eternity, one and the same divine *person*, who nevertheless, as incarnate and made man, subsists in two distinct *natures*, divine and human. Now, (1) the " nature " includes the will and the consciousness ; and we are here (the critics tell us) postulating in the human Christ two wills and consciousnesses, lying (so to speak) side by side in the same person— a very impossible conception—whereas in the Gospels what we are witnesses of is one person, Jesus the Christ, with one will and consciousness, the consciousness and will of a Son, in presence of another will and consciousness, that of His Father who is in heaven ; and there is no suggestion of a dualism of wills or consciousnesses in His own person.

(2) The identity of the divine personality throughout seems to involve the idea of Christ's manhood

as "impersonal." So the theologians have constantly called it. But it is a wholly unacceptable
idea. It is precisely in Jesus, "the Son of Man,"
that we seem to see all the characteristics of human
personality at their highest.

Now it must be acknowledged that these are
very important criticisms which, as we hear them,
strike home with a powerful sense of truth. And
there is another of a different kind which urges
that the Councils were in their definitions, by the
use of such words as "substance," "person,"
"nature," tying the Christian religion to a temporary phase of philosophy which is past and gone,
and from which it had better now shake itself
free.

I would seek to give these criticisms, what they
clearly deserve, the most candid consideration,
which shall be quite free, that is, shall at present
quite ignore the questions of the ecclesiastical
authority claimed for these decisions.

1. The only true and historical way of regard-
ing these dogmatic decisions is to regard them as
primarily *negative*. Their motive was not any
positively felt need of interpreting or defining the
faith as a thing good in itself, but simply the
pressing necessity for excluding certain very power-
fully supported intellectual theories which were
at work and which were calculated to undermine
the traditions of faith worship and practice which
the Church was set to maintain—what it called
"the tradition." It must be admitted that the
love of intellectual definition for its own sake took
possession to a dangerous extent of the Church
both in East and West. But these "intellectual
exercises" have not crystallized as disciplinary
decrees. It is important to notice that Athanasius,
and the Fathers generally, take a very restricted
view of the legitimate functions of the Church with

regard to Christian doctrine. Athanasius contrasts it with its functions in respect of discipline. In this latter region it claims to issue directions on its own authority. Thus the Council of Nicaea with regard to the Easter festival said simply that " it seemed good (ἔδοξε) " to the bishops to give such and such directions. But with regard to doctrine it is much more modest. " With reference to the faith they wrote—not ' such and such things were determined,' but ' thus the Catholic Church believes.' And they added immediately the statement of their faith, to show that their judgment was not new but apostolic, and that what they wrote was not any discovery of theirs, but was what the apostles taught." [1] And, as a matter of fact, St. Athanasius in his almost endless argumentations hardly ever refers to the decision of the Council, but prefers to conduct all his argument in the region of scripture and the necessities of practical religion and reason. And in this he is not singular. It is so with almost all the Fathers. A dogmatic decision was for them certainly a regrettable necessity, only justifiable under extreme need.

2. But I think that, for reasons already given, we are bound to admit that in the case of each of the four great councils the decision at which it arrived to exclude certain lines of teaching or proposed explanations of the person of Christ was a necessary decision—really necessary if the faith of the New Testament was to be maintained. As I have said, to admit as tolerable the Arian explanation of Christ as in effect a demi-god, and thus to repudiate the whole basis of strict monotheism, which inspires both Old and New Testaments, would have ruined Christianity, by assimilating it to insurgent Paganism. It was just as necessary, if the faith of St. Paul and St. John was to be maintained,

[1] *De Synodis*, c. 5.

decisively to exclude any teaching which fundamentally distinguished the person of Jesus from the person of the Son of God, and thereby converted " incarnation " into "indwelling," and substantially assimilated Christ to prophets and saints. In the other direction it was certainly as necessary to exclude the ideas which would have rendered Christ's manhood fundamentally unreal, especially in respect of just those regions of mind and will and spirit in which man is distinctively man. It was, in fact, in view of the ecclesiastical tendencies of the day, a miracle of grace that the Church took so firm a stand against Apollinarius and the Monophysites, though it is precisely this that involved it in the postulate of the two natures to which we shall return directly. I see no reason to doubt that if St. Paul and St. John could have had the situation explained to them, they would have accepted the necessity for the definitions.

3. Though, as I have said, we constantly read highly critical and even contemptuous estimates of the terminology of the Councils, I do not see that they could have found at the time better words in which to embody their decisions, nor have I ever seen any better modern terms suggested. In fact the critics do not generally suggest that the work was badly done for its time, but they suggest that the Councils used (as they were bound to use) the philosophical categories and terms of their day, and that these categories and terms have been outgrown.

But it is very necessary to protest that the Church was not professing to act philosophically. It chose the term " of one substance " to exclude the idea that Christ was not *really* God and then to exclude the idea that He was not *really* man. As the Church used the term it was acting with practical statesmanship and discrimination, rather than with philosophical accuracy : for it is plain that " unity of substance " is used in rather different senses when it is applied to describe (1) the relation of Christ to the Father and (2) His relation to His fellow men. Its aim was practical. So again it was practical necessity which led to its doing the world a great service—that is, selecting an old word which hitherto had meant no more than " substance " (i.e. *hypostasis*) and stamping it with the distinctive meaning of " person," an idea for which hitherto Greek and Latin philosophy had had no term. Once more, if it was, as I think it was, essential that the Church should maintain that the Creator and His creatures —God and man—belong to kinds of reality which are essentially different, I do not see that it could have chosen a better word to use than " nature," when it affirmed in Christ's one person two " natures," the one original and the other acquired. I do not see then how the way in which the Church did its defensive or self-protective work, so far as the choice of its terminology is concerned, could have been bettered. Nor do I see how the terminology in question could be bettered to-day, so long as it is granted that the idea to be expressed is that of the incarnation in a real and full manhood of one who belonged to the eternal being of God, as a Son with His Father. On the contrary it has always appeared to me fairly evident that what the critics want is not better terms to express the same idea, but the substitution of a different idea —either the substitution of what is fundamentally the pantheistic conception of God, according to which God and man are parts of the one substance, in place of the essentially different Biblical idea of God the Creator distinct from His creatures, or the substitution of the idea of a God-indwelt man for that of the incarnate God.

Of course, I know that there is a philosophy which deprecates the whole idea of the existence of real objects or things having distinctive qualities or natures, created by God and in a measure really knowable by us, and of persons made in the image of God, and therefore having a different nature from mere things and animals, and of God as the only self-subsistent and self-complete being, the Creator of all that is. What this philosophy suggests to us as the ultimate reality is (to use Lord Balfour's language) " an identity wherein all differences vanish, or a unity which includes, but does not transcend, the differences which it somehow holds in solution." But this sort of philosophy is not the only Idealism. And it has to reckon with the sort of Realism which the common sense of mankind as well as the theology of the Bible postulates. And granted the sort of Realism which believes in real objects having distinctive natures, and in real persons, and in a real God the Creator, I do not think the terminology of the councils can be easily bettered.

4. But the best things can be most lamentably abused ; and it is manifest in history that the Greek genius, which exercised itself rightfully within the Christian Church in defining and protecting the fundamental faith of Christendom, became enamoured of its own intellectualism and to a lamentable extent distorted the true character and estimate of the Christian religion. For the Christian religion is a way of life—" the way " was the first name for the Church. This " way " involves and depends upon a certain self-disclosure of God and certain ideas about the destiny and capacity of man and his sin and need of redemption. Thus it requires a Creed, and it is idle to regret the necessity. It must perforce have formulated and defended the intellectual principles on which its way of life depends. But it ought always to have presented itself to mankind first of all as a way of life. While in fact, under the dominant influence of Greek

intellectualism, the interest in the intellectual propositions and formulas became the foremost interest, and the Church presented itself to the world, not as a society called to live a life, but as a society maintaining a very elaborate system of doctrines, the propagation of which was its chief business. This is the impression we get in history of the later Greek Church, though the impression made by its mystics and saints must not be forgotten. And a similar intellectualism may be charged against the Western schoolmen, even though Erasmus and his friends did not by any means judge them fairly.

Under such conditions the misuse made of the definitions of the Church is of this kind. They ought to have been regarded as simply warning men off certain misleading and one-sided lines of logical development, leaving them to get their positive picture of Christ from the Gospels, and their positive theory from the books of the New Testament. That, as we have seen, was the real intention of Athanasius and others of the Fathers. They talk very little about the definitions. All their argument—good and bad—is upon the ground of Scripture and occasionally of tradition, and of the meaning of the sacraments and the requirements of the spiritual life. But another tendency is also apparent and in effect prevails. The dogmatic decisions become premises to argue from, and Christ is represented not as He was, but as, it was thought, He must have been. Thus, because it is laid down that there are to be recognized in Christ the two distinct natures, divine and human, what it is not unfair to call a fancy picture of Christ is drawn, as acting now in one nature and now in another, now as God and now as man, which does not really correspond to the picture in the Gospel. Again, it comes to be argued that because He was God, therefore He *must have been* continuously omniscient, and such a plain statement as " Of that day and that hour knoweth no one, no, not the Son," is explained away to mean that He did not choose to reveal what He really knew. " The truth," as Theodoret grimly observed, "tells a lie." Later all that belongs to human limitations—mental growth, anxiety, faith, hope, even prayer in the real sense—is excluded from His consciousness as inconsistent with His Godhead. The intellectual dogmas, instead of serving their original and legitimate purpose, have become the premises from which conclusions are drawn as to what the Incarnate must have been, which practically obscure the picture in the Gospels. So we feel it to be with the later scholastic theologians. The reality of our Lord's humanity, so far as the life of His soul was concerned, becomes almost obliterated.[1]

Or again, because the dogmatic decision against Nestorius laid it down that there was one continuous personality and that divine, the phrase becomes current that the humanity of Christ was " impersonal," [2] whereas in the Gospels we feel that we have a picture of the Son of Man intensely individual and unmistakably personal in His manhood.

5. But the abuse of a thing does not prove that it has no use. The definitions of the Councils were no doubt misused, but we have seen reason to believe that they were necessary, and that the lines of thought which they were intended to exclude were really destructive of the foundations of the Christian faith. The best way to test their legitimacy is to inquire whether, accepting them as limits to our thinking, we are able to accept at its full value and fairly interpret the picture which the Gospels present to us of the Son of Man. As we have seen, it is not the picture of a mere man with a merely human consciousness or a merely prophetic claim. It cannot

---

[1] See on all this my *Dissertations*, pp. 154 ff.
[2] I quite recognize the truth which the phrase is meant to convey (see below, p. 227). It is not used in the formula of Chalcedon.

be so interpreted in any one of the Gospels. Only the incarnation doctrine of St. Paul and St. John can really interpret it. On the other hand, the divine person in the Gospels is certainly presented to us as growing in wisdom, as being tempted, as asking questions, apparently for information, as praying, as overwhelmed with anxiety, as asking upon the Cross the great question of the perplexed and dismayed all the world over, and finally, as, at least in one respect, asserting His ignorance. And, negatively, He never shows any sign of transcending the knowledge of natural things possible to His age, country, and condition. How can these facts be reconciled with His personal Godhead ?

I see no help in solving this question so great as is supplied by two phrases in which St. Paul characterizes the act of the Son of God in taking our manhood[1]—" he beggared himself " (or "made himself poor "), and " he emptied himself " or " annulled himself." St. Paul, in using these words, is not thinking of any particular aspect of the human life of Jesus, such as the limitation of His knowledge ; but he regards the Incarnation in itself as having involved in some sense the abandonment of " riches " which belonged to the previous divine state of the Son. It is when we look at the facts in the Gospel that we are led to welcome St. Paul's words as giving us the clue to what we see there. The divine Son in becoming man must, we conclude, have accepted, voluntarily and deliberately, the limitations involved in really living as man—even as sinless and perfect man—in feeling as a man, thinking as a man, striving as a man, being anxious and tried as a man. Jesus does not indeed appear in the Gospels as unconscious of His divine nature. He knows He is Son of the Father. He " remembers " how He came from God and would go back to God. But He appears none the less as accepting the

[1] 2 Cor. viii 9, Phil. ii 7.

limitations of manhood. And St. Paul, I say, gives us the hint which directs our vision. This was no failure of power. God is love, and love is sympathy and self-sacrifice. The Incarnation is the supreme act of self-sacrificing sympathy, by which one whose nature is divine was enabled to enter into human experience. He emptied Himself of divine prerogatives so far as was involved in really becoming man, and growing, feeling, thinking and suffering as man.

No doubt such a conception raises questions to which we can find no full answer. Thus—Is the self-emptying to be conceived of as a continual refusal to exercise the free divine consciousness which He possessed, or as something once for all involved in the original act by which He entered into the limiting conditions of manhood ? And I think if we are wise we shall not attempt to answer the question. We have not the knowledge of the inner life of Jesus which would make an answer possible. Or again, we are asked how we relate this " limited " condition of the Son as incarnate with His exercise of all the cosmic functions of the eternal Word— what the New Testament calls " the sustaining " or " bearing along of all things " or the holding all the universe of things together—and again I think we had better give no answer. All that appears evident is that it was the eternal Son who was manifested in human nature as Jesus of Nazareth, and that *within the sphere and limit of His mortal life* He appears as restricted by human conditions ; and we thankfully accept this supreme example of humility and self-sacrifice, without attempting to relate it to what lies outside our possibilities of knowledge.[1] We do well to be agnostics, if we put our agnosticism in the right place.

[1] I have endeavoured to enter at greater length into this question in *Dissertations*, ii, where I have also given full quotations from the Fathers.

Now the recognition that the Incarnation involved this limitation in the exercise of divine faculties, *within its sphere*, is quite consistent with the terms of the ecclesiastical definitions. We are bound to recognize the nature of God and the nature of Man as both belonging throughout to the person of the Christ, and as in their essence distinct. Only that power of self-limitation and self-adaptation in God which we have already recognized as in a measure involved in creation, and especially in the creation of free spirits,[1] we should here, in Jesus Christ, recognize again as brought to bear with a fresh intensity to make the Incarnation really possible, spiritually as well as physically. Just as we believe that now in the heavenly places Christ is still truly man, but that the manhood is all radiant with Godhead : so in His earthly state we should believe that Christ was really God and so knew Himself, but that Godhead was submitting itself to the limitations of manhood. As St. Cyril puts it : " He suffered the limits of humanity to prevail in His case." [2]

But we must surely repudiate that mode of speech which prevailed at the time of Chalcedon and later, whereby the life of Christ on earth was represented as containing two consciousnesses and two wills, so to speak, juxtaposited in distinction the one from the other, so that He thought and spoke and acted now as God and now as man. We should repudiate this, because we feel that the Gospels present us with one who is, and knows Himself to be, always and in all things the Son of God, but who is throughout existing, acting, and speaking under the conditions and limitations of manhood.

Also we should deprecate the unguarded use of a phrase which became current among theologians— we mean the phrase which describes Christ's man-

[1] See *Belief in God*, pp. 115–17. [2] *Dissert.*, p. 146.

hood as " impersonal." All that this really means is that the manhood had no *separate* personality. There was only one person—the eternal Word— who exists eternally in God, who was active in the whole universe, and who at last was incarnate in Jesus Christ. But when He took the manhood, complete in all human faculties and activities, He became to it the centre of personality. He made it personal. Thus the humanity of Jesus in the Gospels has nothing of abstract universality about it. It is no mere veil of the Godhead. It is, indeed, intensely individual. And if man, in distinction from all other creatures, was originally made in the divine image and likeness, we can understand how the divine person can become the ego or subject of the manhood in Jesus without its thereby ceasing to be human.[1]

I do not then think that the Chalcedonian formula, summarizing the decisions of the Councils, requires revision in itself ; but if we would justify it, we must recognize very frankly that the purpose of the dogmas was negative—to exclude certain fundamentally misleading interpretations of the person of Christ— and we must insist that for our positive conception of the person of Jesus we need constantly to study with unembarrassed eyes the picture in the Gospels and the doctrine of the Epistles.

Note A, see p. 198

(1) " *The Shepherd* " *of Hermas.*
(2) *The* " *Didache.*"
(3) *The* " *Odes of Solomon.*"

(1) " *The Shepherd* " *of Hermas.*—Undue attention has, I think, so far as his theology is concerned, been given to this interesting prophet of the early Roman Church. He is interesting as a prophet—interesting on

---

[1] See further appended note B, p. 230.

account of his visions, which he and others believed to be inspired, and on account of the enthusiasm which he threw into the message from God given him to deliver. His importance lies in the ethical region. He shows that the Church, or that part of the Church which accepted him as a prophet, still clearly viewed the Christian religion as " the way." Its main interest was moral. The theological background of Hermas' visions was not apparently scrutinized. If we do scrutinize it, it must be confessed that his theology is confused and confusing. He certainly believed in the incarnation of the Son of God, Who " was older than any creature," through whom all things were made and in whom they are sustained. He is thus certainly no Ebionite or humanitarian in his estimate of Christ. But he is very confusing in the language he uses about the Holy Spirit and holy spirits, and about the relation of the Son and the Spirit, whom he sometimes seems to identify, and he may be accused of " Apollinarian " language about the flesh of Christ. I think the best account of him is still Dorner's. But the fact is he was no theologian, and his careless language is such as must almost inevitably have occurred before the days when doctrine was formulated.

(2) *The teaching of the Twelve Apostles* still appears to me to be a very early and very Judaic document which must represent some group of Christian communities quite outside the main streams of Christian influence, who must, moreover, have lost contact with the main streams early, and remained uninfluenced by the ideas of St. Paul and St. John. Its ethical teaching is not like that of St. James. It barely deserves to be called Christian. The document does not supply any clear indication of a doctrine of Christ's person. But it includes the direction to baptize " in the name of the Father and of the Son and of the Holy Ghost," which implies the doctrine of the Son as a divine person.

(3) *The " Odes of Solomon."*—The beautiful mysticism of these odes, which Dr. Rendel Harris discovered and published some fourteen years ago (Cambridge Press), implies (see especially Ode 41) a quasi-Johannine doctrine of Christ (see p. 76).

16

(4) As has been already remarked, *the Ebionites, i.e.* that obscure section of Judaistic Christians who definitely rejected the doctrine of Christ as a divine person incarnate, represent a later deterioration. They cannot be quoted as if they represented the belief of St. James: see Hort, *Judaistic Christianity*, p. 200 ; and B. I. Kidd, *History of the Christian Church* (Oxford, 1922), i, pp. 85–103.

NOTE B, see p. 228

The Term " Enhypostasia "

We should be very grateful to Dr. H. M. Relton for his most suggestive and excellent *Study in Christology*, and to Dr. Headlam for his preface to that study. Dr. Relton has done good service in seeking to familiarize us with the term *enhypostasia*, to which Leontius of Byzantium sought to give currency, to express the idea that the manhood of Jesus found its personality in the personality of the Son of God. Leontius holds a very important place in the sixth century as resisting the current tendency to monophysitism, even inside the orthodox church. I have tried to bring this out in *Dissertations*, iii (see quotation, p. 277, and references in index under the heading *Leontius*). May I venture, however, to deprecate the attempt of Dr. Relton to revive the idea of Apollinarius that we are to ascribe an eternal humanity to the Word, before His incarnation. I suppose that there is some deep sense in which it must be true that all created things have their eternal counterpart in the Word, and humanity amongst them. But this applies to all created things. And we do well not to be " wise above that which is written." There is nothing in Scripture suggesting an eternal manhood in God—nothing at least that is not more adequately represented by the idea that man pre-eminently was made in the divine image. And this is enough to explain how God could take our manhood.

CHAPTER VIII

THE IMPLIED DOCTRINE OF THE HOLY TRINITY

I

IT has already become apparent that the Christian faith in Jesus as the Son of God or Word of God incarnate involves a belief that the being of God is not so " simple " as the Jews, with their less intimate knowledge of God, had supposed. He is still the " one Lord and His name one " ; but this unity is found to contain a distinction within itself—first of all the distinction of Father and Son, which had not been made evident at first.[1] God had, so to speak, come nearer to men in Jesus Christ, to redeem them, and more of His inner being had shown itself to the discerning minds of men in the process. It is very important to take note that belief in the Holy Trinity was not the result of any philosophical or speculative movement among the Christians.

There have been in the world speculative philosophies which have arrived at some sort of Trinitarian belief. Thus we read of an Indian Trinity— Brahma, Vishnu, and Siva—and of a Trinity in the later Greek (Neo-Platonist) philosophy—The One,

[1] Whatever anticipations of Trinitarian doctrine have been discovered by Christian theologians in the Old Testament were certainly not apparent to the Jews. I have already had occasion to speak of the development in later Jewish thought of the "wisdom" or "word" of God, as alive and operative in nature, in terms almost suggestive of distinct personality. But this suggestion never became explicit among them.

231

Reason, and Soul. The former of these doctrines of Trinity was an intellectual attempt to construct a bridge between the Absolute One and the many gods of popular belief, and also an attempt to harmonize hostile cults[1]; and the latter was the result of a purely philosophical attempt to analyse existence into its elements. But the Christians, without any philosophical intention at all, and without any speculative interest, found themselves believing in Father, Son, and Holy Spirit, as a result of their experiences as the disciples of Jesus. The name of God had become for them " the name of the Father and of the Son and of the Holy Ghost." As a consequence of the way in which they came so to believe, it follows that the doctrine at first presented no intellectual difficulty to their minds : for in fact mankind experiences no intellectual difficulty in believing anything which comes to it as experienced fact, though the intellectual analysis of it may prove it to be as mysterious as possible, and the explanation of it wholly baffling. So it appears to be at present with the ultimate elements with which physics deals, and indeed generally with the ultimates of every science.[2] The difficulty of explanation and analysis does not carry with it any difficulty in believing that the facts are so and so. So it was at last with the Christians, when the need of explaining themselves became urgent, and their speculative interest was awakened. They found the idea of the Trinity most mysterious, and its formulation in words most difficult and always finally

[1] See De la Mazelière, *Evolution de Civilisation Indienne,* ii 72 : " De fait la *trimurti* n'est pas la conception de trois hypostases, mais la réconciliation de trois cultes hostiles."

[2] This is what Huxley means by protesting that he was not so foolish as to reject Christianity because it is mysterious. " The mysteries of the Church are child's play compared with the mysteries of Nature. The doctrine of the Trinity is not more puzzling than the necessary antinomies of physical speculation " (see my *Bampton Lectures,* lect. ii, note 15, pp. 246-7).

somewhat unsatisfactory; but, before they made
any attempt to understand or to formulate, they
would have said that in their experience of Jesus
and His Spirit the true God had unmistakably
revealed Himself to them and laid hold upon them
in a novel way. So that, as I say, they found
themselves believing in Father and Son and Spirit;
and the subsequent difficulty they found in explaining to themselves or to others the mystery
involved in their belief did not disturb their faith
in the fact.

How the belief came about we can easily understand. They came to believe in Jesus as being the
Son of God. And reflecting on what His own words
about Himself implied, and also on what was implied
in His divine sovereignty as Lord of all, they
recognized in Him, as we have seen, one who had
come into the world from the Father and who
belonged to His being, as Son with a Father. Then
again they were led to expect from Jesus, the
Christ, the outpouring of the Spirit of God. And a
few days after He had finally left them, the Holy
Spirit actually came, taking them as it were by
storm, and possessing their souls with an almost
intoxicating force. And the Spirit dealt with them
like a person controlling them, and guiding them,
in the most unmistakable ways. So we see in the
Acts and Epistles how the thought of God was
modified by their experiences, and the Name of
God became to them the threefold Name of the
Father and of the Son, or Lord Jesus Christ, and
of the Holy Ghost. It is very interesting to watch
how the very complex and difficult idea of Trinity
in Unity passes into their experience, and we will
seek to follow the process in some detail. But the
result is manifest prior to any reflection upon the
intellectual problem which it presents. You see
what had happened when St. Paul prays that " the

grace of the Lord Jesus Christ, and the love of God, and the fellowship of the Holy Spirit may be with you all " ; or when he writes about the " same Spirit " who pours out the manifold gifts in which the Church rejoices, and the " same Lord " who presides over its manifold ministrations, or the " same God " whose presence is felt in all its various activities ; or when, enumerating the grounds of Christian unity, he makes mention of the one Spirit, one Lord, one God and Father of all [1] ; or when St. Peter writes to the Christians of Asia as those who feel upon them a divine election according to the predestinating choice of God the Father, in sanctification of the Spirit, unto obedience to Jesus Christ and purification through His blood [2] ; or when St. Jude bids Christians to build themselves up in their most holy faith, praying in the Holy Spirit, keeping themselves in the love of God, looking for the mercy of our Lord Jesus Christ.[3]   In all these cases the name " God " is reserved for the Father.   It was only slowly that the Son and the Spirit came to be freely called God, though both St. Paul [4] and St. John do so call the Lord Jesus.   The reason for this reserve was, no doubt, that the instinct of monotheism was against such a use, and nothing was more important than to preserve the monotheistic standing ground of the Old Testament against the surging Paganism around.   But there is no question that the gracious activities of the Son and the Spirit among men were, to their believing minds, properly activities of God. Thus, whether it be the case, as St. Matthew's Gospel relates, that our Lord actually named the Threefold Name to the disciples before His departure, or whether, as so many critics suggest, it was rather that the Palestinian editor of the first Gospel was so familiar with the formula as to attribute it to

---

[1] 2 Cor. xiii 13, 1 Cor. xii 4–6, Eph. iv 4–5.   [2] 1 Pet. i 2.
[3] Jude 20–21.   [4] See above, p. 86.

our Lord, we understand how inevitable it was that the Name of God should have come to be so named ; and when, toward the end of the first century, Clement of Rome wishes to repeat the solemn affirmation of the old prophets " as the Lord liveth," we understand how natural it was that it should take the threefold form—" as God liveth, and the Lord Jesus Christ liveth, and the Holy Spirit." [1] That is what " the living God " had come to mean.

II

Now we must examine more in detail how the distinctions in the being of God emerge.

(1) *The three distinguishable Persons.*—That the Son of God, as He was on earth, was a person distinguishable from His Father is evident. He spoke of His own intimate fellowship with the Father as person with person. We have traced the steps by which the first disciples were led to the conviction that this fellowship of Son with Father was superhuman and belonged to God's being before the world was—that is to His eternal being.[2] We have seen no reason to doubt that St. Paul occasionally calls the Lord Jesus by the title God, and St. John evidently does so. This is the new thought of God—that the Father was never without His Son, or God never without His Image or Word—subordinate to the Father as He who receives to Him who gives, but belonging to His Being. So far the

[1] Clem., *ad Cor.* lviii 2. I do not cite 1 John v 8—the text of the three heavenly witnesses—because, of course, it is not authentic. We may be thankful that Roman Catholic scholars are now allowed to acknowledge this.

[2] Dr. Rashdall says (*Jesus Human and Divine*, p. 50) that St. John does not call the pre-existing Word " Son," but surely he does in John i 18 (if the right reading is " God only begotten," it carries the same meaning) ; cf. iii 17. Also Jesus asserts that His Self—He who now speaks as man—was pre-existent (viii 58, x 36, xvi 28, xvii 5).

New Testament plainly implies a distinction of persons in the Godhead.

Again the Christ, who is the Son, was to bestow the Spirit, in whom He Himself lived. In the Synoptists our Lord very seldom is represented as speaking about the Spirit. Once He seems to speak of the Spirit, who dwells in Him and in whose power He acts, as a person who can be blasphemed, and again He promises that He shall dwell in His disciples and inspire them to speak right words.[1] But we have noticed that the intensity of the belief of the earliest Church in the Spirit would suggest that our Lord must have spoken more on this subject than the Synoptists would suggest, and certainly in the fourth Gospel there is much more. There certainly our Lord speaks of the Holy Spirit as of a distinct person, " another paraclete " or helper, who is to take His own place. In these last discourses, though the Greek noun for Spirit is neuter, He is always referred to by the masculine adjective "He."[2] He is described in decidedly personal language as guide, interpreter, remembrancer, witness and judge, convicting the world.

Thus it does not surprise us to find the earliest Church in Jerusalem and in its further extension speaking of the Holy Ghost as of a person possessing the Church. To lie to the Church, as Ananias and Sapphira did, is to "tempt" the Holy Ghost and to "lie" to Him, that is to God. He is a person being "resisted" by the Jews. He gives directions, speaking in the heart of individuals, to do or not to do this or that, to go here or there. He "carries off" Philip the Evangelist. He is joined to the apostles and elders at the Council in Jerusalem in

[1] Mark iii 29, xiii 11. But in the Old Testament once at least the Spirit of God is momentarily distinguished from the Father, as sending the Righteous Servant, "The Lord God hath sent me and his Spirit" (Is. xlviii 16).

[2] John xiv 26, xv 26, xvi 8.

giving their decision. He directs the appointment
of particular missionaries and appoints presbyter-
bishops.[1] From time to time the Lord Jesus appears
to Stephen and to St. Paul, or speaks to the latter,[2]
but such appearances or messages appear to be
thought of as quite distinguishable from the ordinary guidance given by the Spirit : that is to say,
" the Spirit of Jesus " is not confused with the Lord
Jesus.

So in St. Paul's Epistles the Holy Spirit is spoken
of as a person. He intercedes with groanings for
the Church, as dwelling at its heart, and the Father
recognizes His mind, because He intercedes accept-
ably. He bears witness within the heart of the
Christian to his human spirit. He can be grieved
and disappointed.[3] Constantly in St. Paul He is
spoken of as " the Spirit " or " the Spirit of God "
or " the Spirit of Christ," so as to be plainly distinguished from Christ, though in one passage Christ
in His glorified manhood is spoken of by St. Paul as
having become " quickening spirit,"[4] and once " the
Lord " and " the Spirit " appear to be identified.
This passage, and the various uses of " spirit " in
the New Testament, are examined elsewhere in some
detail.[5] But for the present I will content myself
with a protest. To say, as " the critics " are so
fond of doing, without more ado, that St. Paul
" identifies " the glorified Christ and the Spirit, on
the strength of *one* phrase,[6] while in some thirty
passages he distinguishes them, is unreasonable and
as far as can be from the spirit of legitimate criticism.
St. Paul is not a writer who is precise in his use of

---

[1] See Acts v 3, 4, 9, vii 51, viii 29, 39, xiii 2, xv 28, xvi 7, xx 28.
[2] Acts vii 55, ix 41, xviii 9, xxiii 11.
[3] Rom. viii 16, 26, 27, Eph. iv 30, 1 Thes. v 19.
[4] 1 Cor. xv 45.
[5] 2 Cor. iii 17. See appended note, p. 253.
[6] And even here, according to the MSS., he also speaks of " the
Spirit of the Lord," thus drawing a distinction.

terms. But he is a writer who, without such technical precision, has a remarkable power of making his meaning clear on the whole. He uses " spirit " in a great variety of senses. But on the whole he leaves no doubt in our mind that he thinks of the Holy Spirit dwelling in the Church as a self-conscious and willing agent, distinguishable from the Father or God and from the glorified Christ. There is " one God and Father," and " one Lord," and " one Spirit." That is the total impression.

Thus I think we shall give a true account of the doctrine of the Bible as a whole about the Holy Spirit if we say that in the Old Testament the Holy Spirit of God expresses the activity of God in the world, and especially His activity in " inspiring " exceptional men and most conspicuously the prophets ; and that He is promised as the special endowment of the future Messiah and of the " servant of Jehovah," and thereafter as the endowment of all men in the Messianic kingdom. But in all this there was very little tendency to speak of the Spirit as a person distinguishable from God. In the New Testament, however, this tendency becomes very marked. The Spirit is still the active energy of God. But there is a very marked tendency to think of Him, lodged as He is in the heart of the Church and in the heart of the individual Christian, as a person—a self-conscious subject—distinguishable from God and from Christ, the Lord or the Son of God, who sends Him.

On the whole I hold it as unquestionable that the Church at the end of the Apostolic Age is found believing, as a result of its experience of Jesus and His Spirit, in three distinguishable agents : (1) God, whom they now know as the Father ; (2) Jesus, the Christ and Lord, whom they believe in as the Son or Word of the Father, who for their sakes had been made man, and in that manhood glorified and spiritualized had gone into heaven and had sent down upon the Church (3) the Holy Spirit, His own Spirit and the Father's, to be their helper, strengthener, guide, and intercessor ; and their thought of the one God includes that of the three " persons."

(2) *Their mutual inclusiveness*.—But so far we have given but a very one-sided account of the theology of the New Testament. It is true that they believe in one God the Father, and one Lord the Son, and one Spirit of the Father and the Son, each conceived of as divine and personally distinct. But this suggests three Gods, and that is not by any means the total picture. So close a unity is suggested that each *involves* the others. This impression is conveyed quite without the appearance of conscious intention, but very subtly, both in St. Paul and in St. John. In St. Paul the Holy Spirit possesses the Church and its members, so that the Church as a whole and the body of each member of the Church is His temple (1 Cor. iii 16, 17, and vi 19). But the presence of the Holy Spirit, that and nothing else, implies and carries with it the presence of Christ. He treats the Spirit dwelling in us, or our having the Spirit, as equivalent to Christ dwelling in us (Rom. viii 9, 10). And the Spirit (or Christ) dwelling in us implies or involves God dwelling in us (1 Cor. iii 16, 17). Each involves the others. So again it is the Spirit that binds the body, which Christians are, into one, and diffuses in it His manifold gifts. Therefore it is the body of Christ—even Christ Himself—and He also is described, not only as the head of the body, but the all-pervading source of its life and unity (1 Cor. xii 11–13 and Eph. iv 15–16), and the " fullness of Christ " into which it grows is also called the "fullness of God " (Eph. iv 13, iii 19). Though the Three are spoken of as personally distinct, each by His presence and actions involves the presence and action of all.

The three are one. So in St. John the promised
coming of the Spirit involves Christ's coming : " I
will come unto you." The " other paraclete " is to
be no substitute for His absence but the security for
His presence. And as He abides in the Father, and
the Father in Him, so His coming will be the Father's
coming : " We will come unto you " (St. John xiv
16–23). So in creation and the sustentation of nature,
Christ is the agent—through Him are all things, and
in Him all things consist. For that very reason all
things are " through " God as well as from Him and
unto Him (Rom. xi 36). This subtle thought appears
constantly. The three are by no means *separate*
persons. There is, it seems, in the three but one
being, one mind, one activity.

The common idea of human persons attributes to
them a mutual exclusiveness. They have been described as " impermeable." This impression, however, is largely derived from the separatedness of
human *bodies*. When we get to the spiritual self of
a man, we find that personality is radically social
and deeply permeable.[1] Nevertheless, the impression
given us of the mutual interpenetration of the divine
Three suggests a unity to which the closest conceivable
fellowship of human persons could not approach.
It would seem as if the Father can do nothing except
through the Son or Word and by the Spirit, and the
Son nothing except from the impulse of the Father
and in the Spirit, and the Spirit nothing except from
the Father and the Son, bringing them with Him in
His action.[2]

---

[1] See especially Canon Richmond's *Essay on Personality as a
Philosophical Principle* (Edwin Arnold, 1900)—a very valuable
book which has never received sufficient attention.

[2] It is to be noted, however, as I have mentioned before, that
barely a word is said in the N.T., as far as I can ascertain, of the
activity of the Spirit in nature or in the conscience of men in general,
or anywhere at all except inside the Church. The gift of the Spirit
is represented as poured out upon Christ and, through Him, upon

All this has a more absorbing interest because it appears so unintentionally. It all emerges in the process of man's redemption (save so far as cosmic functions are also ascribed to the Son).[1] But it would seem as if, in the process of redemption, we necessarily get some glimpse into the eternal being of God. This appearance of a trinity in unity— as Father and Son and Spirit co-operate in the work of redeeming man—suggests necessarily what God is in Himself. The secret of His being is, as it were, in a measure, overheard. The Church, through its experience of redemption by Father, Son, and Spirit, found itself believing in a trinity of divine persons and (none the less) in the unity of God.

III

It was with this equipment of faith that the Church went out into the world which we have already described as full of intellectual curiosity and the love of abstract discussion, as well as full of a deep sense of spiritual need, which prepared it to welcome any real or pretended revelation from the unseen world. It was required to explain its faith to the outside world, and it found the necessity equally urgent to

His Church. "The Spirit was not yet" till Christ poured it out, and, except in the channel of the Church, not a word is said suggesting His activity. This silence surely does *not* mean that the Spirit is not the "giver of life" wherever life is. And we are surely right to argue that where the fruits of the Spirit in human goodness appear, there is the activity of the Spirit. But it is very notable that, while the Word of God is said to be the Light which lightens every man, nothing of the sort is suggested about the Spirit. Our attention is solely directed to His action in the Church—so far as the New Testament is concerned.

[1] It is worth noting that we can know nothing (save by very fallible conjecture or reasoning) about the inner relations of the being of God except what is reflected in the original experience of the Church. Thus the ground for belief in the eternal procession of the Spirit from the Father through the Son lies simply in the fact that He did so "proceed" when He was poured out upon the Church.

explain itself to itself.   And the stimulus to explanation lay chiefly in various suggestions or theories which might be more or less plausible, but which the Church felt would undermine its faith and its tradition, or were contrary to Scripture—" Scripture " meaning first the Old Testament books and then, as the Gospels and St. Paul's Epistles and the other books of the New Testament were gradually " canonized," the New Testament books also.

As has been already explained in connection with the doctrine of the person of Christ, the Church teachers made many mistakes. The " prophet " Hermas in the Roman Church was widely believed in as a real prophet who received symbolic visions which really came from God ; and his moral message was full of edification ; but he had no instinct for theology, and his utterances, so far as they concern the doctrine of God, are confused and confusing.[1]

So also some of the apologists, in their attempts to expound the Christian faith in terms of current philosophy, use expressions which were afterwards repudiated by the Church, as when they seem to represent the divine *Reason* as an eternal quality in God which *became* the personal Word or Son only when proceeding forth from God in the act of creation.[2]   Inasmuch as the individual teachers were certainly not infallible, mistakes were inevitable. But St. Paul and St. John, when they look back to the beginning before the world was, suggest to us no such idea, but the thought of one who in that eternity already was the Son and the Word of God, with God as His offspring, but distinct from Him.

---

[1] He seems to confuse the Holy Spirit with the eternal spiritual being of our Lord ; and Justin Martyr's teaching about the Holy Spirit is unsatisfactory, as judged either by Scriptural or later Church standards (see Dr. Armitage Robinson, *The " Apostolic Preaching " of St. Irenaeus*, S.P.C.K.; and Swete, *The Holy Spirit in the Ancient Church*, pp. 25–39).

[2] See Dr. Kidd, *Hist. of the Church*, i 359–71.

" He (the Son) is before all things." " In the beginning was the Word, and the Word was with God, and the Word was God." [1]

On the whole the difficulty proved to be to avoid, on the one hand, language which suggested Tritheism —*i.e.* the belief in three Gods rather than one, or one God who was the source of two others, the Son and the Spirit, or who was the source of one other (the Son) and an influence called the Holy Spirit— and, on the other hand, to avoid what came to be called Sabellianism, or Modalism, which sought to describe Son and Spirit as only aspects, phases, or manifestations of the one God and not distinctive persons. On the whole, the danger was greater in the Tritheistic direction than in the Sabellian, for the Church was keenly alive at least to the distinctive being of the Son who was incarnate. One difficulty was that, to start with, there was no word current in Greek or Latin to express " person." You could, of course, describe a human person by calling him a man, or a spirit by calling him an angel or demon or God, and you could talk of mind or soul, but for a person as such—whether God, or angel, or man— there was no current word. It was, in fact, the Christian sense of the value of personality which disclosed the need of such a word. Origen, in describing the " tradition " of the Churches derived from the apostles, which all Christians are bound to hold, describes it as a belief in the one God, the Creator of all that is, and the author of the Old Testament as well as the New, who before all creation was the Father of Him, the Son, through whom all things were made, and who in these last days, emptying Himself, was incarnate and was made man, by a birth of the Virgin and of the Holy Spirit, being and continuing to be God : and in the Holy Spirit as associated in honour and dignity with the Father

[1] Col. i 17, John i 1.

and the Son.[1] This account of tradition manifestly leaves open questions, especially about the Holy Spirit, which Origen would have men solve by diligent investigation of the Holy Scriptures. Finally, however, it was decided that the Three must be regarded as " of one substance," that is to say, as belonging to the one eternal being of God, and that each must be distinguished as eternally a person— the words chosen to designate " person "—that is, the conscious subject—being the Greek word, "hypostasis," which hitherto had been used in the general sense of substance, and the Latin word " persona," which, meaning first the actor's mask, and then his " part " or the character which he represented, and then the part which anyone is called to play in life, was already trembling on the verge of meaning what we mean by a person. The Fathers are profuse in their apologies for the inadequacy of these terms. Man has no celestial language, but God has revealed Himself so distinctly that we must find the best words we can to describe and guard the revealed reality. After a time, of course, as always happens when a new terminology is adopted, people got used to the terms, and the apologies are not so much heard. The Church doctrine is that God subsists as three persons in one substance or reality. " Deus Pater, Deus Filius, Deus Spiritus Sanctus. Et tamen non tres dii : sed unus est Deus." But it was again and again affirmed that the term " person " is not used of God in exactly the same sense as it is used of human persons. The Three are one in a fuller sense than could be true of three human individuals.

Harnack and others have laid great stress upon certain differences of a metaphysical kind which appear to distinguish the way of thinking about the Trinity which we find in the great Greek teachers (Origen and, later, the Cappadocians, Basil and the

[1] *De Princip.*, i 4.

Gregories) and Latins like Tertullian, from what we find in Athanasius at Alexandria and Augustine in the West. The truth is that the former teachers begin, on the whole, from the thought of the different persons, and then seek to give intellectual expression to their unity, while Athanasius and, especially, Augustine, begin from the unity, and then within the unity are at pains to be true to the distinctions also. There is a difference; and doubtless it would have become considerable if these Church teachers had been merely philosophers pursuing abstract truth. But they had, all of them, behind them the faith of the Church in the one God the Father, and the eternal Son who was incarnate in Jesus Christ, and the Holy Spirit who had inspired and guided in such and such ways the people of God, and who could only be described as " persons," and who yet belonged to the being of the one God. Granted this, their metaphysical differences, in the extremely rarefied air in which a discussion of the eternal being, whom we know only in part and discern only in a dim reflection, must necessarily proceed, are not, to most of us, of much importance, and easily admit of being exaggerated.[1]

Amongst us, however, Dr. Rashdall has been constantly appealing to the teaching of Augustine and later of St. Thomas Aquinas as if they did not really maintain the distinct and eternal *personality* of Father, Son, and Spirit, but were content to believe in one God in whom " Father," " Son," and " Spirit " are names only for qualities or activities within the one divine mind and being, which are not distinguishable persons at all.[2] Now it is quite true of St. Augustine that, deriving his philosophy from Neo-Platonism, partly through the medium of

[1] See Tixéront, *Histoire des dogmes* (Lecoffre, Paris); vol. ii gives a very fair account of these differences (pp. 67 ff. and 261 ff.).
[2] Rashdall, *Jesus, Human and Divine*, pp. 24 f., 61 f., 67.

17

Victorinus Afer, he is jealous above all things for the maintenance of the unity of God. And the human analogy which he loves best as pointing upwards to the divine being is the analogy of the distinct *functions* in the single human person—the fundamental *Self* (mind or memory) with its expression in *Thought* (or word), and then again in *Will* (or love); and it is quite true that this analogy of itself would not suggest three persons in the Godhead. It is a manner of thinking the issue of which would be Unitarian, no doubt.

Thus if Dr. Rashdall had said that St. Augustine (and later St. Thomas) uses an analogy which suggests something much less than three persons, he would have said no more than the truth. St. Augustine himself is careful to point this out and correct the impression.[1] For St. Augustine's faith and doctrine is as far as possible from resting on this analogy or on any argument. It rests in the revelation of God contained in Scripture and taught by the Church. And there is no doubt how St. Augustine conceives this revelation, and what his doctrine is. It is familiar to us in the *Quicunque vult*. It is the doctrine of one God in three " persons "—for we must use the term person for lack of a better name. The divine being is one—one substance, one mind, one will. But this divine being exists in three persons, each of whom is whole God, in each of whom the divine mind and all the divine attributes exist personally. You may, of course, say that St. Augustine's doctrine is not intelligible, or you may say that his favourite analogy[2] does not tend to prove his doctrine. But there is no sense in appealing to Augustine as if he did not hold that each of the

---

[1] *Epist.* clxix. 6.

[2] He also uses an analogy which suggests distinction of persons—the analogy of the *Lover* and the *Loved*. Then he tries unsuccessfully to make " Love " suggest a third person (*De Trin.* viii 14).

three persons, of Himself, is whole God, or as if he would tolerate any kind of "reduced" Trinitarianism.[1]

So it is with St. Thomas Aquinas. He, too, begins from the divine unity. He, too, like Augustine, derives his philosophy of God partly through Neo-platonist channels—the medium being the unknown thinker who wrote under the name of Dionysius, the Athenian disciple of St. Paul, and who was uncritically taken throughout the middle ages to be really that apostolic man. Thus, like Augustine, he seeks to represent to himself the distinctions in the Godhead after the manner of internal relations within a single thinking and willing subject. No doubt this manner of thinking taken by itself would lead to a Unitarian conception of God. But Thomas, no more than Augustine, contemplates the possibility of such a conclusion. He knows that the Christian doctrine of God was not the product of human reasoning, but of divine revelation. He knows that human reasonings could never substantiate the doctrine of the Trinity, though they may be able to approve it, and cannot disprove it. He himself receives the doctrine of the Bible and the Church without a shadow of question. In article after article of his *Summa* he asserts, like Augustine, that the Divine being subsists in three eternal and co-equal persons. The relationships in God are not qualities but persons. Godhead is in essence one and indivisible, but each of the persons in whom it subsists is a distinct person (*alius*) from the others.[2]

---

[1] " Tantus est solus Pater, vel solus Filius, vel solus Spiritus Sanctus, quantus est simul Pater et Filius et Spiritus Sanctus " (*De Trin.* vi 9).

[2] *Summa Theol.* pars 1*a*, qu. xxxi, art. 2 : "Personaliter alius Pater, alius Filius, alius Spiritus Sanctus." "Cum nomen *alius*, masculiné acceptum, non nisi distinctionem suppositi in natura [a distinction of subject in nature] significet, Filius alius a Patre convenienter dicitur." "Neque tamen dicimus *unicum Deum*, quia pluribus Deitas est communis." "Pater est *alius* a Filio, sed non *aliud*. Et e converso dicimus quod sunt *unum* sed non

It requires indeed a philosophical microscope to distinguish in final outcome the doctrine of the Cappadocians who begin with the Three from the doctrine of Augustine and Aquinas who begin from the One. Both with the like emphasis believe in the one God in three persons.

But I am not writing in the main for those who can move freely in the high air of metaphysical speculation. Probably most of us entertain what seems to us a well-grounded scepticism as to the powers of the abstract reason. But we very earnestly seek to know whether—apart from subtle differences —the traditional Christian doctrine of one God as existing in three persons, Father, Son, and Spirit, is for us believable. It is to this question that I must address myself, without raising any question of ecclesiastical authority.

I think the experience of the disciples must be, in some sense, repeated in us. I have already called attention to the fact that the doctrine of the Trinity is clearly there—implicit certainly, and in great measure explicit—in the New Testament, especially in St. Paul and in St. John. It emerged simply in the process of believing in Christ as the Son of God incarnate and in the realized activity of the Holy Spirit—the Spirit of God received from the ascended Christ. I do not think my readers can question this. To believe in Christ, as the first Christians came to believe in Him, involves us necessarily in the thought of God as not a solitary monad. There in the ultimate being is Father and Son—God and His Word or self-expression. There already is the distinction of persons. Perhaps we should have been disposed to think of the Spirit

unus." Cf. qu. xxx, art. 1: "Cum in divinis sint plures res subsistentes in divina natura, plures quoque personas ibi esse necesse est." Cf. qu. xxix, art. 4: "Hoc nomen *persona* dicitur ad se, non ad alterum ; quia significat relationem, non per modum relationis, sed per modum substantiae quae est hypostasis."

as only the influence or activity of God in the souls of men. But we must acknowledge that this will not account for the language of the New Testament or the language of Christ, if we believe that He really uttered the discourses in the Fourth Gospel, which it is very hard to ascribe to any lower speaker. Certainly the first Christians felt themselves in their relations with the Holy Spirit as in contact with a person, and so spoke of Him. And if we are constrained to admit distinctions or mutual relationships in God, it seems absurd to originate a hitherto unheard-of doctrine of Duality for the originally Trinitarian belief, when plainly we have no new facts to go upon. Let us see then whether this doctrine of the Trinity commends itself to our reason.

I think we shall probably agree with Huxley that the foundations of things are always mysterious and the doctrine of the Trinity not more mysterious than the ultimate principles of physics or biology. To feel that a belief is rational we must feel—not that we could demonstrate it *a priori*—but that it is grounded in experience and that it interprets experience. It was a true saying of Dr. Hort, who was certainly one of the greatest men of the last generation, that the evidence for the truth of the Christian revelation is shown, not so much in any light which it receives, as in the light it gives.[1] What commends the doctrine of the Trinity is the light it throws on some otherwise dark problems.

1. It alone enables us to think of God as in Himself " the living God " apart from and independently of creation. We have seen at an earlier stage of our argument that the " unassisted " speculative reason of man arrives, with sufficient assurance, at a belief in God, who is the " Wisdom and Spirit of the Universe "—that is at what is called the Higher Pantheism; but that it does not seem to carry us

---

[1] See *The Way, the Truth, and the Life* (Macmillan), p. 11.

with any security to a belief in a God prior to and independent of the world. God appears to be as dependent upon the world for self-expression as the world is on Him. He realizes Himself in the world. Perhaps He only attains self-consciousness in the self-consciousness of men. We also saw plainly enough that from a religious point of view such a conception falls wholly short of what men—what most men—need. The religion of the prophets of Israel and of our Lord gave a profound stimulus to human life just because it represented God as a person, perfect and complete in Himself, having the characteristics of a person, wisdom, justice and love in a supreme sense ; having a will and purpose for men, who were made in His image, but alive in Himself before ever the world was, the Creator of all that is and the judge of all rational beings. We satisfied ourselves that we must accept the message of the prophets and of our Lord as a genuine self-disclosure of God. But we find ourselves intellectually paralysed when we try to give any meaning to this idea of one self-existent being, alive in Himself with the fullness of life before the world was. For life, as far as we can see, involves relationship, and rational or moral life the relationship of persons. How can we think of an eternal will without an eternal effect or product of this will, or of an eternal consciousness without an object of this consciousness adequate to itself, or of an eternal love without an eternal object of love ? To say that God *finds* Himself first in nature is disastrous for religion. But how can He live and love alone ? Now, as we have seen, the idea of the Trinity was not evolved in response to any such intellectual questionings. No difficulty appears to have been felt by the Jews or first disciples in believing in God who is one only person. But they found themselves, in the way we have described, as a consequence of their experience of Christ and of the Spirit, believing in a trinity of persons in the one God. A glimpse into God's eternal life seems thus to have been given to men. And the relief to the intellect is great. Now we can see how God can be alive with the fullest life we can conceive of—will and reason and love—because His own being involves in itself a relationship of persons. In the eternity which we cannot with our finite intellects conceive He was productive, and found His object of knowledge and object of love in His eternal Word or Son and in the Holy Spirit. As I have said, this apparent necessity of thought carries us much more completely to the conviction of some relationship of persons than to the specific conception of Trinity. Perhaps it does not surprise us that we do not find our rational powers go far enough to discover God as He is. We shall be content to accept God's self-disclosure as it has been given. But the intellectual relief is great when we find ourself authorized to think of the very being of God as a movement of life in which the Father is eternally expressing Himself and knowing and being known, loving and being loved, in the Son and the Spirit. There is at once the fullness of life in God, for the one eternal being is a fellowship of persons, one with an intense unity, but alive with the movement of a perfect life. I could not have discovered the Trinity. But it is only the disclosure of it which enables me to think about God with any satisfaction as alive and personal in Himself.

2. I am quite able to see that the higher I go up in the scale of creation the more complex does the living organism become. The nature of man is the most complex unity in the world known to us. If I seek to rise to the source and penetrate to the ground of all life, and find this source and ground to be a living God perfect in Himself, the upward soaring train of thought leads me to postulate that

this Eternal Being must be something quite different from a monotonous unity. When I admit the disclosure of Trinity—that is multiplicity in unity—it is only what I should expect in the perfect and absolute being. And I can dimly conceive how there in the eternal Word and the Spirit was the counterpart, under conditions of eternity and perfection, of all that wealth of life which is gradually evolved on a lower plane in the process of creation.

3. Again, only when I am a believer in the Trinity do I seem to lose the sense of bewilderment which the old thinkers of Greece experienced in bringing the One, the Unchangeable and the Eternal, into any relation to a world of which the very being lies in movement and change. The moving world and the unchanging, immobile God seemed not merely to belong to different grades of being, but to be in no possible relation to one another. Does not creation involve movement? Does not God move in the moving world which He sustains in being, and live in its life? But now I am delivered from all this horrible imagination of a God who is absolute immobility. For God is eternally alive—eternally moving out into self-expression. He has the whole movement of absolute life within Himself. Thus to create and to begin to live and act on the lower plane of gradual and progressive creation is no unnatural thought to associate with a God who eternally is life in Himself, because there is in Him what is dimly descried as the eternal generation of the Son and the procession of the Spirit.[1]

4. Finally, is it not a delight to believe that the ultimate reality is not monotonous unity, but a unity which contains in itself a fellowship of persons —one with a unity which can never be realized

[1] This idea is developed by Victorinus Afer, whose importance n his influence on Augustine has not had enough made of it (see art in *Dict. of Ch. Biography*).

among human persons, but which at the same tim
assures us that personality and personal life essentially
involves fellowship? In man personality emerges
out of fellowship and always involves fellowship.
The idea of personality as primarily individual and
fundamentally selfish we have learnt to be false.
It is only in fellowship we begin to realize ourselves,
and the more widely we expand into fellowship the
more we realize ourselves. And it is with delight
that we see the ground of this law in the Supreme.
For there the eternal being is fellowship. There
is no priority in Him of unity to multiplicity, and
no priority of multiplicity to unity. The Eternal
is one in many and many in one—one God, Father,
Son, and Holy Ghost.

"If reason," says Lotze, " is not of itself capable
of finding the highest truth, but on the contrary
stands in need of a revelation, still reason must be
able to understand the revealed truth, at least so
far as to recognize in it the satisfying and convincing
conclusion of those upward soaring trains of thought
which reason itself began, led by its own needs,
but was not able to bring to an end." [1]

Is not this a good description of how reason stands
towards revelation in this matter of the doctrine of
the Trinity?

NOTE.

On the New Testament uses of " spirit," and especially on
2 Cor. iii 17 ; see above, p. 237.

"Spirit" is used in a variety of connected senses in
the New Testament, not always easily distinguishable :
(1) Of *God* (John iv 24, " God is Spirit ") to express His
utter freedom from conditions of place or form. As
pure spirit He seeks only spiritual worshippers. (2) Of
created spirits, good and bad. In almost all cases such

---

[1] Lotze, *Microcosmus* (Eng. trans.), ii 660.

spirits are spoken of as persons, but in one or two places
" spirit " is used in a sense not unlike ours when we speak
of the spirit of the age (see my *St. John's Epistles*, pp.
168–9). (3) Of the human spirit, markedly distinguished
from the flesh and from the Spirit of God, see especially
1 Cor. ii 11, 2 Cor. vii 1. (4) Of the whole manhood of
Christ, as spiritualized and glorified in heaven. See John
vi 63, " The things that I have been speaking to you of
—my flesh and blood—are to be thought of as the flesh
and blood of the ascended Christ, and therefore as spirit
and life, not unprofitable flesh." Burney, I am glad to
see, supports me in this rendering, *Aramaic Origin of the
Fourth Gospel*, p. 109. So in 1 Cor. xv 45, St. Paul
says, " The last Adam became life-giving spirit " (5)
Of the Holy Spirit of God which dwelt pre-eminently in
our Lord, and after His ascension is given as His own
Spirit no less than His Father's, to the Church.

Now the question is whether St. Paul in 2 Cor. iii 17,
" The Lord is the Spirit," *identifies* Christ the Lord in
heaven with the Holy Spirit, contrary, as I have said, to
his constant custom of distinguishing them. I think it
is very difficult to suppose this. And the passage seems
to me to suggest a quite different interpretation. According to the MSS., it runs (ver. 16) : " But whensoever
the children of Israel shall turn to the Lord [referring
to Ex. xxxiv 34] the veil is taken away. Now the
Lord is the Spirit : and where the Spirit of the
Lord is, there is liberty." Here the sudden transition
from the Lord who is the Spirit to the Spirit of the
Lord, followed by another transition in the next
verse back again to " the Lord the Spirit " seems
to me to be so awkward as to make eminently probable
the minute emendation[1] of the text proposed by Dr.
Hort and Dr. Chase, according to which we should read,
" Whensoever it shall turn to the Lord, the veil is
taken away. Now the Lord is the Spirit, and where
the Spirit is Lord, there is liberty. And we all
. . . reflecting the glory of the Lord, are being transformed . . . as from the Lord the Spirit." Here St.

[1] An emendation which only involves the change of ν into ν
κυριου into κυριον). Dr. Chase, however, prefers κυριευει.

Paul no doubt in some sense calls the Spirit the Lord.
But I have come to be convinced that it is in this sense:
" The Lord to whom Israel must turn is the Spirit [*i.e.*
the Holy Spirit now given to the true Israel in the Christian Church]. Only where that Spirit is Lord is real
liberty, and it is in the power of this Spirit-Lord that
we Christians are being transformed." It is true that
St. Paul does not elsewhere call the Spirit Lord, but I
think he is led to do so here by the suggestion of the
narrative in Exodus: and it appears to me that there is no
violence or improbability involved in this supposition, viz.
that as St. Paul constantly calls the Father the Lord,
and Jesus Christ the Lord, so once he should have called
the Holy Spirit the Lord—for obviously He is Lord in
Christian souls in the same sense as the Father and as
Jesus. This seems to me much more intelligible than
that St. Paul should confuse Christ and the Spirit by
saying " The Lord Jesus is the Spirit " while he elsewhere so clearly and constantly distinguishes them. It
is quite intelligible that St. Paul should once call Christ
in His glorified manhood " quickening spirit," as having
become wholly spiritual and the source of life to His
Church, but surely not that he should call Him " the
[Holy] Spirit " with the definite article, contrary to his
constant practice.

CHAPTER IX

SIN AND THE FALL

WE are now occupied in considering certain ideas and doctrines which are involved or implied in the New Testament doctrine of Christ. And one of the most obvious of these is the idea and doctrine of the sinfulness of humanity. For among the most familiar of the titles of Christ is that of the Redeemer or the Saviour—who "shall save His people from their sins"—and that of the Reconciler, who by making atonement or propitiation reconciles us to God, and that of the Second Adam who inaugurates a new humanity regenerated and renewed in Him. These titles mean that mankind are in a state of unnatural bondage to sin or to the power of evil, and need to have their freedom restored to them by the act of God; and that they are alienated from God and their true good and need to have a new status of sonship conferred on them by the grace of God; and that they belong to a race under condemnation and need incorporation upon a new stock. I suppose no one would be disposed to question that the Bible as a whole views men as being to start with in this unnatural condition, and as needing to be saved from it, and as unable to save themselves. This assumption is stated in a striking form by St. John when he says that "if we say we have not sinned, we make God a liar." For, as Westcott interprets the phrase, "all the communications of God to men presuppose that the normal relations of earth and heaven have been interrupted. To deny this is not to question God's truth in one particular point, but to question it altogether."

I

This is the point then. The Bible is the record of a Gospel of redemption. It is a proclamation of good tidings from God. It holds out to man the highest and most glorious possibilities in Christ Jesus. But it does so on the assumption that in humanity as it stands there is something radically perverted, in view of which it needs for its salvation something quite different from mere example or encouragement to make the best of itself—it needs fundamental reconstruction by Him who originally created it.

I have just said that it will hardly be doubted that this is the Biblical assumption, but we had better examine the assumption a little, and especially we had better examine our Lord's estimate of His brother men.

This estimate, like everything else in our Lord's teaching, is given on the Old Testament background. The Old Testament is full of the picture of mankind within and without the chosen people as a wicked world, in which God is profoundly disappointed and which lies under His just and inevitable wrath. On this dark background there is the radiant picture of the righteous who " walk with God " ; but, as the sense of the individual spiritual life develops, even the righteous man appears as sinful and confessing his sinfulness. "There is no man that sinneth not." [1] The record of God's dealings with His saints, Moses, Aaron, and Samuel, is that they are not only " heard " but also " forgiven " and

[1] 1 Kings viii 46 ; cf. Eccl. vii 20, Job iv. 17 (R.V. marg.), xiv 4, xv 14–16.

" punished." [1] Isaiah confesses his own sinfulness
as well as his people's. "I am a man of unclean
lips and I dwell in the midst of a people of unclean
lips." [2] The penitent psalmist acknowledges sin
as inherent in his nature even before his birth.
" Behold I was shapen in iniquity and in sin hath
my mother conceived me." [3] This is the tone of
the Old Testament. Thus when John the Baptist
summons Israel to prepare for the coming of the Christ
it is by a call to repentance—a fundamental change
of mind—and by a baptism for the remission of
sins, [4] and that is represented as the substance of
the first preaching of Jesus. [5]

There is no doubt that our Lord is very far from
representing human nature as He found it as wholly
corrupt. He showed a vivid appreciation of what
we should call natural goodness, which He found
in those whom the Jews regarded as outcasts at
least as much as within the chosen people. He
values " the cup of cold water " and every act of
natural kindness. He welcomes men who show a
right disposition of mind as " not far from the
kingdom of God." Also He is extraordinarily
gracious to the outcasts. The " publicans and
harlots " of society are assured of ready forgiveness.
He came, He said, not to call the righteous but
sinners. But there is a tendency to misrepresent
our Lord's graciousness. Two things are specially
noticeable in our Lord's teaching about sin. (1) He
dissociated it wholly from physical and ceremonial
associations and placed its seat firmly and only in
the heart of man. [6] And (2) His main emphasis
is on the sins of " the righteous," that is, of those
who were so regarded and so regarded themselves.
Sins of violence and lust were, of course, regarded
as sins and stamped with reprobation in respectable

---

[1] Ps. xcix 8.   [2] Is. vi 5.   [3] Ps. li 5.
[4] Mark i 4.   [5] Mark i 15.   [6] Mark vii 20-3.

Jewish society. But Jesus was at pains to bring to light the even deeper sinfulness of spiritual sins, such as were quite consistent with social respectability and involved no ceremonial pollution— hypocrisy or self-righteousness, avarice, pride, contempt, hatred, spiritual blindness and prejudice, and above all unmercifulness and the neglect of active goodness. "Inasmuch as ye did it not unto one of the least of these my brethren . . . depart from me." Such sins of the spirit He represents as even more dangerous than disreputable sins. "The publicans and the harlots go into the kingdom of God before you."[1]

When our Lord announced the joy of heaven as lying more in the reclamation of the lost than in the righteousness of "the ninety and nine righteous persons who need no repentance,"[2] He was speaking to the Pharisees and scribes who murmured at His receiving sinners and eating with them. They are represented in the character of the elder brother in the parable of the prodigal son, and of the righteous Pharisee in the story of the devotions of the Pharisee and the publican. Thus it is impossible to deny an ironical note in this allusion to "righteousness." It was exactly this righteousness which He came to expose as "a whited sepulchre." On the whole it must be acknowledged that while our Lord infinitely deepened the sense of God's willingness to forgive, and refused to regard the outcasts as "hopeless cases," He also deepened and broadened the sense of sin. He appears to assume its universality. Thus it is noticeable that, speaking to His new flock in the Sermon on the Mount and reminding them of the natural goodness of men in their love of their children, He says: "If ye then *being evil* know how to give good gifts," etc. He compares men to Satan's "goods" held in

---

[1] Matt. xxi 31.   [2] Luke xv 7 ; see verse 2.

bondage by the "strong man" and waiting for the stronger to deliver them.[1] He claims of men the moral equivalent of self-mutilation[2] as the price to be paid to get rid of sinful inclination; and nothing can exceed the simplicity with which He speaks of hell, with its awful anguish, as the inevitable penalty of tolerated sin, whether sins of omission or of commission. Thus it is quite natural that, when our Lord has in view the kingdom of God which He is inaugurating, He should declare that none can be fit for it without a fundamentally fresh start. "Verily I say unto you, except ye turn and become as little children, ye shall in no wise enter into the kingdom of heaven."[3] And this fundamental turning appears to be inseparable from discipleship to Himself, which means a very thorough faith in Him as the divinely commissioned Redeemer. This is apparent in the Synoptists. And it is profoundly expressed in the Gospel of St. John. There our Lord is represented as holding Himself aloof from men's first enthusiasm for Him. "Jesus did not trust himself unto them, for that he knew all men, and because he needed not that anyone should bear witness concerning man; for he himself knew what was in man."[4] He knew to start with that sad secret of human untrustworthiness, which in slow and embittering experience has in countless cases and in every age turned philanthropists into cynics and made wise men mad. Therefore He demands of men a deep reconstruction. "Except a man be born anew, he cannot see the kingdom of God," "Except a man be born of water and the Spirit, he cannot enter into the kingdom of God."[5]

Certainly this is the spirit in which the first Church

---

[1] Matt. xii 29, Luke xi 21. This applies not only to the "possessed," see verses 23–6.
[2] Mark ix 43–9, Matt. v 27–30, xviii 8.
[3] Matt. xviii 2.   [4] John ii 24.   [5] John iii 3, 5.

in Jerusalem understood its message. It was no announcement to men of a glory which was already theirs, if only they would open their eyes to discern their true nature. Enlightenment was not enough. They needed to embrace by faith a " salvation," now first offered them—offered in a new " name " which was the only name of salvation—and the gateway to this salvation was baptism, which conveyed to them what they could not otherwise receive, the forgiveness of their sins, and prepared them for the new gift of the Spirit.[1] Even the saintly Gentile soldier Cornelius, though the effective appeal of his "prayers and alms" to the ear of God is fully recognized, and though God in merciful manner gives the Holy Spirit to him and his company, is not thereby dispensed from the entrance into the Church by baptism. Like everybody else he needs the new standing ground " in the name," and the forgiveness of his sins.[2]

I do not think the New Testament can be accused of any pretension to expound the secrets of divine justice for the satisfaction of our intellect. It does what is much better. It assures us of the character of God and thus enables us to feel quite confident that He will deal in justice and love with every human soul He has created. But it exists to record a Gospel—a salvation for men, publicly proclaimed, and divinely covenanted; and this Gospel is based on an assumption that what humanity needs is something other than development or enlightenment. It needs fundamental reconstruction—a fresh start, a new birth, forgiveness and renewal,— and of all this there is only one source—the Prince of the New Life, the Saviour, the Redeemer Jesus Christ : and this fresh start is offered, so to speak, objectively, as membership in the new community,

---

[1] Acts ii 38–40, iii 19–26, viii 14 ff., xix 4–6.
[2] Acts x 43, 47.

to those who seek this great deliverance as sinners who need to be saved.

I do not think I need pursue the enquiry through the New Testament. Everyone recognizes in St. Paul the strongest and most vehement maintainer of the corruption of the " natural " man and his need of redemption through faith in Jesus Christ. We will come back to St. Paul directly in connection with the idea of the Fall. I would only say in passing that I think he has been too exclusively judged from the early chapters of the Romans. And even in that Epistle he contemplates " Gentiles who have no law " and yet " do by nature the things of the law "—who " by patience in well-doing seek for glory and honour and immortality," and who find what they seek, whether Jews or Gentiles : and he speaks of men of old who " had not sinned after the similitude of Adam's trans-gression."[1] Elsewhere he bids the Christians look for and appreciate (apparently in the world at large) a standard of truth, honour, justice, purity, and virtue.[2] I do not think St. Paul would have been blind to goodness of character wherever found, or would have doubted its acceptableness to God. He is not a systematic theorizer, blind to what does not seem to square with his theory. He is stating a general impression of the Gentile world; and if he paints it in lurid colours, he seems to think that those he writes to will not find the language too strong.[3] Similar language is used by St. Peter to Gentile Christians in similar circumstances : and St. James' estimate of human nature as it is found among the Jews is not less severe.

---

[1] Rom. ii 7, 10, 14, v 14.   [2] Phil. iv 8.

[3] The Ephesian Stoic, who about the middle of the first century wrote " letters " under the assumed name of Heracleitus, speaks quite as severely of Ephesian society.   See my *Ephesians*, p. 253.

II

The kind of estimate of human nature which we find in the New Testament, both in its optimism and its pessimism—that is, its glorious estimate of what humanity is intended by God to be and is capable of becoming, and its dark estimate of what it has in fact, by rebellion against God, made itself to be—was not out of harmony either with the general sentiment in the period of the Roman Empire when Christianity first spread, or with the general sentiment of the middle ages. In both periods it was natural to men to feel that the world was a very evil world, that nothing that men could do for themselves would make it better, and that they must look for redemption to God and a spiritual world above. But what characterized the early Renaissance, and what reasserted itself [1] in the spirit of industrialism and in modern movements as a whole, at least before the Great War, was a sense of human power—the power of man to redeem himself by his own initiative, especially by the instrument of knowledge in general and the science of nature in particular, which was at his disposal and which he could manipulate in the cause of his own advancement. This is the gospel of the Kingdom of Man. And this gospel has seemed beyond question to make the language of the Bible sound out of date— as if it disparaged the " God in man " which is the only kind of God congenial to this modern spirit.

It is not that the modern estimate of human nature as it is, or as it has actually been found in experience hitherto, is higher than the old orthodox estimate—apart from some mediaeval and Calvinistic exaggerations. Rousseau and Byron and Shelley

[1] Reasserted itself, I mean, against Lutheranism and Calvinism, which crossed and half-extinguished the spirit of the Renaissance.

are as emphatic as the writers in the Bible that
"our life is a false nature —'Tis not in the harmony
of things." And now-a-days we hear no more
of Rousseau's idealizing of natural or primitive
man. He is involved in the same condemnation
with civilized man. All around us to-day a cynically
low estimate of man seems to prevail in ordinary
literature—a low estimate of his capacity to restrain
his lusts, or to maintain unselfishness, honesty and
truthfulness in industrial life or in politics or in the
law courts ; and the spirit of idealism is fluctuating
and weak. What seems to be lacking, where the
characteristically modern spirit, in any one of its
many forms, prevails, is the readiness to welcome
the idea of redemption as the gift of God, or the self-
revelation of God which is incidental to redemption.
We seem to want a God who is so fully to be identified
with *ourselves* that either He must take us as we are,
and not judge us or condemn us for our sins, or else
(in the case of the more enthusiastic and reforming
spirits) that we can find Him sufficiently in our own
enlightenment and our own strivings after progress.

But, after all, we are not in very good spirits about
progress and world-redemption. There are a great
many people, even among agnostics, who are feeling
that there is something in the old language about
the need of a return to God. What is greatly to
be desired in ordinary men is the courageous determination to think for themselves. They have
been led captive by the prophets of the modern
spirit so as to take it for granted that the Bible
religion is antiquated. Now, of course, the
traditional religion had become encrusted with
antiquated ideas in stagnant ages. And an age
which is an age of real and progressive science justly
demands of religion correspondence with science
rightly so called. But when the matter in hand is
the interpretation of human life, which science has

not hitherto shown any profound power to interpret or to redeem, it is surely not too much to ask people to reconsider frankly for themselves whether their own reason warrants them in rejecting the estimate of human life and its needs which is undoubtedly Christ's, and the offer of divine redemption which He makes. And it is certain that the optimism of Christianity, its glorious appreciation of human capability and destiny, is bound up with its pessimism —with its profound sense that mankind has set itself by its own sin on the wrong road and needs redeeming by God, who alone can redeem it as He first made it, and can give it the light and stimulus and direction by which alone it can recover itself and realize itself afresh.[1]

When I hear contemptuous rejections of the Biblical estimate of man as he is, as if it were dishonouring to human dignity, I often think of the man who of all the characteristic spirits of the Renaissance had the profoundest genius as an interpreter of man—our own great Shakespeare. No one ever had deeper interest in humanity or a higher estimate of man's capacity.

" What a piece of work is a man ! how noble in reason ! how infinite in faculty ! in form and moving how express and admirable ! in action how like an angel ! in apprehension how like a god ! the beauty of the world ! the paragon of animals ! "

No one moreover ever contemplated humanity with less of the spirit of the prophet and the reformer. He was a typical man of the Renaissance. He stood utterly and marvellously aloof from the keen

---

[1] I find these suggestive words quoted from Dr. Joh. Weiss, *Das Urchristenthum*, p. 188 : " Strange as these things have become to us, we cannot too earnestly make ourselves familiar with the thought that the old Christianity understood the new life not merely as a new mode of thought and moral conduct, but as a wonderful equipment with new powers, the work of God."

and bitter religious controversies of his time. He seems to know and care nothing about them. He would approach mankind, with all his unmatched genius for understanding and representing it, purely and simply as the spectator—willing to be fascinated and delighted with humanity as he found it, " good and bad together." But, so approaching mankind, one fact about human life appears to arrest him and absorb him and terrify him—the fact that men are not free, as they would boast themselves— that they are enslaved by passion and obsessed by delusion. This note becomes conspicuous first per- haps in the somewhat morbid atmosphere of the Sonnets—in the marvellous 129th Sonnet about lust, where he exclaims—

> " The expense of spirit in a waste of shame
> Is lust in action."

Then its violence and deceitfulness and its miserable issue is described with intense realization, and the sonnet ends :

> "All this the world well knows ; yet none knows well
> To shun the heaven that leads men to this hell."

In the great tragedies this seems to become the one theme—the obsession of men. It may be by lust, or by vanity, or by ambition, or by jealousy, or by pride and the contempt of common men ; it may be by the paralysis of too much thinking; but in all cases what is presented to us is the same spectacle of a man obsessed. All the world can see it except he himself. But he, obsessed, is also blinded, and so blinded is driven forward by an inevitable fate to his doom, and only by the violence of the tragedy can the stage of human life be set free again for life to go on its way. This spirit of the tragedies seems to possess Shakespeare. One of our best recent interpreters of Shakespeare—

Walter Raleigh [1]—speaks as if even that mighty mind nearly lost its balance in gazing into the awful gulf. And he seems to have recovered himself in his last period—that of the Romances—by refusing to think any more about it. In one of his last utterances, in which the man himself seems to speak through Prospero's lips, he gives up human life as a riddle without an answer, a dream which has no eternal significance. Certainly he never shows any signs of becoming interested in the faith in divine redemption. But when I hear people reject St. Paul's estimate of human life as a piece of " morbid pathology," I think of Shakespeare and what he seems to have seen in his marvellous mirror.

For myself I make my profession. I have tried honestly and freely to know myself and to study human life all around me and in the record of history ; and I know no interpretation of human life which is adequate both to the rays of glory which I see there and the encompassing gloom, except the estimate of the Bible. Man is made to be a king, but he is " a discrowned king " : and no one can put him again on the way of honour except his God who made him and would redeem him.

III

The Christian idea of sin was not developed as a philosophy by reflection, but appeared as part of a teaching about God and man which claimed to be a divine message given that men might know how to live. Nevertheless it involves a philosophy in that it places the seat of sin in the will and finds its essence in disobedience or violation of a law known to be divine. So the Bible looks out upon a disordered and miserable world and finds the secret of the disorder and misery simply in the refusal

[1] See his *Shakespeare* in " English Men of Letters," pp. 210–12.

of God by men and other free spirits dimly seen in the background.

So the nature of sin is vividly represented in the marvellous story of the fall of Adam and Eve, which dates, we should remember, before any of the prophets whose writings remain to us. So it is in the Law and the Prophets and the Psalms. So it is finally defined at the end of the New Testament period in the First Epistle of St. John in the phrase " Sin is lawlessness "—the Greek words implying that the two terms are convertible—that there is no sin which is not the breach of law by a rebel will, and nothing else in the world which breaks the law of its being except sin (1 John iii 4). It is this doctrine which gives its peculiar hopefulness to the Bible, in spite of its stern view of actual conditions. For there is nothing as God made it which is not good and meant to serve a good end. There is no evil substance. The grossest sins are but the misuse of faculties good in themselves. And however much evil habits may have engrained vice into our nature, let but the will be again replaced in love to God and obedience to His will and the whole nature can be recovered. That is the radical meaning of St. Paul's doctrine of justification by faith ; for faith as he uses it means the surrender of our being to God in Christ ; and when that is gained God can work freely upon us to accept and to renew. " All things work together for good to them that love God." Thus the world, if it were converted to God, would again become a paradise. And at the last issue all evil wills are to be either converted or subdued, and God is to come into His own again in His whole creation.

This Biblical idea of sin may be put in contrast with three other explanations of it which challenged the Church at its beginning and still challenge it.

(1) In the Hellenistic world in which Christianity spread, the prevalent tendency was to find the secret

and source of sin in the flesh or in the material world. The spark of the divine, which is the soul of man, is imprisoned at present in the body with its corrupting passions and influences, and is subjected to the mysterious tyranny of the material world. What it must hope for is to be released from the body and delivered from the material world, and so be free to resume its place in the pure being of God. And there were a hundred mysteries and doctrines which offered to secure to the initiated soul emancipation at last and passage into the divine. But Christianity stoutly resisted this tendency to fix the blame of sin in the wrong place. To believe that matter is evil and the source of sin—whether as the creation of an evil or inferior God, or as something eternally existing and intractable—is to despair of the world and of our present life in the body.[1] And the Christian's determination to plant and promote the kingdom of God in the world and to consecrate to God every element in nature, including his own body, depends on the belief that there is nothing bad in the world but a bad will, and that man's body as well as his soul, and the whole material creation, are the subjects of divine redemption.

2. It is opposed also to the more modern interpretation of sin, which came into fashion with the dominance of the idea of development, as imperfection which is gradually being outgrown. It is "the tiger and the ape" still surviving in man, which are gradually being subdued to the spiritual

[1] The belief that the material is the evil accounts for the way in which the Gnostic movements, where this doctrine prevailed, swung between an extreme asceticism and an extreme license. To believe in matter as evil begets the desire to be as free from its bondage as possible—that is the source of oriental asceticism. But after all we cannot be free from the body. To eat and drink, in whatever moderation, is as bodily an action as drunkenness. So arises the idea that all bodily acts belong simply to the temporary envelope of the soul and are morally indifferent. And hence the rebound into license.

or rational purpose. The history of man is the history of a gradual—if slow and interrupted—progress towards perfection. There is, of course, an important element of truth in this conception. Certainly there is a great deal of evil which is ignorance and imperfection, which gradual enlightenment can cure and which itself affords the stimulus to progress. If we try to think of a comparatively sinless world and what its development might have been, we should imagine it as gradually outgrowing its childish ignorance and youthful mistakes—as gradually gaining control, and passing on to perfection in the maturity of its powers. But this is precisely to leave out the very thing which sin is. Sin is the refusal of allegiance to God and rebellion against the law of our true being. It is the selfishness which places our being and its efforts upon a false centre and so disorders our whole world. And sin, rightly so defined, shows not the slightest trace of being outgrown in the process of civilization. There is sin as much in modern London as in ancient Britain, though the sin is of a more or less different kind. Advanced civilization certainly presents a parody of the divine intention for man as much as barbarous societies. Progress no doubt represents the divine purpose, but the reason why progress has been so broken, so fragmentary, and so liable to reversals and catastrophes lies just in the thwarting, disturbing, destructive power of sin, from which neither education nor refinement of itself has the power to redeem. Perhaps to-day the kind of optimistic delusion that I have been describing is one into which we are less liable to be betrayed than our fathers or grandfathers.

3. The Christian doctrine of sin is rooted in the conception of mankind as really free and responsible, and has its roots cut by the doctrine of determinism. According to this latter doctrine, all that has

occurred in general or in detail has been at the last analysis inevitable. There is strictly nothing that need not and ought not to have been. The doctrine is so alien to fundamental human instincts that while it abounds in the schools of philosophy, it does not adventure itself much into the ways of common life. It could not, in fact, really apply itself to life without moral disaster. To believe that I am and always have been and always must be inevitably determined to do what I have done or shall do, would, beyond all question, as it appears to me, destroy the springs of moral action. I have endeavoured, in the previous volume, both strictly to limit the sphere of human freedom and to maintain its reality,[1] and I will not recur to the subject here. I should like, however, to record a remark which I twice heard made by the late Master of Balliol, Dr. Jowett, which seems to me to be true. He noted that theologians like Augustine, and (strictly speaking) St. Thomas, and Calvin appeared to be able to maintain an ultimate and absolute determination of human actions by God, as a sort of remote mystery of religion, without its interfering with the practical moral appeal of Christianity. But he observed that it would not be so with modern scientific determinism. That is no remote mystery hidden in the inaccessible depths of the divine being and incomprehensible by men. It claims to be a requirement of science, its action is in the field of observed experience, and its effect is wholly intelligible. It is to make all our sense of responsibility and personal guilt—all that is really meant by the sense of sin—an illusion and to establish the conviction that we cannot help being just what we are. I am thankful to believe that science is

[1] But I will call attention to what seems to me an admirable article in the *Hibbert Journal* for July 1922, by Captain H. V. Knox, entitled *Is Determinism rational?*

becoming much more conscious of its limitations and may retreat from this truly irrational position.

IV

There is one difficulty presented by the Christian doctrine of sin which, since the principle of evolution entered into control of our imagination, has appeared and still appears as most formidable—I mean the doctrine of the Fall. Christianity has not been content with asserting that men in general or universally have proved themselves individually sinners. It has attributed to humanity an organic unity, by descent from a common origin—our first parents, Adam and Eve—and has, in part at least, accounted for the prevalence of sin by attributing the disordering of human nature or its partial corruption to the inherited effects of their fall, as it is described in Genesis.[1] There is hardly any allusion

---

[1] I am here only dealing with the doctrine of sin incidentally as involved in the doctrine of Christ's person. Thus (1) I am giving the go-by to all the questions raised about the exact nature and effect of the Fall—whether positive or negative: and to the Augustinian and Calvinistic exaggerations : and to the Protestant conception of the imputation of Adam's sin to his posterity ; though I may remark in passing that I do not think any doctrine of *imputation* can be legitimately attached to St. Paul except in the sense that God sees things not as they are but as they are becoming. This is the *real* way to see things. Thus faith is imputed as the righteousness it is not yet, because faith does, in fact, contain in itself the whole root or principle of righteousness, by retransferring our nature to the allegiance of God in Christ ; and Christ's righteousness may be said to be imputed to us, though St. Paul does not say so, because as His members we are in Him and on the way to become more and more interpenetrated by Him. *Non quales sumus sed quales futuri sumus Deus nos amat.*

(2) I am giving the go-by to many interesting questions connected with the Hebrew story of Paradise and the Fall, and its influence in later times. In this connection Ezek. xxviii, which suggests a different idea of paradise from Gen. iii, is very interesting. Also it is interesting that in the later apocalypses it would appear that that unique fragment of unassimilated mythology, Gen. vi 1–8, was exercising more influence than Gen. iii. But I am only concerned here with the idea of the Fall and of its consequences in general outline.

in the other canonical books of the Old Testament to this primaeval fall, and though it became a subject of interest in the later Jewish schools and we see the fruit of this in the books we call " apocryphal," yet the ideas there presented are confused and contradictory; and there is nothing about the fall of Adam in the New Testament except in two famous passages of St. Paul's Epistles. But these two famous passages have exercised an enormous influence on theology, so that a modern Roman Catholic writer on dogmatics says, hardly with exaggeration, that " the whole dogmatic system of the Church revolves upon the two poles of sin and redemption, the old humanity and the new, *Adam and Christ*."

The contradiction between the religious tradition and the scientific conception as popularly stated took this form—that the Bible taught that mankind " began at the top " and fell from his high estate into continually deepening degradation from which only " the elect " are redeemed by the act of God, while science teaches that mankind began at the bottom in a brutish condition, hardly differentiated from the apes, and has gradually climbed upward by his own efforts through the period of some half a million years during which something which can be identified as our race appears to have been on the earth. Here is a startling contradiction indeed. But the statement requires serious revision. It was only the imagination of theologians in a very unscientific age, and especially in England the influence of Milton, which begat the idea of Adam and Eve as created in the full-blown glory of intellect and virtue. Genesis does not in any way suggest it. It suggests for Adam and Eve something like the complete ignorance, as well as the innocence, of childhood. All the beginnings of the arts appear after the fall, and in the line of Cain's descendants.

And the story of Genesis iii makes almost no impression on the rest of the Old Testament, which is throughout the story of a divine purpose for man pursuing its gradual way to its goal, but constantly thwarted and baffled by human sin. This is the impression which the early Christian teachers received. They answered the question whether man was created perfect in the negative. " He was not created perfect, but only in a condition to attain or receive perfection."[1] So we may restate the position thus : " The Bible teaches that man was created free to correspond with a good purpose of God for him : and his advance towards the realization of his heritage of sovereignty in the world might have been inconceivably more glorious and unimpeded than it has been but for his constantly renewed and perpetuated disloyalty to God and disobedience to the law of his being. It is to this that his misery is due. And as he was made for constant dependence upon God, so he cannot hope to rescue *himself* out of his bondage, but only to be rescued by God when he will return to Him in penitence and surrender." Now I am not aware that such a revised statement brings us into any collision with science. We must not speak as if science could bring human origins into the clear light. The emergence of the distinctively human faculties, and the place and the manner of such emergence, are still involved in impenetrable obscurity.

But this at least seems to some of us to be certain —and to make a great difference between us and our grandfathers—that we have ceased to be able to treat the story in Genesis as history at all. We see there neither a record preserved in human

---

[1] So Clement and, in effect, Irenaeus. The Fathers also knew that death was a law of the world before man ; and that man was created mortal by nature.

tradition, nor a revealed history of what happened at the beginning. We are not disposed to think that mankind began in a single pair sharply differentiated from the lower animals. We find it very difficult to form any mental conception of how things happened " in the beginning." We are inclined to think that about the beginnings and endings of the world and of mankind—about things which lie outside the possibility of experience or investigation by us—we can be taught only in parables or symbols. So we are ready to attach the highest value to the early chapters of the book of Genesis, taking the stories they contain as symbols, not history. We see in them the clearest traces of divine inspiration. We see there true ideas about God and His mind—about the world and man's relation to the world and his relation to God, about the origin and nature of sin and its consequences, and about God's dealings with man both in judgment and mercy—all so vividly expressed that a child can understand them and the imagination of mankind can never get rid of them.

But, granted all this, we need to ask ourselves whether the language of St. Paul about the effect of the sin of Adam in letting loose the forces of death, and constituting mankind sinful, can still be used by us; and whether generally the idea of the Fall and the antithesis of the Old Adam and the New has still really for us the equivalent of its old meaning.

I think so in this sense.

1. Sin—*i.e.* disobedience to God and the law of our being—essentially and always is a fall. Indirectly it may be through sin that we make discoveries about ourselves and the world. So sin may be a condition of progress. But not a necessary condition. We could have gained the fruit of the tree of knowledge without sin, for sin is always a perversion and a loss. It puts us in a wrong relation

to ourselves and to our fellows and to God. Everywhere, in all its forms, and in every case sin is lawlessness and therefore is a fall. We are fallen by
our iniquity. Thus Adam and Eve stand for every
man and woman, and the story of their fall is the
true story of humanity and of what has been its
ruin in every individual case. And over against the
Old Adam, which is sinful humanity, stands the Last
Adam, which is the sinless humanity. Thus in Jesus
Christ I see humanity both restored to its true basis
and its true relations, and not only restored but perfected in God. And I apprehend the true character
of my redemption only when I grasp it as a radical
transference of my fundamental allegiance, and so
of my whole being, from the stock of the Old Adam
to that of the New.

2. I do not think we shall be driven to accept a
merely individual account of sin. I do not think
that more accurate science will make us hesitate to
say with the Psalmist, " In sin hath my mother conceived me." Whatever science ultimately teaches as
to the "monophyletic " or " polyphyletic " origin
of mankind, I think it will continue to authorize us
to regard mankind as constituting one race which
can be dealt with, whether barbarous or civilized,
as having certain fundamentally identical spiritual
capacities—that is, intelligence (as distinct from instinct), the moral conscience, and some measure of
moral freedom, capacity in some measure for enlarging fellowship and progress, and capacity for God.
It appears to me that anthropology and the science
of religions work on the basis of the assumption that
humanity of all periods and in all countries is one
race, and continually tend to justify the assumption.

Further, it seems to me that psychology tends to
emphasize what is the Christian tradition that a
man's soul, or self, is not purely individual. He is an
individual with the responsibilities of an individual,

and progress towards the ideal will deepen and intensify his individuality. But that mysterious and elusive thing he calls himself carries within it elements and qualities which are inherited and not personal, and which make him the representative of something much wider and much older than his individual self —of his family, his race, nay of humanity as a whole. In his unconscious mind he carries (so it appears) instincts and memories which are racial and not personal. If this is so, it would be very bold to deny that there may be, or must be, some inheritance of sin, in its weakening and perverting effect upon the spiritual nature, in those roots of our being which lie below the beginnings of personal consciousness.[1]

. . . .

In this book I am only concerned to justify a certain attitude towards man, as fallen and needing to be redeemed, which appears to be inseparable from the appeal of Christianity—which appears to have been the attitude of Christ Himself. This appeal takes shape in St. Paul's language which bids us die to the Old Manhood that we may live in the New. It treats us as belonging to an old manhood— the Old Adam—which is corrupt according to the deceitful lusts, and would have us regenerated or grafted upon a new stock—the sinless humanity of the Second Man. It would have us believe that by natural inheritance our old manhood came to us

[1] I think it is important to note that " original sin " is a fault or defect or disorder in our inherited nature, which admits of more or less. One man's nature is more disordered to start with than another's. And the fault or defect can be diminished by self-restraint or deepened by indulgence. Also, it is important to notice that there is nothing in the New Testament which justifies our using the word " guilt " of this inherited taint. No doubt it disqualifies us as it stands for the fellowship of God ; but nothing is guilty except the action of a rebellious will. The defect of nature in itself is an appeal to the divine compassion to redeem us, not an occasion of His wrath against the individual personally.

19

more or less weakened and impaired by Adam's sin, but that it admits of being restored and renewed in Christ. No doubt St. Paul believed in Adam as a person and we cannot easily do so. Nevertheless, I think that there is very little or nothing in St. Paul's language which will not hold good for us if we take the Old Adam, not as an historical person, but as the symbol of our race as it has made itself by sin, to which by our birth and natural tradition we belong. And there is no force in the strange argument that if the First Adam is symbolical, so may be the Second. We are driven to treat the first as symbolical because we cannot penetrate the mists of ages. But the Christ stands in the light of history. We know that He understands our nature, and we believe He has the will and the power to redeem it.

In the volume which preceded this I have dealt with the New Testament accounts of the Birth of Jesus as from a Virgin and therefore miraculous. I have there endeavoured to make it plain that this history was not the *product* of any theological demand. It shows in both its forms—both in St. Matthew and St. Luke—the signs of a date far earlier than any such theological or Christological development as would have made the demand effective. I have given what seem to me sufficient reasons for trusting the story ; and I can only refer my readers back to what was said there. But I have also pointed out that already in the Fourth Gospel, where the story in the Synoptists is no doubt assumed as familiar, Christ's birth of a virgin appears to be referred to as lying behind and interpreting our new birth. St. John, that is, here as elsewhere, assumes what is in substance St. Paul's doctrine of the Second Adam ; and he suggests that the miraculous conditions of the birth were appropriate or necessary for the incarnate person who is to be fount of the new sonship. I cannot but repeat here that what

St. John suggests and the Church has emphasized does appear to me to hold good, viz. that any one who grasps the contrast between the sinless Christ and the sinful world—the world in which the greatest saints are the most conscious of their sinfulness—and who accepts Christ as the Second Adam, the new creation in which our manhood is renewed, so far from finding a difficulty in the Virgin Birth of Jesus will welcome it as in the highest degree acceptable and congruous in His case, if not rationally necessary.[1]

[1] For all this see *Belief in God*, pp. 274–82, and *Dissertations*, pp. 63 ff. See also in this volume, p. 120, and note 1, for St. John's reference (in cap. i. 13) to the Virgin Birth as the basis of our regeneration.

CHAPTER X

THE ATONEMENT

THE idea of atonement made by our Lord for man in the sacrifice of the cross is so prominent an element in the faith of the New Testament and of the whole Christian Church, that it cannot be ignored in any comprehensive treatment of the faith in His person. It has found a welcome as wide and deep as possible in human hearts all down the ages ; but it has also presented peculiar difficulty to the intellect. What is attempted in this chapter is simply to fix attention upon the central idea of the Atonement, as the New Testament presents it to us upon the background of the Old, and to rid it of certain misunderstandings which have been allowed to pervert it. Then I should wish to leave my readers with the feeling— This, at least, is part of the faith in Christ to which my heart and my reason respond.[1]

I

Let us seek to clear the air by certain preliminary considerations.

1. It is plain that the redemption of man through Jesus Christ, which the New Testament has for its theme, is a complex process which admits of being regarded in various aspects or from different angles.

[1] It must be remarked that while the Church did in fact define the doctrine of the person of Christ, it left the doctrine of atonement quite undefined.

Hence there are marked differences in the points of view of the different books. But they all agree among themselves and with the books of the Old Testament in one point : that ultimately redemption can mean one thing only—the actual restoration of men into the moral likeness of God. The kingdom of God, which is the theme alike of the Old Testament and of the New, is to be a perfected fellowship of man with God and of man with man ; and there can be no fellowship of man with God " except they be agreed "—that is, except they be of the same mind or character ; and there can be no fellowship of man with man unless they come together in obedience to God and correspondence with His purposes.

Men are prone to superstition ; and the best definition of superstition is religion which is non-moral. And there has been a great deal of superstition not only in the religions of the world generally, but also among the Jews and in Christendom, both Catholic and Protestant. Wherever men have attributed some kind of power to racial privilege, or to orthodox belief, or to sacraments or charms, or to the prayers of intercessors, which can in any sort of way be a substitute for actual conversion of will—for ceasing to do evil and learning to do well ; wherever men have proclaimed or believed in Christ's atonement, or His righteousness " imputed to us," as if it could be made available for us without our being personally changed from evil to good— there is superstition ; and the teaching of the prophets and of Christ is on no point more emphatic than in condemnation of this sort of superstition. No expedient or device can exist for bringing us into the favour of God except by our becoming actually godlike. " In the rich pharmacopoeia of heaven, there can exist none such." To be and to remain unlike God in character must exclude us from the fellowship of God, however correct our beliefs and elaborate our ritual acts; and, conversely, the Bible as a whole encourages us to believe that there is no external or accidental barrier, whether in the way of intellectual error or hereditary ignorance, which can ultimately exclude from God and His kingdom any man who is really a man of good will. Heaven is nothing else but the home of the godlike; and hell is nothing else but the state of those who have made themselves, by their own faults, radically incompatible with God. There is no substitute for a good will, and no compensation for a bad one. Thus whatever place vicarious atonement, made for us by our Redeemer, may hold in the scheme of the Bible, we must expect it to conform to this fundamental demand for real, personal righteousness.

2. "My song," says the Psalmist, "shall be of mercy and judgment." Such is the theme of the Old Testament and of the New—God's inevitable wrath on the hard and impenitent heart, and His abounding mercy on the repentant. God is forgiving, as being both willing and able to efface sins however heinous. "Though your sins be as scarlet, they shall be white as snow; and though they be red like crimson, they shall be as wool." But only repentance—that is the change of heart and will—can change the face of God towards us. "Wash you, make you clean; put away the evil of your doings from before mine eyes; cease to do evil; learn to do well; seek judgment, relieve the oppressed, judge the fatherless, plead for the widow." Such is the constant theme of the prophetic message. And it is the theme of our Lord's teaching also.

We find Him asserting the forgivingness of God towards the penitent in the most moving language, both parabolic and simple. It is as expressing the Father's mind that He came "to seek and save that which was lost." And we note the stress He lays on the necessity of a changed heart. That is the only evidence that a man is really forgiven. So the unthankful servant in the parable[1] finds that his acquittal, though it had been formal and valid, is invalidated by his showing himself still quite hard-hearted. And on the other hand the woman that was a sinner proves that she has been forgiven by the generosity of her devotion to Christ.[2] Where such love is, forgiveness must have already been given. Here we have the teaching of the prophets intensified. God certainly needs no propitiation to make Him *willing* to forgive; and nothing is needed by the individual to secure his forgiveness by God but the contrite heart which responds to His love.

3. All this teaching about God we are surely meant to apply to the relations of God to all men individually, in whatever ignorance of God they may have been nurtured, for it expresses fundamental principles of His being. Nevertheless, the constant assumption of the Bible from Genesis to Revelation is that men need something besides true ideas about God. They need an activity of divine power to rescue them from a hopeless condition into which rebellion against God has plunged them, and this activity of God is what is called redemption. The Bible is a history of divine redemption, and it is only in the process of redemption that the disclosure of the real character of God is made. As has been shown in the previous chapter, no one can understand the Bible, Old Testament or New, whose imagination is not filled with this conception of man as needing to be not enlightened only but redeemed.

And further this method of divine redemption, though its ultimate aim is universal, proceeds through the election of one people, Israel, to be the redeemed people; and when in the New Testament

[1] Matt. xviii 21-35.   [2] Luke vii 47.

the Church or people of God is freed from all national restrictions, nevertheless it is the society, and not barely the individual, which is both the subject and the instrument of divine redemption. The method of divine redemption is corporate. No doubt this is to trench upon the topic of the Church, with which we are not concerned in this volume. Nevertheless, it is in its most general sense hardly open to doubt ; and it must in some sort be here taken for granted because the idea of atonement has its roots throughout in this corporate method of redemption.

4. This is indisputably so in the Old Testament. God made a covenant with the people of Israel as a whole, and the covenant was inaugurated and perpetuated in sacrifice, the sacrifices of bulls and goats, as being in some sense representatives of the people or substitutes for the men who offered them. The sacrificial system expressed their allegiance as a people to God and His law, and the fear wherewith they were to fear Him. The customs of sacrifice date from a time when the people had no understanding of the moral character of God, and the early prophets appear simply to deride them as worthless. But later, through the teaching of the unknown prophet of Deuteronomy and the mission of Ezekiel, the spirit of prophecy and the law of the sacrifices were conciliated. Thereafter the sacrificial system is made to express Israel's constant need of walking with awe before the face of the righteous God and making constant atonement for its corporate and individual sins ; not for its high-handed sins of rebellion and defiance of God, for which the sacrifices did not avail,[1] but for its sins of carelessness and ignorance. Of course the consciousness never left the deeper minds in Israel that " the blood of bulls and of goats " could not really " take away sin." Nevertheless, the temple worship nourished in the

---

[1] See *Epistles of St. John*, pp. 209 ff.

heart of Israel a deep sense of its constant need of propitiation. There is no question of this. What is questioned is whether this whole system was not by Christ ignored and abolished as meaningless—whether in His eyes it pointed on to anything which He was to fulfil and not to abolish.

5. Our Lord would appear to have said nothing about the temple sacrifices. He denounces the Pharisaic tradition as a misuse of authority and a perversion of religion. But He said not a word against the sacrificial system. Presumably He accepted it as a divine institution though imperfect. But He positively attached Himself to something in the Old Testament—the prophecy of the Righteous Servant—which gave a wholly different idea of vicarious sacrifice and propitiation on behalf of the nation. The Righteous Servant in Is. liii is represented as inaugurating the new Israel of the Restoration by the vicarious sacrifice of himself.[1] He in his innocence bearing the sins of the people offers his life as a guilt-offering to God. And God accepts the offering—the offering of the one for " the many." The righteous victim of unrighteousness becomes the effective intercessor for " the many " ; and they, for his sake forgiven and by his knowledge and instruction made righteous, constitute the restored Israel. He sees in them the travail of his soul and is satisfied.

This moving picture of vicarious sacrifice appears to have made strangely little impression upon the later literature of Israel. But we perhaps have a reflection of it—though it suggests a lower conception of God—in the heroic self-oblation of the Maccabean martyr to expiate the wrath of God upon his nation. His six brothers have been martyred in the persecution of Antiochus, in presence of the tyrant and of their mother, who stands by and exhorts them to

[1] See above, pp. 59 ff.

constancy. Then the youngest, who has seen all his brothers tortured and killed, makes his brave profession, before he follows them : " These our brethren, having endured a short pain that bringeth everlasting life, have now died under God's covenant ; but thou, through the judgment of God, shalt receive in just measure the penalties of thine arrogancy. But I, as my brethren, give up both body and soul for the laws of our fathers, calling upon God that He may speedily become gracious to our nation ; and that thou amidst trials and plagues mayest confess that He alone is God ; and that in me and my brethren the wrath of the Almighty may be stayed, which hath been justly brought upon our whole race." [1]

Whether we have here a reflection of the thought of the later Isaiah or no, we cannot, without a quite arbitrary rejection of well-authenticated texts, doubt that our Lord identifies Himself with the Righteous Servant,[2] and this means that He sees Himself as the inaugurator of the New Israel, and knows that by His voluntary death, on behalf of the people, He is to make propitiation for their sins. Both the crucial texts are, as has been said, stamped with the mark of their origin by the expression " for many." The first (Mark x 45, Matt. xx 28) is the phrase " The Son of man came . . . to give his life a ransom for many." The actual words used only lay stress upon the price of His life which He must pay to set His people free. The idea of an offering for sin made to God lies in the prophecy referred to rather than in the

---

[1] 2 Macc. vii 36–8. In 4 Macc. vi 28–9 (an Alexandrian book) the martyr Eleazer is represented as praying " Be propitious to thy race, being satisfied by our punishment for them. Make my blood an expiation ($\kappa\alpha\theta\acute{\alpha}\rho\sigma\iota\upsilon$), and my life ($\psi\acute{\upsilon}\chi\eta\nu$) a substitute ($\dot{\alpha}\nu\tau\acute{\iota}\psi\upsilon\chi\upsilon\nu$) for theirs." And the author concludes (xvii 22) that " through the blood of these pious men and their propitiatory death, the divine providence saved Israel."

[2] See above, p. 61, where the point is argued.

words taken by themselves.[1] The other passage, at
the Last Supper, is much more explicit: "This is my
blood of the covenant, which is shed for many,"[2] or
" This cup is the new covenant in my blood." [3] These
phrases suggest unmistakably a reference not only to
the sacrificial death of the Righteous Servant " for
many," but also to the sacrifices of animal victims
which inaugurated the covenant of Sinai, " Behold
the blood of the covenant." [4] This is our Lord's
only reference to the animal sacrifices of the Old
Covenant; and He declares that the New Covenant
is to be inaugurated also in blood—the blood of His
own self-sacrifice, by which the many are to be given
their new standing-ground before God. In winning
this new standing for His people, He, we should
gather, is their vicarious representative. He is acting
for them, without any co-operation on their part.

There is here no contradiction of the teaching, so
often given by our Lord, of the free forgiveness of
sins by the Father wherever He sees a penitent
heart. But it supplements it. God is still to deal
with men, not as isolated individuals, but as a people.
It is the new Israel which is being inaugurated, and

[1] The figure of the " ransom," by suggesting the thought of a
bandit or tyrant who held the prisoners, became the basis of the
strange theory, common in early and mediaeval days, of a trans-
action between Christ and the devil, in which the devil, by putting
Christ to death, took more than his " rights " of the Sinless One,
and so had no further claim on men. But we can never rightly
press either a metaphor or a parable beyond the special point of
comparison—in this case the greatness of the price needed to set
men free. It was by a similar misuse of a metaphor that
" propitiation " was made to suggest that God's mind towards
man needed to be changed, on which see below, p. 295.

[2] Mark xiv 24. St. Matthew adds (xxvi 28) " unto remission
of sins."

[3] This is the phrase used in the earliest account of the Last
Supper which St. Paul received " from the Lord," doubtless
through the older apostles.

[4] Exod. xxiv 8. In other passages of the New Testament the
sacrifice of Christ is regarded as fulfilling the Passover, the Day of
Atonement, and the Sin Offering (see Sanday and Headlam, *Romans*,
p. 92).

the new Israel must be inaugurated in sacrifice—not now the sacrifice of animal victims of which God had no need, but the self-sacrifice of the Man, which knows no limits and goes even to offering His life-blood. That is the basis of the New Covenant.

6. If we are to trust the Fourth Gospel, we must believe that John the Baptist had anticipated this function of the Christ when he called Him " the Lamb of God which taketh away (removeth by expiating) the sins of the world." But whether or no " the critic " can bring himself to trust the Fourth Gospel at this point, he must acknowledge that the expiation wrought by the self-sacrificing death of Christ is taken for granted in the whole of the New Testament which looks back upon Him. It is taken for granted in the first Jerusalem Church, as appears when St. Philip interprets of Jesus the sacrificial language of Is. liii. It is implied when baptism " in the name of " Jesus or " by calling on His name " appears as the condition of the forgiveness of sins; for this means that His merit alone avails for re-mission [1]; and this belief pervades the New Testa-ment. It is in popular estimation specially attri-buted to St. Paul. But it was already in " the tradition " as St. Paul received it at his conversion.[2] He places it, no doubt, in a special light, but that is all. On this special light, however, in which St. Paul views the doctrine of Atonement we must say a word.

7. St. Paul, then, especially in the Epistle to the Galatians, is occupied with the claim of the Judaizers who would have insisted on the perpetual obligation upon Christians of the Jewish Law, as represented by the rite of circumcision. And still in the Epistle to

---

[1] Acts ii 38, viii 16, 32–5, x 43, 46.
[2] 1 Cor. xv 3, " That which also I received, that Christ died for our sins according to the scriptures." See Dr. Rashdall, *The Idea of Atonement in Christian Theology*; quoted below, p. 303.

the Romans their claim occupies the foreground. As against such a claim he represents the Jewish Law as a temporary expedient to convict the Jews of sin and to prepare them for Christ. This conviction of sin he presses to the full. The Jews, no less than the Gentiles, find themselves involved in sin and unable to endure the tremendous judgment of God. They need to be saved. They cannot save themselves. God must save them. And that is what He has done in Christ. It is a salvation full and perfect that God has provided for men in Christ, and which the apostles are sent into the world to proclaim, and it is wholly the work of God in Christ, an act of divine grace and good favour which man has not merited, and to the accomplishment of which he contributes nothing. On the whole, St. Paul never leaves us in any doubt that the salvation which is offered us of God's free bounty is nothing else than real deliverance from the power of sin into actual goodness or moral freedom, by the full co-operation of all our powers with the purpose of God. But in the beginning of the Epistle to the Romans, which Protestantism has unduly isolated from the whole of St. Paul, he presses to the full—even to the point of letting it appear arbitrary — the initial stage of the divine " plan of redemption "—that is, the new status—the ac- quittal (" justification ") or forgiveness of sins—won for us by the " propitiation " of Christ. Wholly without any regard to our merits or our demerits, wholly out of the bounty of His free grace, without any co-operation of ours, God has provided in Him who is the Head of the New Race, the Second Adam, Jesus Christ, a " making amends " for all the guilty past. His unqualified sacrifice of Himself—unto death and the shedding of His blood—is accepted as something which sets free the love of God to flow out in the full stream of redemptive bounty. Let a man, Jew or Gentile, only believe—that is, let him surrender himself to God in Christ and accept His grace, in utter humility and the response of faith to love—and he is acquitted, wholly without regard to the magnitude and multitude of his sins. He is given a fresh start, a fresh status in Christ—of which baptism is the instrument—to live the new life of sonship to God and brotherhood in the community of the redeemed, the Church.

On St. Paul's special teaching about the Atonement I must make two remarks.

(1) St. Paul least of all men admits of being judged by single texts. He does not guard himself in argument. He must be judged on the whole. And so judged, there is no possibility of questioning that St. Paul meant by faith a moral response and not merely an intellectual acceptance. It is self-surrender; it is the response of will to love; it is love inchoate. He explicitly says (within a year of writing the Epistle to the Romans) that faith which does not involve love is worthless.[1] He always assumes that faith involves baptism, and baptism is entrance into the new life. He never contemplates belief without discipleship.[2] This becomes overwhelmingly clear in the epistles of the captivity. But it is clear from the time when he wrote to the Thessalonians. Only in his Epistle to the Romans, he is determined to make men see their own worthlessness apart from God— that their only hope is in Him and His unmerited grace—and that the salvation won for them was, in its initial stage, an act done wholly without their co-operation and *for* them.

(2) The reason suggested by St. Paul, quite incidentally, why God should have needed such a "propitiation" before He could let the proclama-

[1] 1 Cor. xiii 2 ; cf. Gal. v 6.
[2] I think Dr. Rashdall, *op. cit.* p. 116, is justified in saying that "at bottom the Catholic theory of justification finds more support in St. Paul, and is far nearer his real thought, than the Protestant theory in its strict traditional form."

tion of His free-flowing grace go forth among mankind, is apparently[1] that it was necessary to safeguard the reality of the divine righteousness at the moment when it was showing itself as mercy. This is secured if the act which is the instrument and occasion of divine acquittal is an act which placards before men's eyes the awful price by which their redemption was bought. But we will return upon this suggestion.[2]

8. It is remarkable that, though St. Paul won an undisputed victory over the Judaizers, yet his special arguments in the Galatians and the Romans about the relation of law to grace, and about justification by faith, produced little impression upon the Church as a whole. Part of this argument was taken up in a perverted form by Marcion; much of it again by St. Augustine. But it did not generally colour the theology of the Church. On the other hand, the doctrine of atonement won by the self-sacrifice of Christ, or the shedding of His blood, is equally present as a central point of faith in almost all the books of the New Testament,[3] and in the Church as a whole.

It is the recurrent theme of the First Epistle of Peter that that which " redeemed " the Church was a ransom of infinite value—" precious blood, as of a lamb without blemish and without spot, even the blood of Christ " (1 Pet. i 18, 19)—" because Christ suffered for you " (ii 21)—" bare our sins in his

---

[1] Rom. iii 25–6.

[2] On special phrases of St. Paul, see appended note B, p. 304.

[3] It does not happen to be mentioned in the very brief Epistle of Jude, nor in the Epistle of St. James, which is purely ethical. But even here I think Dr. Hort is probably right in translating St. James v 6 (cf. iv 4) " Ye condemned, ye murdered, the Righteous One. Is He not become your adversary ? " If so, " the Righteous One " is probably a reference to Is. liii; cf. Acts iv 13–14, " Jesus his servant, the holy and righteous one," whom " ye killed." And this would probably indicate that the idea of Atonement through the Righteous Servant's death lay in the background of James's mind.

body upon the tree " (ii 24)—" suffered for sins once, the righteous for the unrighteous, that he might bring us to God " (iii 18).

Again the point of view of the great Alexandrian teacher who wrote the Epistle to the Hebrews is that of the High Priesthood of Christ. For, pre-existing as the Son of God, He took our nature, soul and body, that in our nature, but with more than human power, even in eternal spirit, He might offer to God the perfect sacrifice for sins, even Him-self—the sacrifice of perfect obedience consummated in the shedding of His blood—and so enter into the heavenly places to be our High Priest, our effectual intercessor, and to " cleanse our consciences from dead works to serve the living God." Here again the whole status of the Church is made to depend upon the sacrifice of the cross.

Again in the Apocalypse the same dominant idea reappears in the new song of the redeemed which the heavenly beings sing to " the Lamb standing as it had been slain in the midst of the throne." " Thou wast slain and didst purchase unto God with thy blood men of every tribe and tongue and people and nation, and madest them to be unto our God a kingdom and priests." Here again it is to the sacrifice of the cross that the status of Christians as a body is attributed. And finally in St. John's Gospel, though very little is said about atonement, yet Jesus must die for the people of God before He can save it and enlarge it (xi 51, 52), and in the First Epistle, "He is the propitiation for our sins, and not for ours only, but also for the whole world " (1 John ii 2 ; cf. iv 10). It appears to have been a subject, like the final " coming " of Jesus, which St. John thought was sufficiently familiar in the common tradition of the Church, so that he could lay his emphasis where it was more needed. But he plainly took it for granted.

II

This book is not a treatise on the Atonement, and it would lengthen it unduly if I were to attempt to review the history of the doctrine in the Christian Church. The most learned recent analysis of this history which we have is Dr. Rashdall's. He is quite right in calling attention to the extent to which the moral appeal of the death of Christ is emphasized by the Fathers and schoolmen, and to which the aspect of atonement in the work of Christ is, by some theologians, merged in the general doctrine of the Incarnation and its effects. But he labours in vain, as it seems to me, to dislodge from its position in the Christian tradition the belief which, as we have seen, is so prominent and indisputable throughout the New Testament—that, prior to all appropriation by men, through the ministry of the Holy Spirit, of the fruits of the Incarnation, there had been on the part of Christ, as the Redeemer of men and the Inaugurator of the New Manhood, a sacrifice offered to the Father, a sacrifice of obedience unto the shedding of His blood, in virtue of which God was enabled freely to justify, or acquit, those who belong to Him, and to give them a new standing ground as sons of God and members of Christ. Everything in the New Testament appears to depend on this initial sacrifice of atonement, reconciliation, and propitiation.

I do not, as I have said, propose to follow the various theories which by Origen and Leo, by Abelard, by Anselm, by the Calvinists, by Dale and Denney, by McLeod Campbell and Moberly, have been elaborated to explain the Atonement and account for its necessity. But in no district of theology is the contrast so marked between the hesitating and critical attitude displayed towards these intellectual

20

theories of atonement which individual scholars
have striven to formulate, and the whole-hearted
acceptance of the fact by the great body of the
faithful in all ages. Everywhere where Christianity
has spread animal sacrifices, and indeed everything
which men had been accustomed to call sacrifices,
have ceased, because in becoming Christians men
have learned about the one, full, perfect and sufficient
sacrifice, which renders all others needless and gives
to the idea of sacrifice a new meaning. The popular
appeal made by the Eucharist or Mass in Catholic
Christendom is more than half to be accounted for
by the fact that there, by universal acknowledgment,
is presented to God, as covering all our approach to
Him, the one availing sacrifice. It is a quite modern
hymn which bids us pray :

> " And now, O Father ! mindful of the love
>   That bought us, once for all, on Calvary's tree,
>   And having with us Him that pleads above,
>   We here present, we here spread forth to Thee
>   That only offering perfect in Thine eyes,
>   The one true, pure, immortal sacrifice."

It is a modern hymn, but it expresses in language
at once devout and accurate what the heart of the
worshipping Church throughout the world has
believed and welcomed with adoring love : and the
whole purport of the hymn-singing of Protestant
Christendom, and the whole strength of the appeal
of revivalist preaching, has witnessed to the un-
dying power of the doctrine of the Atonement. It
is hard to believe that anything not grounded in
truth could have made such an appeal and received
such a world-wide welcome. We isolate ourselves
from the " general heart of man " if we ignore its
power or deny its necessity. The instinct which
welcomes it has its roots in Hebrew Scriptures,
but it has its roots also in the various theologies

of almost every non-Christian tradition. The beliefs may be crude or barbaric,[1] just as the later theories of atonement in the Christian Church may be morally or intellectually unsatisfying; but it is almost impossible to believe that God is at work in all the widespread instincts of men without also feeling that the instinct which has led men to seek in sacrifice atonement with God is a divine instinct, which Christianity must have expressed and satisfied if it was to be what it claims to be—the religion for all mankind.

What I propose to do is to consider the chief moral and intellectual scandals which have been found in our time in the doctrine of the Atonement as commonly preached, to see whether they really belong to its essence, or to its scriptural presentation : and then to consider whether we can find such a rationale of the doctrine as shall make it welcome to our intellects as well as our hearts.

1. First, then, let us recognize that any presentations of the doctrine which suggest any difference of mind or disposition towards men between the Father and the Son—which represent the Father as Justice demanding punishment for sin and the Son as Mercy, pleading with Justice and satisfying it by offering itself as an innocent victim in place of the guilty—are radically unscriptural. In the New Testament, quite constantly, the mind of the Father is declared to be towards men purely good —the mind of love—and the cost of the sacrifice is represented as the Father's no less than the Son's. " God so loved the world that he gave his only-

---

[1] The story of the sacrifice of Iphigeneia to Artemis, to procure good sailing for the Greek fleet, is taken as the type of the belief in sacrifice at its worst, but it is interesting to see how Euripides (in the *Iphigeneia in Aulis*) half moralizes the story by making Iphigeneia offer herself voluntarily for the cause of Greece, and by making Artemis save her and carry her to Tauris, substituting for her an animal victim, as in the Bible story.

begotten Son "[1]—" spared not his own Son, but delivered him up for us all." [2] Wherever we find the necessity for the sacrificial death to lie, we must utterly refuse to find it in anything in the Father's mind making Him unwilling to forgive, or distinguishing in any way His mind in the matter from Christ's. The essential wrath of God over sin is Christ's as much as the Father's, and the pardoning mercy the Father's as much as Christ's. It is a great step to get this fully and utterly recognized. It emancipates the Christian doctrine from the most revolting aspect of propitiatory sacrifice, as it is found all the world over and in the earlier stages of the Old Testament. And there is no doubt that the New Testament excludes it.

2. Secondly, we need to distinguish the ideas of vicarious sacrifice and vicarious punishment[3]; and I think we shall find that we can repudiate the second while we welcome the first. We can do this by appealing to the facts. All that came upon Christ in the way of suffering came simply from His life of obedience and sympathy. He never sought pain,[4] as if to witness pain would please the Father, or taught men to seek pain, except so far as service and self-discipline involve it. All that He suffered came simply out of His obedience to His Father's mission, and of His speaking the truth and rebuking sin; out of His standing stoutly against wickedness in high places, and out of His boundless sympathy with men. This constituted His mission. " He rode out because of the word of truth and meekness and righteousness." And as the world was, it brought Him to His death. There is not anything here which suggests any " punishment " devised

---

[1] John iii 16 ; cf. 1 John iv 10, " Herein is love . . . that . . God . . . sent his Son to be the propitiation for our sins."

[2] Rom. viii 32.

[3] See Rashdall, *op. cit.* pp. 98–9, 151.

[4] Except in the minor form of the voluntary fast in the wilderness.

by the Father for the Son. All that is said of the Father is that He did not interfere to spare His son —that He let sin take its course, and show its real nature in this supreme example. The Father, in the divine providence that governs the world, made our sins—and the sins which crucified Christ were the normal sins of men—light upon Him, in exactly the same sense as all the world over the sins of men are vicariously borne by their victims—the sins of parents by their children, of children by their parents, of rulers by their people, and of people by their pastors. The Father simply sent the Son into the world, and under the normal action of its moral laws, and did not interfere.

There was a horrible story of that unhappy boy Edward VI having a whipping companion attached to him ; and when the young king did wrong the child - companion was said to be vicariously, and doubtless very unwillingly, whipped. And divines were so misguided as to quote this outrageous instance of substituted punishment as an illustration of the Atonement. It fails as an illustration in two ways. The sacrifice of Christ was voluntary : it was *self* sacrifice : and there was no kind of " punishment " devised for Christ except what was involved in His doing right—in His obedience and His sympathy.

On the other hand there is a punishment for sinners, and it is of two kinds. There is the eternal punishment—that is, the alienation from God which sin involves and which has eternal consequences, and this Christ never bore. There is not the slightest trace of sin-consciousness in Christ ; nor, as far as I can see—be it spoken with all reverence to Dr. Moberly—any trace of what can be called vicarious penitence. The Agony in the Garden has been viewed as if it were a shrinking from the experience of the Father's wrath upon the sins of men with which Christ was to be identified. But this is simply groundless imagination. Neither the Agony in the Garden nor the great question upon the Cross appears to suggest any consciousness on our Lord's part of being identified with human sin. Purely and simply they suggest the agony of a righteous soul— conscious as neither Job nor the Psalmist could be of perfect innocence—finding itself, in a world which it knows to be God's world, exposed to ignominy, failure, outrage, and death, while God remains silent and does nothing. That Christ should have asked the great question—" My God, my God, why didst thou forsake me ? "—and received no answer is, for all who feel the like trial in whatever degree, a cause of profoundest thankfulness. But I cannot see any reason for believing that He experienced in His spirit the sense of the Father's alienation from the sinner.

This spiritual and eternal penalty of sin is gone at once as soon as the sin is gone out of the soul. And, as far as we can see, Christ not being a sinner did not bear it. There is another penalty of sin— the temporal punishment which wrongdoing brings with it, and from this, as far as we can see, Christ does not deliver us. Our absolution does not necessarily or usually ward off from us any of the natural consequences of our repented sins. Only it gives us the right spirit in which to bear them, and it turns them into healing penances. To be absolved is not to be let off. " Heard, forgiven, punished " was the record of God's dealings with His saints under the Old Covenant, and it is the record of His dealings with us under the New.[1]

Thus, as far as I can discern, there is in the case of Christ nothing which can be called vicarious punishment, nothing which was inflicted upon Christ instead of us. The doom on unrepented sin remains and the healing chastisement for repented sin remains.

[1] Ps. xcix 8.

Christ's sacrifice purchased for us forgiveness—that is all we are told—in the sense that it enabled the flood of the Father's mercy to flow freely in the channels of the New Covenant. Why such a sacrifice should have been needful for such an end to be attained we shall consider directly.

3. Lastly it has been an abundant source of scandal that the Atonement—"Christ for us," acting in our stead—has been isolated from "Christ in us," renewing and recreating our characters. It is noticeable how, in St. Paul's teaching, faith in Christ, our atonement, merges itself, even in the Epistle to the Romans, and much more in his later Epistles, in the faith which appropriates and lives in His life. "Christ for us"—our sacrifice of reconciliation—gives us our fresh start, but it is but the prelude to "Christ in us." Our absolution is simply what gives us our admission into the new life. "I will run the way of thy commandments, when thou hast set my heart at liberty." Again and again in the New Testament the effect of the atoning sacrifice is stated in terms of actual righteousness, because this is its only purpose. "How much more shall the blood of Christ, who through eternal spirit offered himself without spot to God, cleanse your consciences from dead works to serve the living God?" What you were redeemed from "with the precious blood ... of Christ" was "your vain manner of life handed down from your fathers." "Thou wast slain and didst purchase to God by thy blood men of every tribe, etc., and madest them to be unto our God a kingdom and priests; and they reign upon the earth." (The consecrated life is the end and effect of atonement.) "His own self bare our sins in his body on the tree, that we having died unto sins, might live unto righteousness." This is the language and purport of the whole New Testament.

There are, in fact, three relations in which our Lord

stands to us in the New Testament. There is *Christ in front of us*, who sets before us the standard of the new life—in whom we see the true meaning of manhood. That is to kindle our desire. Then there is *Christ for us*—our propitiation or atonement— winning for us, at the price of His blood-shedding, freedom from all the guilt and bondage of the past, the assurance of free forgiveness and the fresh start. Then there is *Christ in us*—our new life by the Spirit, moulding us inwardly into His likeness, and conforming us to His character. And the three are one. Each is unintelligible without the others. The redeeming work of Christ lies in all together. We may dwell now on one and now on the other, but we can never really isolate one from the others without altogether distorting the meaning even of the one.

III

We have been at pains, by reviewing the New Testament, to understand how central and essential to the Gospel it announces is the conception of the Atonement with God won for us by the sacrifice of Christ. And we have laboured to disencumber the idea of His Atonement of scandals which have been suffered needlessly to disfigure it. Now let us contemplate it in its legitimate outline, and see whether it commends itself to our conscience and our reason.

Christ stands as the Inaugurator of the New Manhood, perfect and complete in the midst of our sin-stained and weakened race. He sets the perfect standard of human life while He is on earth, so that none henceforth can doubt what perfect manhood means, and from the heavenly places to which He has passed He supplies the power of the Spirit that men may have wisdom and strength to live the good life according to His example. But between the example and the outpouring of the Spirit there stands intermediate another mode of action on our behalf. As the New Man, on behalf of all those who shall give themselves to His allegiance, He offers to the Father a great act of reparation—the sacrifice of obedience consummated in blood and agony upon the cross. Over against all our selfishness, our impurity, our dishonouring of God, He makes that great act of reparation; and in virtue of it the Father bestows upon all those who, by faith and incorporation, are united to Him a new standing ground in His presence, and the gift of free forgiveness ever renewable, so that their past sins are no longer reckoned against them, the guilt and the burden of them is gone, and they can run the way of God's commandments unimpeded, seeing He has set their hearts at liberty.

Even here in this sacrificial action we must not isolate Christ from His people. To present ourselves to God, in soul and body, as a free-will offering is *our* reasonable service, and it is the law of humanity that sacrifice is vicarious as well as individual. We suffer for one another and redeem one another by suffering. St. Paul dares to speak of " filling up in his flesh that which is lacking in the sufferings of Christ for his body's sake, which is the church." And the New Testament constantly speaks of the Cross as our example as well as our propitiation. Nevertheless, as in all that concerns the relation of Christ to His people, that which in us is dependent and imitative, in Him is original and creative. His sacrifice won for His new humanity a boon to which they contributed nothing, which they must receive from Him or in His name simply and solely by faith, the boon of being forgiven; and over all their imperfect strivings and sacrifices that one full perfect and sufficient sacrifice abides—perpetually pleaded

—to give adequacy to what is imperfect and expiate what is sinful.

Christ we believe was one in nature with the Father. His self-sacrificing love is God's love. Why then we ask should God have needed this expiation ? Why should not free forgiveness have simply been announced as a word of God ? Or, to put it otherwise, if obedience, under the conditions of the sinful world, involved death, and all that Christ gave was obedience even to the point of dying at the hands of men, why should it have assigned to it this propitiatory or expiatory value ? So far as we can find an answer to this question at all, we can find it perhaps best on this line—we can reflect how our thought of God would have suffered, if the great act of reparation had not been made by our Representative, acting on our behalf, doing *for* us what we could not do for ourselves. We should have been without that sense, which nothing has conveyed to the conscience of men like the sacrifice of the Cross, of the outrage which sin is upon the majesty of God, as measured by the price which it cost to redeem us. The gift of free forgiveness, the freedom of a fresh start, was not simply given us by God, but bought for us at a great price. This, I suppose, lies at the heart of that rather obscure phrase of St. Paul's— which is the only passage in the New Testament which even suggests the need of an explanation of the Atonement—where he contrasts " the passing over of sins done aforetime, in the forbearance of God " with the great act, at the crisis of redemption, when God " set forth Christ Jesus " upon the great stage of the world " as a propitiation taking effect in his bloodshedding, to be made available for us by faith, for the exhibition of his righteousness at the present season that he might be just (righteous) and the justifier (or acquitter) of him that hath faith in Jesus." Divine righteousness can now show itself freely as mercy, because man, in Christ Jesus, has on the great scene of the world made the perfect act of reparation and borne the uttermost witness to the sovereignty of God by obedience unto death.

Is there not an immense difference between the effect upon men's minds of a mere announcement of free forgiveness and the effect upon them of a covenant of free forgiveness bought at so tremendous a price as the death of the Son of God ? The reason for the fearful price being paid to win forgiveness seems to be found rightly by St. Paul in the necessity for guarding the revelation of the divine mercy from all associations of easy-going indulgence or indifference to sin. It was guarded by the Sacrifice ; and it was God Himself who paid the price.

Note A

Dr. Rashdall's " Idea of Atonement in Christian Theology"

This is a most learned and instructive work, for which every student must be grateful. But it seems to me, in some very important respects, extraordinarily arbitrary. Thus Dr. Rashdall rightly notes (p. 75 ff.) that the doctrine of the Atonement wrought by Christ's sacrifice is not due to St. Paul. " That view is rendered absolutely impossible by a single sentence in one of the practically undisputed Epistles of St. Paul himself, ' I delivered unto you . . . that which also I received, how that Christ died for our sins according to the Scriptures.' The belief that in some sense Christ died for sin—in order that sin might be forgiven and removed —was thus quite certainly part of what St. Paul received. It was already an article of the Church's traditional creed when the apostle of the Gentiles was baptized into it." Cf. also p. 104 : " That God had forgiven sins through Christ, and pre-eminently through His death, was common ground between himself (St. Paul) and his opponents. It was part of the common faith of the Church." But (very arbitrarily, I think) Dr.

Rashdall is disposed to deny that the tradition was due to our Lord's own teaching. He thinks that the idea " resulted from the reflection of the Church in the interval which elapsed between the Crucifixion and St. Paul's conversion—which cannot have been more than a very few years " (p. 76). It was accepted " simply and solely on authority " (pp. 80, 82)—the authority of the Old Testament scripture. " They found it, as they thought, distinctly foretold that He should do so (die that sins might be forgiven), in books which they regarded as in the most literal and plenary sense inspired writing. In that fact I believe we can discover the historical origin of the atonement doctrine " (p. 78). But there is no passage which would have suggested the doctrine at all obviously except Is. liii ; and that our Lord identified Himself with the Suffering Servant of this passage seems to me to be manifest (see above, p. 61). And the two great words of our Lord about the sacrificial value of His death, which are referred to above, both are grounded on this passage. This alone accounts for the undisputed position of the Atonement doctrine from the first.

I think that one great omission which is conspicuous in Dr. Rashdall's conception of Christ is—what is involved in His being the Christ—that He came to inaugurate the new Israel, and that He acts accordingly as the representative before God of the Church of the believers in Him which is yet to be—which by His death and resurrection and the coming of the Spirit He is to bring into effective being, and which is to be the old Church reformed on a new basis, on the basis of a new covenant by sacrifice.

Note B

Two phrases of St. Paul which have been needlessly misinterpreted (see p. 291).

(a) 2 Cor. v 21, " Him who knew no sin, he made to be sin on our behalf." I believe that " sin " here is the equivalent of " for sin " in Rom. viii 3 (" an offering for sin," R.V.). In the LXX, following the

Hebrew, the same word stands for sin and sin-offering (ἁμαρτία, translating *chattath*). Thus Lev. iv 21, " It [the bullock] is the sin, *i.e.* the sin-offering, of the assembly " ; 24, " It [the goat] is a sin " ; 29, " He shall lay his hand upon the head of the sin " ; vi 25, " This is the law of the sin," *i.e.* sin-offering ; viii 14, " The bullock is the sin " ; cf. Hosea iv 8, " They feed on the sin." St. Paul means, I think, simply that " God made him who knew no sin to be the sin-offering on our behalf."

(*b*) Gal. iii 13, " Having become a curse for us." The argument is—Those who struggle in their own strength under the law end under condemnation or a curse. There is a better way—not of saving ourselves, but of being saved. Fruitful faith in Jesus can do what fruitless struggle cannot. He brought us out from under the curse by His self-sacrifice. He was made a curse for us, *i.e.* treated as a malefactor, that we might not have to be treated as malefactors. We note that St. Paul is quoting a text of the Old Testament, Deut. xxi 23, which is " Cursed of God is everyone that hangeth upon a tree [gibbet]," but he leaves out the words " of God." It was the world, not God, which treated Christ as a malefactor.

CHAPTER XI

SUMMARY AND CONCLUSION

THERE are, no doubt, other ideas and principles which the doctrine of the Incarnation implies, and which might fall to be considered here. Thus the affirmation of *the Word made Flesh* involves, as against all the tendencies of Hellenism, the dignity of matter and of the material world, which indeed is implied alike in the Christian idea of creation, of sin, of the Incarnation, of the Church and the sacraments, of the resurrection of the body and the redemption of the whole creation. But we will defer the consideration of this principle until the sacraments and the resurrection of the body have been discussed in the next volume. Again, we have found ourselves close up against the question of Authority as involved in the idea of a divine message or revelation, but that again shall be deferred for discussion in connection with the Church. Once more we shall probably have been led already to feel the coherence of the various elements of the traditional faith which centres in Christ, and this solidarity of " the articles of the faith " has over against it in our days a like solidarity in the sequence of ideas which are grouped as " Modernism." A certain philosophy appears to lie behind each sequence of ideas. But again we shall be able to bring this out more effectively when the whole cycle of rival ideas has been passed in review. So at this point we will summarize our argument and draw it to a conclusion.

Starting from the Jewish background, whence the first disciples started in the company of Jesus—the background of the distinctively Jewish belief in God and the expectation of the Messiah and his kingdom [1]—we observed how profoundly Jesus transformed the Jewish expectation, as His contemporaries held it, even while He accepted the title of Messiah —turning His back on political and nationalist ideals, and building up, out of the materials of prophecy, one profoundly unified and spiritual conception of the Christ, manifested, suffering, dying, rising, glorified, and to come in judgment. And we noted how, quite apart from any question of names and titles, by the unexampled spiritual authority which He wielded, He absorbed the attention, the faith, the devotion of His disciples, so that He came to be as God to their souls. This is the feature in the Gospel story which overwhelms us as we read it. But contrary to this deepening attraction of His person, and pulling in the opposite direction, there was the horror of the impending Cross, and the overthrow which it involved of all that had been associated with the Christ and his triumph.[2] We watched the tragedy of the disciples' failure under the strain of these contending feelings, and then their recovery under the experience of the Resurrection and the Ascension and the effusion of the Spirit. But still we noted that all their faith centred on the risen and glorified Lord, the man whom they had known, full of the Spirit and power, whom they had deserted, whom they had seen crucified, now exalted to the throne of God, who had sent thence upon them the Holy Spirit. It would have seemed as if they were on their way to deify their human Master after the Greek manner. But that could not be.

[1] Cap. i.　　　　　[2] Cap. ii.

In the providence of God it was the bitterest of
their opponents who was to interpret to them the
meaning of their faith. This Saul—in the days
when, as he said, he was "thinking with himself
that he ought to do many things contrary to the
name of Jesus of Nazareth," [1] and was "punishing
his disciples ofttimes in every city and compelling
them to blaspheme"—must have known a good
deal about Jesus. Doubtless he learned more after
his conversion, at Damascus and Jerusalem, about
"the tradition" of the Christian society. But he
was certainly convinced that it was nothing less
than the action of God in his own soul that had
"revealed his Son" in him; and this—the Divine
Sonship—becomes the keynote of his teaching about
Jesus. The man born of the seed of David
according to the flesh, who after living and dying
as man had been exalted to the divine glory and
to the supreme Lordship—before He was born of a
woman to His human condition, aye, before ever
the world was, was the proper Son of God, a Son
with His Father, through whom all things were
made and in whom all things have their consistency.
This is the doctrine of the Incarnation. And we
noted that this doctrine, which interprets the person
and glory of the ascended Jesus upon the background
of Jewish monotheism as the coming of God's
own Son in the flesh, and not the deification of a
man, seems to have been without controversy
accepted throughout the churches. [2] There is, as
we saw, no Adoptionism, properly so called, to be
found in the New Testament. And we discovered
in the Synoptic records of Jesus several solemn
sayings which are most certainly original and which
can only be interpreted in the sense of a trans-
cendental, superhuman Sonship. They do not differ
in real implication from the more emphatic utter-

[1] Acts xxvi. 9.   [2] Cap. iii.

ances about pre-existent Sonship ascribed to Jesus in the Fourth Gospel. That Jesus so spoke must have been on record in the tradition of the Church, though the force of His words had not been generally realized till St. Paul brought it home to the other apostles in its full force. So only can we account for his doctrine of Incarnation coming so easily into general acceptance.

We analyzed the substantially identical doctrine of the Incarnation of the Son or " Word " of God in St. Paul, in the author of the Epistle to the Hebrews, and in St. John. Besides the words of Jesus Himself, we found the materials for the conception of these first expositors of the person of our Lord in the Jewish phrases " the Word," and " the Wisdom," and "the Abiding Place " of God—phrases expressive of God as He manifests Himself in nature or amongst His people—much more obviously than in any purely Hellenistic sources. But it is to be remembered that Hellenism had already influenced the Jewish tradition, especially at Alexandria, as in the Book of Wisdom; and the Epistle to the Hebrews at least is an Alexandrian book.[1]

If the Hellenistic influence on Christian origins has been much exaggerated by one school of critics, so by another school of critics has the influence of the later Jewish Apocalypses. This was our conclusion when we examined the eschatological and apocalyptic teaching of Jesus and noted its complex character and originality. That our Lord was an apocalyptic seer there is no doubt, but He profoundly transmuted the apocalyptic tradition in adopting it. On the whole, He approximates far more closely in teaching to the prophets than to the later writers of Apocalypses. In particular, we saw no good reason for supposing that He prophesied the immediate coming of the end of the world. On the

21   [1] Cap. iv.

contrary, He appears to have declared explicitly that He had no map of the future spread before His eyes.[1]

Having thus reviewed the thought of the New Testament about Christ, we contrasted its doctrine, which is the traditional doctrine, about His person with the most striking and distinctive modern views, all of a humanitarian and rationalistic type, which have claimed the name of critical reconstructions, and found them not truly critical, in that they are strangely arbitrary in what they accept and what they reject, and even violently contrary in their results. We saw reason to claim that the traditional faith—modified, in view of really critical requirements, but substantially unchanged—is alone able to account for the facts as a whole, the facts of the Gospel story and the convictions of the first disciples, by which alone the origin of the Christian Church can be explained. And we considered the most important types of objection which are made to the traditional doctrine.[2]

Then we studied the later development of the doctrine of Christ's person in outline, and came to the conclusion that the decisions of the Councils, which fixed the doctrine in dogmatic limits, were all of them necessary and justified in their negative aspects, considered as excluding types of teaching fundamentally destructive of the Christian faith ; but that they were open to great abuse when they were made the positive basis on which a picture of a Christ was erected, in some points strangely unlike the picture in the Gospels. We felt the need of insisting that, while the decrees were necessary as hedges or safeguards of the fundamental faith of the New Testament, they should be understood to direct us to the Christ of the Gospels as giving us the positive image, and to the apostolic writers

[1] Cap. v.   [2] Cap. vi.

as giving us the positive interpretation, of His person.[1]

Then we proceeded to consider the main ideas and doctrines which the Incarnation doctrine of the New Testament is found to involve; and first the doctrine of the trinity of " persons " in the unity of God, the sense of which gradually became distinct in the process of experience which the Gospels record, by which the Name of God became to the disciples the Name of the Father, and of the Son, and of the Holy Ghost; and we took note of the profound assistance which the reason finds in this conception of the one divine being as not a monotonous unit, but containing within Himself relationships which human language at least can only describe as a fellowship of persons.[2]

Next we examined the presupposition of all the Biblical accounts of Redemption, viz. that man is universally sinful and that, in order to realize the end of his being in fellowship with God and fellow-ship amongst men, he needs something much more than enlightenment. He needs such a fundamental recreation and renewal as involves the direct action of the God who made him. He must be saved. He cannot save himself. And we examined in outline the meaning of the doctrine of " original (or racial) sin," and found it justified or rather required by the essentially corporate and racial basis of human personality.[3]

Finally we found the idea of Atonement or Pro-pitiation made by Christ before God, on behalf of the New Humanity which He came to inaugurate, to be an idea which the writers of the New Testament and the Church from the beginning assumed for true. We found that it clearly depends upon Christ's own testimony. We endeavoured to rid it of scandals in which, in the current tradition of the Church,

[1] Cap. vii.   [2] Cap. viii.   [3] Cap. ix.

it has become too plentifully involved; and thus
purged, and presented in its original outline, we
found it free from the moral objections which have
been urged against it, and deeply responsive to the
moral reason, which demands reparation to evoke
and justify forgiveness; and we saw that its intellectual justification is inseparable from that
estimate of Christ's person which sees in Him the
representative head of a new humanity, who can
act for His " members." [1]

II

In all this process of observing and thinking we
have found no justification for certain opinions
which are commonly held and propounded as critical,
viz. (1) that the theology of St. Paul and St. John,
which is with little difference the theology of the
Catholic Church, overlays and obscures the naive
theology, if so it is to be called, of the historical
Jesus. In any case you cannot get behind the
apostolic witness. The Epistles are, as a whole,
somewhat older than the Gospels as we have them,
and the earliest Gospel records grew up in the heart
of the Church which the Acts and the Epistles disclose to us. But also in these earliest records we
discern a person who cannot be reduced to merely
human proportions. The picture of Him, which
we feel compelled to take for history and not for
invention, is the picture of the superhuman Son of
God. It justifies and requires the theology of St. Paul
and St. John.

(2) We have seen no justification for asserting
any determining influence of Hellenistic ideas upon
the *origins* of Christianity, upon the Christianity
of the New Testament. It is true that it had a
much greater and deeper influence upon its development, which we shall have to consider in connection

[1] Cap. x.

with the sacramental system of the Church. But it had little influence on its origins, save in so far as it had already influenced Alexandrian Judaism in such a way as the Book of Wisdom represents. Like Christianity, so Judaism showed a marked power at different periods to assimilate foreign elements— from Babylonia and Persia and Greece—and to incorporate them into its own proper tradition in a discriminating spirit which never suffered the essential character of its own doctrine to be impaired or obscured. These elements had come to belong to Judaism before Christ was born. They belong to His background. But they were not considerable. It is substantially only the religion of the prophets and the person and teaching of Jesus which provide the materials of New Testament Christianity.

(3) Nor have we found justification for the exaggerated importance which a good many distinguished teachers ascribe to the Jewish apocalypses, and especially to the Similitudes of the Book of Enoch. We found no trace in the New Testament of the idea of the *Pre-existing Son of Man*, who is neither properly divine nor properly human. I suppose no one believes that such a being ever really existed. He is purely mythical ; and it is astonishing how large an influence even some orthodox theologians seem to allow to this mythical figure, without recognizing that the superstructure of orthodox theology is immensely weakened if myth enters so largely into its foundations. But in fact the conception does not really appear in the New Testament. It is gratuitous to imagine it.[1]

[1] The only sentence which really at first sight suggests it is John v 27, " He gave him authority to execute judgment, because he is the Son of Man." This sounds like the Similitudes of Enoch. But it is impossible to ascribe the idea of a pre-existing *Son of Man* to John. He explains his theology in his preface, and it appears constantly in his Gospel, and there is no room for it. It is the Word or Son of God who pre-exists.

III

Not indeed in New Testament times, but in the succeeding ages of the Church, especially when intellectual life has been keen, the doctrine of the person of Christ has been the centre of bitter controversy, and this controversy has undoubtedly distracted the attention of the Church from what ought always to be its main interest—the following " the way," the living the life, the maintenance of the moral, social witness. The religion of Christ, as He taught it, was to be, first of all, the way. The way was a hard way, and made a tremendous claim for sacrifice upon the heart and will of men. But for the men of good will it does not appear that our Lord intended the doctrinal claim to prove difficult. " If any man willeth to do God's will, he shall know of the teaching, whether it be of God." [1]   But the gravest scandal which Church history presents to many of the best men is that again and again in East and West, among Catholics and Protestants, they see a rigid, controversial, and often merciless insistence on doctrinal orthodoxy, coupled with manifest laxity of moral discipline. The situation in the Church has thus constantly presented features precisely contradictory to the apparent intention of Christ—that is to say, a concentration of interest on precise orthodoxy, coupled with a great readiness to " make it easy " in moral matters for those who are prepared to submit to the doctrinal authority of the Church, and to conform to its required practice. This, I cannot doubt, is the gravest of all the causes of scandal in the Church, and I cannot minimize it or apologize for it.[2]

[1] John vii 17.
[2] I would venture to refer to my " Essex Hall Lecture," *Christianity applied to the Life of Men and Nations*, given by me in 1920, and published by the Lindsey Press, 5 Essex Street, Strand, London, W.C.

But when, in order to remove this scandal, men disparage theology they make a fundamental mistake. However many inconsistencies may be found in all ages between men's lives and their professed beliefs, there can be no question that, in the long run, how men behave will depend upon what they really believe about God and human nature and destiny ; and in particular that the Christian " way " depends for its motives and supports upon a specific doctrine about God and His love and His purposes for man, that is the doctrine of the Incarnation. " Herein is love, not that we loved God, but that he loved us, and sent his Son." No one who has followed with any degree of sympathy the argument of this book will doubt that St. Paul and St. John were right in perceiving that the Gospel requires theological controversy, where necessary to defend a certain original and final doctrine on which it depends. " Though we, or an angel from heaven, should preach unto you any gospel other than that which we preached unto you, let him be anathema." " Whosoever goeth onward and abideth not in the teaching of Christ, hath not God." [1] My last words in this volume shall be an attempt to set in a clear light the importance of maintaining (though never by methods of force) the doctrine about Christ of St. Paul and St. John.

I think the word which best sums up the importance of this Incarnation doctrine is *finality* or *uniqueness*. Let me quote the thoughtful language of Edwyn Bevan [2] :

" The great dividing line, it appears to me, is that which marks off all those who hold that the relation of Jesus to God—however they describe or formulate it— is of such a kind that it could not be repeated in any other individual—that to speak, in fact, of its being repeated in any *other* individual is a contradiction in

[1] Gal. i 8–9, 2 John 9.   [2] *Hellenism and Christianity*, p. 271.

terms, since any individual standing in that relation to God would *be* Jesus, and that Jesus, in virtue of this relation, has the same absolute claim upon all men's worship and loyalty as belongs to God. A persuasion of this sort of uniqueness attaching to Jesus seems to me the essential characteristic of what has actually in the field of human history been Christianity."

Now it is to me evident that nothing but the doctrine of "the Word made flesh"—the doctrine of the Nicene Creed—can interpret or justify this uniqueness and finality ascribed to Christ. Dr. Kirsopp Lake has set before us the opposite estimate of the teaching of Jesus in human history, as contributory but as essentially neither final nor complete.[1] Dr. Lake is regarded as an "extremist." But my contention is, that no "mediating" doctrine, nothing except the full doctrine of the Nicene Creed, which is substantially identical with St. Paul's and St. John's, can either explain or justify the ascription to Jesus of finality and uniqueness in the strict sense. What I mean is this : if that doctrine is true, there is finality. No disclosure of God to man, such as is possible in this world, can be even conceived fuller or completer than is given in Him who is God incarnate—the Word made flesh. He that hath seen Him hath seen the Father. And no relation of man to God can be even conceived closer than in Him in whom the Manhood is taken into God. From Him, so conceived, proceeds necessarily the final and universal religion, for whatever elements of truth are found in the religions of the world, and whatever excellencies in moral ideal, here, in Christ, is necessarily something more complete. And we cannot "look for another" Christ. There can be no other. That person, Jesus of Nazareth, is on the throne of the universe.

[1] See the conclusion of his *Landmarks in the History of Early Christianity*.

On the other hand, no doctrine of Christ, less than this, can justify the claim of finality. If Jesus was a man who began His existence as a person when He was born of Mary—however close the union with God into which He was taken, however full the inspiration of the Spirit granted to Him—there can be no reason in the nature of things why another man, in a later age or in another country, and belonging to another tradition, should not be in the same relation to God and equally or more fully inspired. No form of adoptionist or Nestorian or generally humanitarian teaching can claim finality for its Christ.

It must be remembered that religion is a thing for common men. The refinements of the Antiochene school which lay behind Nestorianism were very subtle; but Nestorianism as vulgarly understood was their inevitable outcome. Common men can understand the doctrine of the Incarnation, and they can understand the doctrine of an inspired man. But I do not think it is open to question that so far as they came to hold the latter doctrine, though they might accept Christ as the best and most fully inspired man who has hitherto appeared among men, they would neither worship Him nor think Him the final revelation, nor His name the one name, nor His religion the religion for all mankind. I cannot conceive how this can be doubted.

Of course there are those who would say that the acceptance of the category of evolution in all departments of life, and in the regions of human religion and morality, renders the very idea of a final religion revealed two thousand years ago, and never to be antiquated, quite unacceptable. But I suppose that this objection is based upon a misconception about evolution which we are outgrowing. Evolution is as compatible with retrogression as with progress, as we were warned by

Huxley long ago. It must accommodate itself to the facts. The facts of human history suggest nothing less than necessary or uniform progress. In the particular region of the history of religion this is especially the case. The highest level in the religion of Persia was attained in the teaching of Zoroaster, three thousand years ago. The highest level in Buddhism is indisputably the level of Siddartha Gotama. It would remain true, even if Christ were a mere man, that though in that case, no doubt, some successor *might* attain a higher level than He, yet in fact He still remained the highest ideal. And these considerations suffice, I think, to prevent our rejecting the idea of the incarnation of God in Christ, once for all, as if it could be repudiated in the name of evolution.

But there is another consideration perhaps more satisfactory. It is that though Christ is final—though He is on the throne of the world and His judgment the final judgment—though St. John can rightly claim of Christians that any " advance " which takes a Christian teacher outside or away from the " doctrine of Christ " is self-condemned—yet that Christ and the doctrine of Christ is so rich and manifold that it will take all races and all ages and all sorts of individual characters to realize all that it involves. That is an idea suggested to us by both St. Paul and St. John: By St. Paul when he bids us see the whole development of the Church catholic as the sphere in which Christ is to be gradually fulfilled : by St. John when he recalls to us that the function of the Spirit is to lead the Church into " all the truth." No doubt this is an often misinterpreted text. It needs to be coupled with the two neighbouring texts where our Lord speaks to the disciples of the Holy Spirit as " to bring all things to your remembrance whatsoever I have said unto you " and " to glorify me : for he shall take of mine and shall declare it unto you." The function of the Spirit is to interpret Christ and not to supersede Him. Nevertheless there is so much to be brought out and interpreted that we are constantly feeling we have only made a beginning of understanding Him, and that as Jew and Greek and Roman and Frenchman and Englishman and German have contributed, so will Indian and Chinese and Japanese. It will take all mankind to understand Him in whom dwells all the fulness of God bodily.

The ascension of Jesus is the symbol of His finality. He passed to the throne of the world. He is to come to judge the quick and dead. His judgment on all men and things is to be the final judgment. But the Ascension, though it is in this sense the great end and there can be no higher summit, yet in another most manifest sense is a fresh beginning. It is but the establishment upon His secure throne of Him who is to be the source of redemption for all men : who by His Spirit is to work throughout the world of men until all men have heard His Gospel in effective power and the kingdoms of the world can become the kingdoms of God and of His Christ.

So understood Christianity is indeed the religion of development or unfolding—the gradual unfolding of all the treasures of wisdom and knowledge which are in Christ.

NOTE ON THE ASCENSION.

There is an idea current that the articles of the Creed, "He ascended into heaven, and sitteth on the right hand of God ; from thence He shall come to judge the quick and the dead " depended upon the old Ptolemaic astronomy which rendered possible a belief in a heaven above our heads ; and that the disappearance of this theory has invalidated this group of beliefs connected

with the Ascension. The same is said to be true of the
belief in the descent into hell. Thus Dr. Glazebrook
says : " The clauses have no literal meaning. except for
those who regard the earth as a fixed centre of creation,
with a hollow space underneath for Hades and a solid
vault overhead." And Dr. Streeter, " The Ascension
implies the belief that heaven is a definite region locally
fixed above the solid bowl of the skies."

But it is a mistake to suppose that all intelligent
Christians of the early ages held such ideas. Plato had
taught the intelligent world of the Greco-Roman Empire
by his myths to accept the principle that about
" the other world " or other worlds we can be taught
for the most part only in figure or allegory. This idea
was widely diffused and Alexandrian Judaism gave it
additional vogue. There is no doubt that ideas about
heaven and hell such as Dr. Glazebrook and Dr. Streeter
refer to did prevail in the world of the first centuries,
outside the Church and inside it. But it is not the case
that they were universal. I doubt whether St. Paul held
any such ideas. When he speaks of Christians being
now with Christ " in the heavenlies " or heavenly
sphere,[1] he cannot have been thinking of it as a defined
locality.   When he speaks of " being caught up into the
third heaven " I suspect he knew quite well that he was
speaking in a figure, as one who sees but a blurred reflection in a mirror, or apprehends but in a riddle.[2] Nor
is it the least probable that when the author of the
Epistle to the Hebrews speaks of our Lord as having
passed through the heavens into the true tabernacle [3]
he was forgetting what he had learned from his Alexandrian teachers, that earthly things are only " figures "
or " shadows " of eternal realities.[4] No one would be
disposed to ascribe materialistic ideas of heaven to
Clement and Origen. But it is more surprising to find
Jerome, when he is interpreting ' foolish speaking "
(on Eph. iii 5),[5] giving it as an example of such nonsense
that Christians dare to say " that heaven is curved like

---

[1] Eph. i 3, ii 6.   [2] 1 Cor. xiii 12.
[3] iv 14, viii 2.   [4] ix 23, x 1.
[5] *P.L.* xxvi 519 f.   Dr. Harris, *Creeds or no Creeds*, called my
attention to this quotation.

an arch, and that a throne is placed in heaven, and that
God sits upon it, and that, as if He were a commander or
judge, the angels stand round to obey His commands and
to be sent on different missions." Plainly for Jerome
the truth and meaning of the Ascension did not depend
upon such " nonsense."

Again the Fathers are many of them at pains to explain that " He sitteth at the right hand of God " was
certainly figurative, seeing that God has no right hand.

Lastly as regards Hades, whether it holds some special
position, as a part of or in relation to the earth, there
was a good deal of discussion in many circles and among
Christians in early times. There again it is hard to
believe that when St. Paul speaks of the dead as " sleep-
ing in Jesus " he was thinking of a pit underground.
There is a long and interesting discussion of the matter
in Gregory of Nyssa's *de Anima et Resurrectione,* where he
seems to follow Posidonius the Platonizing Stoic ; and
he reaches the conclusion " that the soul, being im-
material, is under no necessity to be detained in certain
portions of nature." Hades he explains to mean " the
invisible " (τὸ ἀειδὲς), and " to go to Hades " the translation of the soul into the invisible.

I am not disputing the wide prevalence of merely
physical conceptions of heaven and hell such as Coperni-
can astronomy must have utterly overthrown. I am
only pleading that, even when no one doubted the
Ptolemaic astronomy, intelligent Christians did not fail
to see that heaven and hell were not spatial terms.

I have in *Belief in God* (pp. 272–273) spoken about the
Ascension of Christ as a physical fact which the apostles
saw, and of its spiritual significance, quite irrespective
of changes in our conception of the structure of the universe ; and (pp. 180–182) I have endeavoured to show
how illogical and unreasonable it is to argue that because
in the case of what lies outside possible human experience
we must be taught by symbols, therefore we can apply
the same symbolic interpretation to events, such as the
miracles connected with our Lord's person, which are
stated to have occurred *within human experience* and
have all their significance from having so actually
occurred.

TABLE OF SUBJECTS

INDEX OF NAMES